The Passion Prescription

The Passion Prescription

Ten Weeks to Your Best Sex—Ever!

Laura Berman, Ph.D.

HYPERION

NEW YORK

Library of Congress Cataloging-in-Publication Data

Berman, Laura.
      The passion prescription : Ten weeks to your best sex—ever! / by Laura Berman.—1st ed.
         p. cm.
      Includes bibliographical references.
      ISBN 1-4013-0224-6
      1. Sex instruction.   2. Sex.   I. Title.

   HQ31.B447 2006
   613.9'6'082—dc22

                                                          2005046347

Hyperion books are available for special promotions and premiums. For details contact Michael Rentas, Manager, Inventory and Premium Sales, Hyperion, 77 West 66th Street, 11th floor, New York, New York 10023, or call 212-456-0133.

FIRST EDITION

10   9   8   7   6   5   4   3   2   1

This book is dedicated to all the women I've worked with

for the past fifteen years. You let me into your lives and allowed me

to participate in your journey, and I have learned so much

from each and every one of you.

Acknowledgments

THERE ARE SO MANY PEOPLE who played a central role in making this book a reality. First and foremost, thank you to all of the staff at the Berman Center who have allowed me to realize my ultimate dream: to provide a place where women can get all they need to reach their full sexual potential. Every step in *The Passion Prescription* is based on the work that they do and the skills they contribute every day as we work to make women's sexual lives and relationships better. Most especially I want to thank Dana Demas, without whom this book would never have been possible. Your vision and skill have led this project every step of the way. Thank you also to Bill McDunn, Kathy Monke, Jeanine Ramirez, Suzanne Roth, and Martha Weinfurter. I also want to acknowledge Kerrie Grow who always stepped up to the plate with a smile and phenomenal efficiency to help with research, editing, whatever it took to get this done. Thank you especially to Chef Jeremy Charles and Becky Jeffers who spent so much time contributing their expertise to this book and putting into words the phenomenal work they do every day.

I also want to thank Binky Urban, my agent at ICM, whose wisdom and foresight are invaluable to me. And to my publisher, Hyperion, and my editor, Gretchen Young, thank you for being such a pleasure to work with and for sharing the vision of *The Passion Prescription* with me.

Thank you to the folks at NEWSHE.com, Wendy Claunch, Stan Felder, Myron Murdock, and Mukesh Pitroda, and all the staff of the *Dr. Laura*

Berman Radio Show, all of whom work so hard every day to get the message out there to women. I also want to thank Hayden Meyer, my agent at United Talent Agency, for his enthusiasm and guidance and Greg Suess, Jay Froberg, and Bernie Cahill from Roar for their creativity and direction. Special thanks also to Chuck Sanchez from Emperor Public Relations. Thank you for working so hard night and day to give me my soapbox!

I talk a lot in this book about the importance of finding time to remind yourself that you are not only a wife and mother. I am so thankful to the women in my life who remind me what it's like to be just a woman and help me connect with my laughter and lightheartedness on a regular basis, most especially to: Hope Ashby, Elizabeth Evans, Jennifer Gilbert, Marla Henderson, Niamh King, Saira Mohan, Elise Paschen, and Dana Weinstein. Thank you also to my family: my parents, Linda and Irwin Berman; my sister, Jennifer Berman; my grandmothers, Teal Friedman and Jean Berman; and my sons, Ethan and Sammy (not to mention baby Jackson who has grown inside me while I wrote this book and will be here when this book is published!).

Most of all, how to thank my husband, Sam Chapman? Thank you for all your hard work on this book: reading, editing, and writing, especially the Guy's Guides! You are the world's best partner, in life, love, and work. I am romantically inspired on a daily basis by your smarts, your skills, and your undying respect for me and the work I do. Thank you for sharing my life.

Contents

Introduction

■❯❯❯❯❯❯❯❯❯❯❯❯❯❯■

THE ROAD TO GREAT SEX BEGINS HERE.

I wouldn't be the first to tell you that your sexual satisfaction matters. Whether single, in a relationship, or somewhere in the middle, whether young or old, every woman has the right to a satisfying, electric, *passion-filled* sex life. I mean everything you have always dreamed of and more. I'm telling you it's your right. You just have to believe it to make it happen.

This guide gives you all of the tools you need to renovate your sex life from top to bottom. Its approach is holistic at heart, drawing upon a range of scientific fact, clinical experience, and simple inspired creativity. The hope is that every woman can find her way to the sex life she wants *and deserves*. It may mean improving on what you already have. It may mean starting from scratch. No matter where you are currently "living," it is a ten-step guide to great sex, starting from the beginning.

And the beginning is our bodies. Sex is the ultimate expression of the body. It blends together our primal instincts and the modern, rationally driven parts of ourselves. However, too many women are like strangers in their own bodies—and it is far from surprising. I see this every day in the women I treat at the Berman Center, my sexual health clinic in Chicago. Real communication about sex is sorely missing or even discouraged in many women's lives, making their foundation more than a little flimsy for the bumpy journey that sex inevitably is. During our formative years, most parents try to do their best.

But whether it is because they felt uncomfortable or uninformed themselves, they often fail to give us the information we needed and craved at the time. When it is given, it is decidedly clinical and sometimes even laced with negative judgments. The messages from the media and society are a black-and-white paradox of *good girls don't,* but *sex is power.* All of which is a far cry from the pleasurable, intimate, and complex act that sex is. The result is that many women arrive at their sexuality with little idea of what to expect, much less how to get the sexual satisfaction they want and deserve. This book aims to fill in the information gap by explaining how women's bodies work and what can be expected during "good" sex. It also, by its very nature, puts sex squarely on the table so that every woman can begin navigating through her past and moving in the direction she wants to go. Learning about your body, and awakening and relishing in its potential, is every woman's starting point for a healthy, confident sexuality.

Naturally, we all confront sex as novices—men and women alike. However, a woman's more complex sexual response sets her up to believe that something is wrong with *her*. After our earliest sexual encounters, many of us are left with feelings ranging from *Is this it?* to *What's wrong with me?* This experience, for better or worse, adds to an already flimsy foundation. While it often gets better with time and experimentation, feelings of inadequacy and uncertainty can persist. Especially since, in general, men are able to respond sexually more quickly and easily than women—as adolescents and also as we age. Men's orgasms and subsequent ejaculations provide a measure of their sexual success. Women, on the other hand, have no such measure. Sometimes this can set the stage for a lifetime of women compromising on their sexual pleasure. In reality, the problem is likely in the approach or a host of other logistics that women, for one reason or another, never thought to ask about. Through this book, you will discover the tangibles and intangibles you need for sexual satisfaction. By understanding what you need and why, you feel more empowered to ask for it. Every woman is inspired to take back the reins of her sexuality and leave the silence, mystification, and shame in the dust.

The definition of women's sexual *satisfaction* itself has been dragged through the mud for centuries. For much of history, women were told that it was "in their heads" if sex wasn't working right. As recently as the 1970s, a woman was considered abnormal if she could not have orgasms from penetration only. Statistics now indicate that from 50 to 70 percent of women do not have vaginal orgasms from penetration alone, which, ironically, makes *it* the norm. The male-focused ideal of sexuality that prevailed for so much of history is finally being modified to include what has so sorely been missed in the past: women.

Lackluster sex is simply something you don't have to accept. Likewise, the catch-all solution is not necessarily talking it out in therapy. Rather, lackluster sex continues to be an issue because women have grown too accustomed to placing their sexual needs on the back burner. An act as rich and complex as sex has equally rich and complex causes when it is not working. Therapy is one solution, but an array of physical interventions, lifestyle changes, and sexual practices are just a few of the others—all of which you will learn about in this book. Women are realizing more and more every day that it is their right to be happy, fulfilled sexual beings. This book is about keeping that momentum going. The unrealistic pressures that stand in the way of a happy sex life are being thrown under the microscope, picking up where Betty Dodson, Helen Singer Kaplan, and others like them have helped us arrive. Like their work and the work I've contributed previously, I can only hope this book offers women a new and further developed lifeline in rediscovering the truth— their truth—on the path to sexual wholeness. Then the focus can turn to exploring and finding ways to bridge the fundamental difference in the ways that men and women approach sex. Because in the end, it's the coming together that makes sex the sweetest.

Like many parts of life, women need to feel their way through it. There will be pain and ecstasy along the way, soul-mating and heartbreaking. But the journey is what makes the woman—in life and in love. This particular leg of it is sensual, emotional, intellectual, and spiritual, all at the same time. You will go down many different roads to reclaim your sexual satisfaction, but I promise that the reward will be worth it in the end.

It takes commitment—I am not going to try to downplay it! Both emotionally and logistically, you must be willing to give this guide the energy it demands. But the benefits are real for your sex life and your relationship—whether now or for the future. This innovative guide empowers you to tackle your sex life from every possible angle so that a new sexual you emerges upon its completion. It's a ten-week, ten-step program designed to revolutionize your sex life.

Each chapter focuses on a different part of your sexuality. In it, you learn everything you need to know to rediscover your own rapturous pleasure. Some exciting areas you will explore include:

- ☐ Your pelvic floor and why it is one of the most important muscles in your body for sexual satisfaction.

- ☐ How you can intercept the cycle of dwindling passion and attention from your partner.

- ☐ What blood flow does for your sex life, including the medical factors that can affect it and how to get it pumping. Plus, how to deal with your doctor.

- ☐ Results of two groundbreaking new studies. Why vibrators are a must for every woman *and* every couple and the impact genital self-image has on your sex life.

- ☐ A comprehensive vibrator and sex toy guide.

Every chapter ends with a list for you and a list for your partner. Both are designed to make the book work its best for you. Your list is called your **Prescriptions for the Week,** which consist of weekly homework activities based on what was discussed in the chapter. This is where the commitment comes in. You are going to be asked for time, as well as emotional and physical investment, to complete the activities. The more you put into it, the more you will get out of it. Some of the homework will be one-time activities, such as going through your medicine cabinet, while others will be long-term, such as making sure you are masturbating regularly. All have been carefully chosen to deliver you to a better understanding of your sexuality and, ultimately, to sexual satisfaction. The goal is a worthy one, so try to remember this as you progress. Once you have completed the ten-week program, you can evaluate what elements were most helpful. Maybe you will want to revisit some at another time in your life. However, I suspect that much of what you learn will find a lasting place in your sex life.

The list for your partner is called the **Guy's Guide**. It contains the key points from each chapter, so he can learn what he needs to know about your sexual satisfaction, in a condensed version that can keep his attention. After all, it takes two to tango and sex is always a couples issue. We've made it easy—the guides are one-page synopses, so your partner can get on board. And don't forget to tell him that there are all sorts of fun activities you will be trying out together as you take this journey. The benefits are for him, too.

So are you ready to get started? Here's to better sex; you deserve it!

CHAPTER ONE

Self-Discovery

Time to Get in Touch with Yourself

▮⟩⟩⟩⟩▮

THE THOUGHT OF SEX STIRS up all kinds of feelings: desire and need, excitement and anxiety, nostalgia and fantasy. A woman's sexuality is ultimately a combination of the experiences she's already had along with the untapped potential that still lies within her. Past relationships, childhood messages, and her own unique personality—all conspire to create the female sexual identity. Since the beat of our lives is always changing, our sexual needs are constantly in flux as well.

It's no surprise, then, that good sex varies greatly from one woman to another, as well as from one encounter to the next. Good sex can be hard to come by. At its best, sex is a meaningful way to connect with another person, to share affection and love. It can be a way to make up or let loose; it can be thrilling or touching, intense or mellow. Bad sex can be the result of boredom, stress, or a mismatch of sexual needs.

The more women learn about their own sexuality, the more important it becomes for them to achieve satisfaction. And it's time for every woman to learn exactly what her pleasure is all about, starting here.

The Basics of Self-Stimulation

They say that your body is your temple. All too often, an important part of women's bodies remains unfamiliar to them: their genitals. Whether out of fear, shyness, or simply not getting around to it, many women have never learned about the sexual parts of their bodies outside of intimacy with a partner. It's often the case that a man is more familiar with a woman's sexual anatomy than she is! Women *really* need to get to know their genitals, especially if they want good sex.

Knowing what structures are where and how they work is a prerequisite. I am talking about a basic understanding of your sexual anatomy. Each part plays a unique role in the female sexual response. The more you understand, the more you can use the information to your advantage during sex, and also to understand when there may be a problem.

What's the best way to begin this process of discovery? Masturbation. There, I said it. Now that I've gotten it out of the way, I'll admit it's not the easiest thing to talk about. But in my business, masturbation is one of the most important ways to cure what ails you sexually. Learning about your anatomy, looking at your genitals and discovering the *how, what, why,* and *where* of pleasure will change any woman's sexual reality. Plus, it's probably the cheapest, easiest method of treatment I can think of, and it's delivered by someone who cares about you!

Every woman benefits by exploring her body and discovering what she likes. Learning about what feels good and what doesn't establishes a pleasure baseline to work from during partner sex. It puts the focus back on you, whether you want to reconnect with yourself, overcome sexual trouble with your partner, or simply add a new dimension to your sexual awareness. Self-stimulation is the starting point for any woman.

Vibrators are a valuable part of self-stimulation. However, it is most important first to get in touch with your body using two things: your fingers and a mirror. Any woman looking to change herself sexually must become familiar with the tools of her trade. Learning about your anatomy is the absolute first step. The vibrators come later (both for you and in this book).

Masturbation is a natural form of self-exploration. It has a place for the single and the married, the old and the young, and almost everybody does it. A recent study by the Berman Center, which you'll learn more about in Chapter 2, found that 61 percent of women reported that they had masturbated. Other studies have reported similar numbers.

Self-stimulation provides outstanding sexual benefits, to women in particular. By learning how to please yourself, sexual enjoyment increases. It also primes you to show your partner what works, which leads to better sex for both of you. In fact, once you become comfortable, masturbating in front of your partner is an excellent way to turn up the intensity and deepen your intimacy. It gives your partner a window into what brings you pleasure, increasing his confidence and your chances of enjoying sex. So with no further ado, the road to sexual satisfaction begins here.

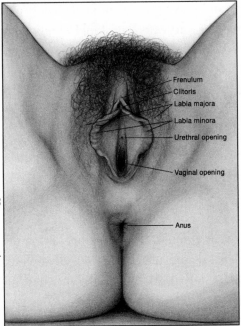

Frenulum
Clitoris
Labia majora
Labia minora
Urethral opening
Vaginal opening
Anus

©2005 Dawn Danby and Paul Waggoner

Fig. 1. Female Sexual Anatomy

Taking a Look

All women need to understand their anatomy. Even if you have been having sex for thirty years, you may be surprised to learn that you do not know everything you should, especially if you have never seen your genitals. I understand that some women might be squeamish about taking a good look at their genitals in a mirror, but it really is the best way to know exactly what they look like and, more important, how they work. Think of it as looking at things from your partner's perspective, which is exactly what you will teach *him* to do later. The female genitalia are illustrated in Figure 1.

Set aside a time when you will either be at home alone, or in a room or area that you feel confident is private. Though it may sound silly to arrange to explore your genitals, it really is no different from organizing intimate time with your partner. It is the first step in rediscovering your sexuality and the foundation for better sex with your partner. Women who know how to please themselves are more responsive in bed, since they know what they want. They are also better equipped to provide guidance to their partners.

So, you get yourself a mirror. This can be a handheld mirror, or you can sit on a towel or blanket in front of a floor-length mirror. Either way, make sure you are comfortable. The next step is to get a decent view by opening your legs.

Again, think about looking at things from your partner's perspective. Once you are in position, take one or two of your fingers and feel the outside of your genital area. Press your palm to your pubic bone and move it around. Sometimes simply rubbing the outside of the vulva can bring a woman to orgasm. But we are still exploring your anatomy, so don't do that just yet!

Next, take your fingers and feel underneath, exploring the difference between the labia majora and labia minora. Notice the difference in sensation and texture, as well as the color, shape, and size. Spread your labia majora and you'll find the clitoris under the frenulum, or little hood of skin. Frenula come in all different sizes and shapes, but its main purpose is to act almost as a foreskin, intended to protect the clitoris. Some women enjoy direct clitoral stimulation by pulling this foreskin back. For others it is too intense and more indirect stimulation is preferred. The urethra is just below the clitoris and similarly can be a source of pleasure for some women, while not for others. So explore the area and experiment with different kinds of touch to see what works for you.

Below the urethra is the opening to your vagina. The vagina is just one part of a woman's sexual anatomy, *not* the entire package. Women are mistakenly taught that the vagina means their genitals. In reality, the vulva is the correct term for describing your external sexual anatomy, minus the breasts. The vulva consists of the labia, clitoris, and all other genital structures, including the vagina. So now that we've cleared that up, massage the area around the opening of the vagina, noting any pleasurable sensations. Believe it or not, the vagina really doesn't have much sensation except on the outer third, or entrance, which is rich in nerve endings and where you'll find your G-spot.

Yes, the famous G-spot. Does it really exist you ask? Of course! It just takes some work and skill to find it. The easiest way to

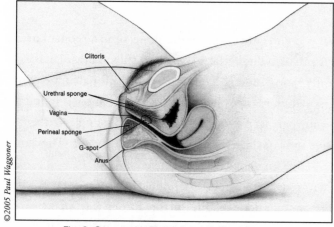

Fig. 2. G-spot with Perineal and Urethral Sponges

©2005 Paul Waggoner

locate your G-spot is by leaning or lying back, while you insert a finger into your vagina (see Figure 2). Your finger should be shaped in a hook, almost like you are gesturing someone to come closer. If you feel around about one or two inches in from the top of the vagina, you should find a spongy bump that feels different from the rest of the vaginal tissue. Many women say it feels almost like touching the tip of your nose. Some women may feel the urge to urinate when the G-spot is stimulated, but this feeling usually passes. Keep moving your finger around the inside of your vagina to get a better sense of its structure and texture. Feel the warmth and moisture, and the soft ridges in the skin.

The vagina, like the clitoris and labia, changes with sexual arousal. Note the color and shape of your vulva as you explore your genitals. Every woman's vulva has a different shape. Like breasts, a woman's labia are often two different sizes. During arousal, the labia majora become flatter and thinner, and raise upward and outward. The labia minora increase in size and may protrude above the labia majora. The clitoris becomes swollen. And the inner two-thirds of the vagina lengthens and becomes engorged.

At the top of the vagina and the bottom of the uterus is the cervix—another area of your sexual anatomy that is rich in nerves and arteries. Some women enjoy cervical stimulation during intercourse or self-pleasuring, while others find it uncomfortable or even painful. If you are feeling particularly explorative and adventurous, there are some great at-home tools that allow you to explore your internal anatomy and actually see your cervix. One is called the *Pleasure Periscope* from California Exotic Novelties. Like a regular periscope, it uses light and a series of mirrors to allow you to see inside your vagina. It also doubles as a vibrator, which can be useful for understanding changes to the vagina during arousal.

Once you feel you have a good enough understanding of your anatomy, it is time to get comfortable and continue stimulating any areas that feel pleasurable. You may need to do something to get you in the mood. Some effective ways to do that include fantasizing—about your partner, the mailman, or Brad Pitt, whatever it takes—popping in a sexy video, or taking a bath. The idea is to let your mind wander toward whatever arouses you. There is nothing wrong with getting turned on by something other than your partner. After all, it's fantasy, not reality!

Good masturbation usually begins with unlearning old techniques and

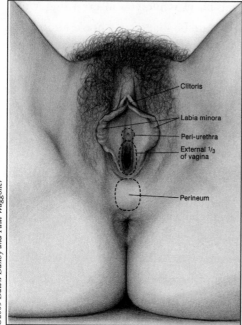

©2005 Dawn Danby and Paul Waggoner

Clitoris

Labia minora

Peri-urethra

External ⅓
of vagina

Perineum

Fig. 3. Hot Spots for Self-stimulation

learning new ones. Like partner sex, it's all about the right technique and the right mind-set. Many women start off slow and warm up by caressing other parts of their body—the breasts, thighs, abdomen, and buttocks can all be erogenous areas. Try massaging different areas of your body while closing your eyes and fantasizing. Don't worry if you feel stilted in the fantasy department; you can learn all about it in Chapter 4. Just lie back and focus on quieting your mind of any worries and enjoying the sensations. This is all about finding your pleasure spots and what works for you. It's a process of exploration.

Return to touching your genitals. Check out Figure 3 for some potential hot spots. As I said, rubbing the outside of the vulva can be very pleasurable, as can direct contact with the clitoris, labia, or vagina. Cup your palm over your pubic bone and rhythmically apply pressure. This is a great way to stimulate the clitoris gently and ease your way into arousal. It's similar to making out with your lover before the clothes come off! Move your hand around until you start to feel ready to go further. Next, take two fingers and gently stroke the inside of your labia majora. If you need some lubrication, add a little lubricant or wet your fingers with some saliva. Rub the clitoris, either indirectly or directly, depending on what you like. Experiment with different kinds of touching until you begin to feel aroused. Try using your fingertips or the entire length of your fingers. Move your pelvis whichever way feels most natural, close your eyes, and keep your fantasy going.

Start massaging the opening of the vagina, which is full of nerve endings, in a circular motion. If you want to, insert a finger into your vagina to stimulate yourself internally. You can rub against the G-spot, or use several fingers to mimic intercourse. If you like internal stimulation, keep doing it while you stimulate your clitoris with either your palm or your other hand. If external stimulation feels best, stick with that.

You can also get creative with a pillow or showerhead to see how that feels. Rubbing against a pillow, while lying on either your back or stomach, is an excellent way to stimulate the entire vulva. Experimenting with a handheld showerhead doesn't just feel great, but also gets you into the bathtub, which is relaxing and always a good thing for sexual satisfaction. Try adding some lavender bath oil and lighting a few candles to enhance the atmosphere.

The point is to experiment and discover what feels good. Don't focus on having an orgasm. It will happen once you figure out what you like and keep practicing it. By focusing on what feels pleasurable, along with relaxing and breathing, you allow yourself to discover new sensations. This naturally changes the quality of your sexual experience. You can introduce a vibrator to increase your pleasure, as well as your chances of having an orgasm, which is coming up in the next chapter. Some lubrication can also help, and there are many options out there that make self-stimulation easier and more pleasurable (for a discussion of lubricants, see pages 28 and 29 in the next chapter).

What Turns Women On

Is it hot in here, or is it just me? You've begun exploring some ways to make sex good—whether again or for the first time. Now it's time to understand what happens to make it all possible. When a woman gets turned on, there is a distinct set of physical changes that occurs. Physiologically, the body goes on quite a journey during sex. Knowing what to expect is essential. Understanding what happens to set the stage for arousal is equally important and, in that case, the mind plays the leading role.

Masters and Johnson were the first to put the living, breathing act of sex onto paper, and that didn't happen until 1966. Their observation of hundreds of people having sex in a controlled laboratory setting led to the development of the first human sexual response model. Coming on the heels of the Kinsey Report more than a decade earlier, which reported on the sexual habits of Americans for the first time, Masters and Johnson created quite a stir with their scientific approach to sex. Their model allowed us to understand for the first time exactly what goes on when men and women have sex, beyond reproduction. Though certainly modified since, the four-stage sexual response model still holds true in many ways today. So what *does* a woman having good sex look like physiologically? Here's what you can expect to feel:

❑ **Excitement:** You may notice your heart rate and breathing become more rapid, and body temperature beginning to rise. Your breasts may actually increase in size and your nipples will likely become erect. You may not notice this unless you are having intercourse or engaging in manual stimulation, but during the excitement phase, the walls of your vagina swell and produce lubrication. Your clitoris will become swollen and the inner two-thirds of the vagina lengthen. A warm, tingling sensation can often be felt throughout the genitals.

❑ **Plateau:** You feel continued increases in heart rate, muscle tension, and vaginal swelling and lubrication. In addition to tingling, there may be a feeling of fullness, even throbbing in your entire genital area. The clitoris withdraws slightly and the pubococcygeal, or pc, muscle tightens to narrow the opening of the vagina, creating what Masters and Johnson first coined the orgasmic platform. A flush on your face, chest, or breasts often appears.

❑ **Climax:** You reach the peak of sexual excitement. Intense feelings of pleasure are ushered in, along with synchronized vaginal, anal, and uterine muscle contractions, and a loss of voluntary muscle control.

❑ **Resolution:** Your heart rate, breathing, and body temperature all return to their pre-sex state. Blood flows away from the vagina and your breasts and nipples return to their normal size. Some women go back and forth between the Climax and Resolution stages several times during sexual activity, known as being multiorgasmic.

The Masters and Johnson model was applied to both men and women. It seems logical enough—you get excited sexually, keep it going for a little while, have an orgasm, and then come down from it all, right? Unfortunately, there was something missing from the model that had done so much to open the doors on American men's and women's bedrooms. And it was something that *really* mattered for women: desire.

Dr. Helen Singer Kaplan, a famous sex therapist, was the first to point out that a woman's mind plays as much of a role in her sexual response as her body. She changed our understanding of the female sexual response to include desire as the real prelude to sexual activity. Though Masters and Johnson provided us with a physiological snapshot of arousal and orgasm, it was not the complete picture. Desire is *always* the doorway to a woman's sexual response. As you set out to discover the new sexual you, you will learn everything you need to know about finding the keys to unlock it.

Every Woman's Anatomy Lesson

If you doodled in your notebook during health class, you may have missed out on some of the important sexual anatomy lessons. Even if you were paying attention, the education you received was probably average at best! Unfortunately, sex education is a flash in the pan for most of us. The information about women's genitals especially leaves a lot to be desired. So in addition to getting in touch with yourself literally, take a minute to brush up on your sexual anatomy basics.

Vulva: This describes the entirety of a woman's external sex organs, not including the breasts. Contrary to popular belief, it is not correct to call a woman's genitals her vagina. The vagina (see page 17) is merely one part of a woman's sexual anatomy. The vulva is all of it. The vulva is normally covered with pubic hair, which varies greatly from woman to woman. Some have a light patch of hair, while others have an abundance that continues onto the upper thighs. Grooming choices also affect the vulva's appearance, which you will learn all about in Chapter 7.

Mons Pubis: The soft mound of flesh that sits directly on the pubic bone and is usually covered by pubic hair. If you think of a woman's sexual anatomy as having a V-shape, it lies near the bottom of the V, just above where the thighs come together. The mons pubis has numerous nerve endings, so rubbing or applying pressure can be highly sexually arousing—an often overlooked fact.

Labia: Women have two sets of labia, or lips as they are also called. The labia majora are on the outside and the labia minora are on the inside. The labia majora are larger and often covered with hair. The labia minora are smaller and completely free of hair. Some women's labia minora are completely covered by the labia majora until they are spread apart. For other women, the labia minora protrude in a variety of shapes and sizes. It is totally normal for every woman's labia to look different. Like other parts of the body, the labia vary in size, color, and shape from one woman to the next.

Both sets of labia have all sorts of nerve endings that feel very pleasurable when touched or rubbed. During sexual arousal, the labia become engorged with blood, causing them to expand in size and darken in color. The labia minora tend to open up, making for easier access to the vagina. Since they are attached to the hood of the clitoris, stimulating the labia minora during sexual activity is a great way to stimulate the clitoris indirectly. This can be done either with fingers or the base of the penis during intercourse.

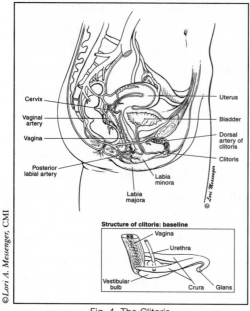

Fig. 4. The Clitoris

©Lori A. Messenger, CMI

Clitoris: Ah, the clitoris! If there is any part of a woman's sexual anatomy that is sure to bring her pleasure, the clitoris is it. Many of you have probably already figured this out. The clitoris is actually a much larger structure than you might think, though most of it is internal. The external part can be found where the labia minora meet. The lips join to form a soft fold of skin, or clitoral hood. Underneath the hood you will find the clitoral glans, which looks like a pea-sized knob of flesh. When most people think of the clitoris, they think of the glans. You can see the entire structure of the clitoris in Figure 4.

Helen O'Connell, an Australian urologist, discovered in 1998 that the clitoris has an entirely different structure than previously thought. Yes, not until 1998. Dr. O'Connell found that the glans is connected internally to a shaft of erectile tissue about two to four centimeters long. Attached to the shaft are two clitoral legs, or crura. These legs measure nine to eleven centimeters long and spread backward into the pelvic region. Two more bundles of erectile tissue, the clitoral bulbs, extend down the sides of the area around the vagina. They are connected back to the glans of the clitoris. All together, the structures of the clitoris add up to approximately four inches in length. Interestingly, the average nonerect penis is around the same length. In fact, the crura and glans are made up of the exact same erectile tissue as the penis.

Stimulation of the clitoris often brings women to powerful orgasms. Pay attention to it and your entire genital area will benefit. During sexual arousal, all of the clitoral structures fill with blood and increase in size, creating pressure that intensifies arousal in the entire genital region. The glans expands and becomes firm. As a woman becomes more aroused, the glans will often disappear behind the clitoral hood and usually briefly reappears just before orgasm. If it does disappear, it's for a reason, and it usually works best if you and your partner don't try to find it. Too much stimulation can be uncomfortable, which is the exact opposite of what you're going for. The legs and bulbs of the clitoris also fill with blood. Since they wrap around the vagina, they contribute to an even greater feeling of fullness in that area. The bottom line is that a well-stimulated clitoris helps all other parts of the female genitals function at their peak during sex.

Vagina: The term vagina has been so widely misused that most women are surprised when they learn it refers only to the canal that accommodates a penis and delivers a baby. The opening of the vagina is external; the rest of it is internal. The vagina is shaped like a banana and tilts upward toward the small of your back. It usually measures between five and seven inches long, though it expands during arousal and childbirth (thankfully!).

The walls of the vagina touch lightly in its normal state. The walls contain a series of folds, which allow the vagina to swell and expand. The first third of the vagina has many folds. The area is also rich in nerve endings, which makes it a pleasurable spot to stimulate. The back two-thirds has fewer folds and is not as sensitive to touch, but may respond to pressure. During arousal, the back portion of the vagina often expands and lengthens, while the opening tightens to better grab on to a penis.

When sexually aroused, the increased blood flow to the vagina and swelling of the vaginal walls cause tiny droplets of plasma to appear that combine together to create lubrication—a process called transudation. The degree of wetness a woman feels depends on a number of factors. Some women simply lubricate more than others as a rule. Wetness can also be related to how turned-on a woman is, while other times it has no tie to arousal and is just based on individual or situational differences. Certain medications, menopause, and childbirth can all inhibit lubrication (in Chapters 2 and 3 you will learn about the many options for treating vaginal dryness). Women who want to be more lubricated should try a water- or silicone-based lubricant. Always remember to test for allergies first.

The vagina also contains two sponges—one on the top and one on the bottom—which can be sensitive to touch and pressure. You can see these by flipping back to Figure 2 on page 10. The top sponge is the well-known G-spot, which is technically the urethral sponge.

The bottom and less well-known sponge is the perineal sponge. The perineum is the area between your vaginal opening and your anus, as described next. The perineal sponge is located on the floor of the vagina, and a good way to locate it is by pushing down after you've inserted a finger into the vagina while lying on your back. This area is rich in blood vessels. During sexual arousal, the perineal sponge becomes engorged and highly sensitive. It is another area that can feel extremely satisfying to stimulate, with either touch or pressure.

The sensitivity of many structures in the first third of the vagina helps explain why penis diameter, or width, matters more than length. When a penis stimulates the front-most vaginal walls, and urethral and perineal sponges, a sensitive area of your sexual anatomy is given attention. Since friction from the penis is also thought to tug on the labia and indirectly stimulate the clitoris, you can see that size matters—just in a completely different way from what you may have thought! If your partner has a slimmer penis, you can help increase friction by tightening your pelvic floor muscles. Squeezing and releasing while your partner penetrates heightens arousal for both of you. In Chapter 6, you will learn all about the pelvic floor, and how to make the most of it for your sexual health *and* satisfaction.

Perineum: The smooth area of skin located below the vaginal opening and above the anus. The perineum is rich in nerve endings, which, again, can make it an enjoyable part of sexual activity. Sometimes the perineum is cut or naturally tears during childbirth to accommodate passage of a baby through the vagina.

Cervix: The fleshy button-like structure that joins the top of the vagina with the uterus. A tiny hole in the center of the cervix allows sperm to pass into the uterus and blood and other fluids to pass out of it. During childbirth, the cervix expands up to ten centimeters wide to allow a baby to pass through. Normally, however, the opening is quite small. The cervical opening is covered by mucus that prevents bacteria from entering the uterus. The mucus plug dissolves and moves through the vagina during ovulation. Many women will notice that their discharge becomes heavier around this time. The cervix may also feel soft in the days leading up to ovulation and hard afterward. This makes sense since a mushier cervix will increase the chances of sperm reaching an egg by allowing more of it to pass through.

The cervix changes position naturally. It depends on where a woman is in her menstrual cycle and also happens naturally during sexual arousal. Since the vagina lengthens in response to arousal, the cervix often moves further back in the body. Depending on the size of your partner's penis, deep penetration is usually necessary if you want to stimulate it during intercourse.

Uterus: The hollow, pear-shaped organ that is also known as the womb. The uterus measures about three inches long and two inches wide and sits behind the bladder. Each month, the walls of the uterus line with endometrium in anticipation of a fertilized egg. If pregnancy does not occur, the lining is shed in the monthly menstrual cycle as a period.

Like the vagina, the walls of the uterus gently touch in its resting state. During pregnancy, the uterine walls are pushed apart by a growing fetus to many times its original size. The walls of the uterus are made of some of the strongest muscles in the body. It is these muscles that open the cervix during childbirth and push a baby through the vaginal canal. The uterus returns to its original size after pregnancy.

The uterus is another part of the sexual anatomy that becomes engorged when a woman is aroused. During orgasm, the uterus involuntarily contracts along with the vagina and anus. Some women who have had a hysterectomy experience a different quality orgasm due, in part, to the lack of uterine contractions; however, many factors contribute to changes in orgasm after a hysterectomy.

Ovaries: The ovaries are about the size of almonds, located on either side of the uterus. They are the primary source of the female hormones estrogen and progesterone, as well as testosterone, all of which play a central role in sexual desire. The ovaries also contain a woman's eggs. A woman is born with all of her eggs—about one million—which degenerate over the course of her life.

At the time of her first period, a woman has about 400,000 eggs left. Each egg is contained inside a follicle. When a woman ovulates, one follicle matures sufficiently for the ovary to release an egg. The egg is released into the pelvic cavity and drawn into the uterus by the fallopian tubes.

Fallopian Tubes: The literal "egg tubes" extend about four or five inches from each side of the uterus. They curve back toward the ovaries. The inside of the tubes is covered with cilia and the ends flare out with tentacles, called fimbria. When an egg is released from the ovary, the fimbria gently sweep it into the fallopian tube. Wavelike contractions of the tube's muscles and movements of the cilia propel the egg toward the uterus. This usually occurs between days fourteen and seventeen of a woman's menstrual cycle. If the egg is fertilized by a sperm, it implants itself in the lining of the uterus in hopes of developing into a fetus.

Eggs that are not fertilized disintegrate and pass during menstruation.

THERE IT IS. GOOD SEX is on the horizon. In the chapters that follow, you will learn everything you need to know to jump-start your sex life or discover new ways to improve it. Every woman, no matter what age, relationship status, or sexual wish she has, will find her way there in the pages to come. Sexual satisfaction is on the way. It's time to make room for it—in your life and in your relationships.

Good sex gives us something to look forward to in the daily grind of our lives. It matters for our minds, our bodies, and our relationships. By carving out a space for it when life seems overwhelming, we make sexual pleasure a priority again. Sometimes, women simply need to learn that it's okay to put themselves first. The bedroom is a great place to start.

PRESCRIPTIONS FOR THE WEEK:
Week 1

✓ Bring your anatomy lesson to life. Get in front of a mirror and identify all of the parts that are in Figure 1. Notice how your genitals are similar to and different from the picture; note the shape, size, and color of your labia.

✓ Try masturbating at least once. Don't make the goal orgasm, but rather an exploration of your body to learn more about what feels good. Go through the exercises explained in detail in this chapter. Touch, rub, and stimulate your genitals in any way that feels good and pleasurable. Remember, this is not a destination—it is a journey!

✓ Try a new technique when you are self-stimulating. . . . Maybe it's using a pillow or exploring the perineal sponge area or the G-spot for the first time.

GUY'S GUIDE:
A Summary of Key Points for the Man in Your Life

1. The clitoris is the key to most women's sexual arousal and orgasm. It's located where the labia minora (her inner vaginal lips) meet. See Figure 1 on page 9. The lips join to form a soft fold of skin or clitoral hood. Underneath you will find the clitoral glans, which is shaped like a pea. When most people think of the clitoris they think of the glans. In reality, the clitoris extends all the way back into a woman's pelvis. When aroused, it primes the rest of her sexual anatomy for sex. This is where your focus should be when trying to arouse your partner to orgasm. Keep in mind: The clitoris retracts when it becomes too aroused, so move to another spot when this happens.

2. Believe it or not, a woman's vagina doesn't really have much sensation, except for the first third, which is rich in nerve endings. This is also where you'll find the G-spot. Yes, it really does exist! The easiest way to find the G-spot is by gently inserting a finger into your partner's vagina and curving it forward, almost like you are gesturing someone to come closer. If you feel around about one or two inches in from the top (toward her belly button), you should find a spongy bump that feels different from the rest of the vaginal tissue. Many women say it feels almost like touching the tip of your nose.

3. Masturbation can be an exciting part of your and your partner's sex life. Encourage her to explore her own body first, learning about her anatomy and what pleases her. Then she can teach it to you! Just give her the space and time she needs to learn on her own first.

4. As you might already know, every woman's genitals look different. Some women's inner lips are completely covered by the outer lips until spread apart. Other women's inner labia protrude naturally. Both sets of labia can have a variety of shapes and sizes. They also vary in size, color, and shape from one woman to the next. Make sure you are up to speed on your partner's sexual anatomy (see Figure 1).

5. Stimulation of the clitoris during intercourse often brings women to powerful orgasms. Later, you will learn about positions and techniques that make sure you are working it—often the clitoris is not naturally stimulated during intercourse.

CHAPTER TWO

The Wonderful World of Vibrators

■░░░░■

Now that you've begun exploring your body, it's time to turn it up a notch, so to speak, and learn about the many benefits of sex toys. Not just for fun, vibrators offer a real boost to your sex life. Improved sexual response—whether going it solo or with a partner—increased novelty, and a whole new world of pleasurable sensations await you with the flip of a switch! Sex toys serve a valuable purpose for every woman, in every situation.

And in case you're reluctant, I don't simply think these things—I know them. To help address some of the taboos associated with sex toys, I conducted a study of nearly 2,000 women ages eighteen to sixty on vibrator use and perceptions. The findings might surprise you. Even you seasoned vibrator users might learn a thing or two.

The Truth About Vibrators

Like masturbation in general, vibrators offer women an easier way to orgasm. However, neither can replace the intimacy of sex between two people. Both vibrators and masturbation put women's sexual pleasure in their own hands, ahem, and also work to enhance sex with a partner. A woman can use a vibrator alone to explore what feels good and learn more about her body. She can also incorporate a vibrator into her relationship to help with foreplay and reaching orgasm or to add some novelty to sex with her partner.

Myths like women becoming addicted to vibrators or men leaving because of them have permeated our thinking and left us conflicted. I say conflicted because I think that most women are curious about sex toys in general but are not exactly clear on how to use them and feel as if they have to keep it a secret if they do. Similarly, I think many men enjoy the thought of a using a sex toy with their partners but may not want to admit it at the risk of appearing inadequate to other men *and* women.

Sex toys have an interesting past but probably not in the way you would expect. Originally developed in the 1880s to treat hysteria, vibrators were not considered sexual devices until the 1920s when they began appearing in the first erotic films. The condition known as hysteria had been around for more than 2,000 years and was not officially removed from the medical diagnostic literature until 1952. Hysteria was thought to result from a disturbance of the uterus. It included a vague mix of symptoms such as excited emotions, unusual sensations, and even sexual fantasy! Not surprisingly, the commonly prescribed treatment was massage of the female genitalia to produce paroxysm, which is defined as a spasm or convulsion. Until the 1880s, physicians used their fingers to bring female patients to paroxysm. The vibrator was invented to help speed along the process and relieve the physicians' tired hands.

Since the use of female genital massage with or without a device did not involve penetration, it was not seen as sexual. Only when vibrators began appearing in erotic films in the 1920s did the medical establishment finally realize, or acknowledge, that paroxysm was in fact orgasm. The failure to recognize this earlier illustrates the male-focused ideas about sex that dominated throughout history. Since penetration by a penis was the only way a "normal" woman could have an orgasm, stimulating the external genitalia was considered medical, like treating any other body part. We now know that between 50 and 70 percent of women do not reach orgasm from penetration alone; for most, some type of clitoral stimulation is necessary. Though hysteria was far from a legitimate disorder, it's no surprise that the treatment of women's symptoms with massage and vibrators made them feel better!

Once vibrators were discovered to bring women sexual pleasure, they were swiftly removed from doctors' offices and went underground. It was not until the 1960s that vibrators were openly marketed to women as sex aids. It's taken a long time, but today with the advent of the Internet and female-friendly erotica shops, purchasing a vibrator is considered almost acceptable. *Almost.*

Vibrators Are Good for You

I wanted to understand more about women's feelings toward sex aids, in particular their responses to popular myths, and also the connection between vibrators and women's sexual satisfaction. To help find the truth about vibrators, the Berman Center carried out a study on a random sample of nearly 2,000 women ages eighteen to sixty. We discovered who uses sexual devices, how they use them, where they get them, what their partners think of them, and, most important, what women think of them—both good and bad. The findings may surprise you.

The best news is that there are plenty of women taking their sexual pleasure into their own hands. In our study, nearly half of women ages eighteen to sixty reported using a vibrator. We found that 29 percent were currently using a vibrator, while another 15 percent had used one in the past. Women ages twenty-five to thirty-four were the most likely to have vibrator experience, at 51 percent. Debunking one of the leading vibrator myths, we found that single women are *not* the ones who use vibrators the most. Nearly 60 percent of women in relationships reported past or present vibrator use versus slighty more than 30 percent of single women.

We found that all women with vibrator experience reported higher levels of sexual desire, more arousal, and easier orgasms. These women also reported higher levels of sexual satisfaction, and, not surprisingly, higher quality of life in general. The bottom line: The use of vibrators is associated with a more sexually satisfied and happier woman.

Among women in relationships, almost two-thirds indicated that their partners were supportive of their vibrator use. In fact, we found that almost half of the women used vibrators with their partners, in addition to using them alone. Not to mention that 4 percent of the men borrowed their partners' vibrators! This demonstrates that men are not intimidated by women using vibrators and may actually enjoy it. It also supports the idea that vibrators have as much a place for couples as they do for singles. Vibrators not only enhance arousal with higher quality, longer foreplay, but also work to provide clitoral stimulation to women during sex. Many women who cannot orgasm during intercourse find that if they stimulate their clitoris with a vibrator while having sex, they do achieve orgasm. Vibrators serve yet another purpose for couples by allowing them to explore sex without penetration. This is useful for couples who have decided to start from scratch to rediscover their sexual connection or for couples dealing with sexual dysfunction.

And how about the notion that a woman will prefer a vibrator to her partner? On the whole, women disagreed with the idea that a vibrator can replace a partner. Women with vibrator experience also reported that they were not addicted to their vibrators and that vibrator use was not the only way for them to have orgasms. Vibrators did not negatively affect their sexual sensation. The women we surveyed considered vibrators to be a complement to their sex lives, not the main event, and definitely not harmful.

As mentioned, we also found that women who were more sexually satisfied reported a higher quality of life. They reported higher levels of happiness, a stronger feeling of purpose, and lower levels of stress. What more could you ask for?

Vibrator and Sex Toy Guide

Now that I've told you about all of the positive ways vibrators can change your life, you may be wondering how to get one and which kind you should get. Purchasing your first vibrator can be intimidating. Many women are unsure of what to buy, where to get it, and how to use it when they get home.

Fortunately, the purchase of vibrators and other sexual aids has become increasingly female-friendly with the Internet and more inviting erotica shops. The difference this trend has made cannot be overestimated. Gone are the days when you had to venture to an intimidating store with blacked-out windows in an unfamiliar part of town to purchase a sexual device. Stores across the country, such as *Eve's Garden* in New York City, *Good Vibrations* in San Francisco, *Toys in Babeland* in Seattle and New York City, *Grand Opening* in Brookline, Massachusetts, and *G Boutique* in Chicago have redefined the erotica shopping experience. The stores are attractive, well-lit, and cater with their product lines to women. They carry everything from trendy lingerie to vibrators and videos to how-to guides. The women who work at the stores are great resources if you are not familiar with vibrators and other types of sexual aids. They can answer questions and provide recommendations based on what you want and lead you in the right direction even if you don't know what you want. If you feel more comfortable ordering online, there are a variety of great Web sites to start exploring and learning and also to order confidentially. The Internet is ideal for privacy when it comes to shopping for sex aids. Check out our Resource Guide at the end of this book for some store and Web site recommendations.

And don't forget about sex toy parties—the new version of the Tupperware party in which a bona fide sex toy expert visits you and your friends in the comfort of your own living room to tell you all about sex toys. These parties are cropping up everywhere and are a great opportunity to learn more about sexual devices in a comfortable setting. Some good ones include Passion Parties, Pure Romance, and Safina Sex-Ed Salons. Check out their Web sites. The women who run the parties are great sources of information. They also have products on the spot, so you can place an order and go home with your new toy that very night!

Remember, sex toys serve a real purpose in making sex better. Whether you plan to use your vibrator alone or with a partner, they offer endless possibilities for exploration and pleasure. Vibrators are also great to take on vacation, since getting away from everyday stress can leave you feeling more romantic and relaxed.

And don't forget the lubricant, which is always a rule of thumb for vibrator and sex toy use. In addition to making things feel more slippery and sensual, lubricants also remedy vaginal dryness. Many factors can cause vaginal dryness, from recent childbirth or menopause to certain prescription and over-the-counter medications. Lack of lubrication is a common source of sexual frustration and there are many options for solving it, which we will discuss in the next chapter. For now, lubricants are your best bet if you are just starting to explore sex toys.

There are three main groups of lubricants: water-based, silicone-based, and oil-based. It is important to choose carefully. Certain lubricants can interfere with latex contraceptives, like condoms, diaphragms, and sponges, while others are not suited for use with certain sex toys. All lubricants carry the risk of potential irritation. They should be tested on a small area of the inner labia before they are used with either a partner or a vibrator. If a burning sensation or topical irritation develops, wash the area with mild soap and water and try another kind once the irritation is gone.

Water-based lubricants are considered to be all-purpose. They are formulated to be nonirritating and safe for use with latex products and sex toys. Some water-based lubricants contain glycerin, which can cause yeast infections in women who are prone to them. In this case a glycerin-free lubricant should be used. Good options include K-Y Ultra Gel, which also comes in a "warming" version, or Liquid Silk. A common disadvantage of water-based lubricants is that they dry up easily. Often, some water or saliva can reactivate the lubrication. A popular twist on water-based lubricants is flavored lubricants, which are edible and designed to be used anywhere on the body. But beware, they often contain sugar and glycerin, which can cause yeast infections.

Silicone-based lubricants are the new and improved lubricants. They stay wetter longer than the water-based formulas, but they cannot be used with silicone sex toys because of silicone-on-silicone reactions. They are still safe for use with condoms and other latex contraceptives, as well as sex toys not made of silicone. Some women are prone to irritation from silicone, so test an external area first. Silicone-based lubricants also tend to stain bedding and clothing more than the water-based formulas. Two excellent silicone-based lubricants to try are Pjur Woman Bodyglide and Überlube. Both have a slick texture that doubles as a sensual moisturizer.

Finally, the oil-based lubricants are the forebears of the water and silicone varieties of today. Examples of oil-based lubricants include Vaseline and vitamin E oil. Aside from being very messy and difficult to clean up, due to their thick texture, this group of lubricants is not considered safe for use with any latex products or rubber sex toys. Oil can break down latex, increasing the odds that a condom will break. Since oil-based lubricants have many alternative uses, for example as moisturizers or healing salves, their appeal is enhanced for some who are in monogamous relationships and don't use condoms or other latex contraceptives. Allergies to vitamin E oil are common, so be sure to test for sensitivity before trying it.

Now, it's time to talk vibrators. Whether you are just starting out or would like to learn more, the following are the most common types, including how and where (anatomically) to use them. Other sex aids, such as dildos, anal toys, and erotic novelty items, are also covered and I recommend my favorites for each.

Vibrators

Vibrators come in an endless array of shapes and sizes. Add to that the variety of attachments available and you may find yourself feeling like a kid in a candy store—overwhelmed and curious all at once. As I mentioned, visiting a female-friendly erotica shop is a great way to find someone who can guide you through the many choices. Web sites are another resource, since they allow you to spend as much time as you need learning about vibrators. The user reviews are also often helpful.

Many vibrators are colorful and whimsical, while others are simple and neutral. Some vibrators are intended to be used externally, but the vast majority can be used internally as well. Some are even curved at the end to stimulate the G-spot. Vibrators for strictly external use often have clever shapes like hearts or animals or more basic designs. Some are much larger and can do double duty as body massagers. Vibrators that are designed to be inserted come in the form of bullets, slender pens, and larger penis-like models. The bullets are usually made of plastic or metal, with silicone or rubber covers that add new texture and mix up the type of sensations you feel. Covered bullets can also be used to stimulate the shaft of a man's penis, the sensitive area at the base of it, or the perineum. This reminds me—I have found that most women I work with prefer their vibrators to be less realistic looking. I guess they want to leave that to the men in their lives!

Vibrators operate either on batteries or by plugging them into outlets. While battery-operated models can have shorter lifespans, they are more versatile since there are no cords or outlets to manage. Some battery-operated vibrators provide an additional bonus of being safe for use in water, though not all models are, so check the packaging.

There are five types of vibrators I typically recommend to my patients; all of them can be used to stimulate the clitoris, vulva, labia, and many other areas of the body. Two of them can be used for internal stimulation, as well. If you're not sure about where to use a vibrator on your sexual anatomy, the descriptions that follow are intended as a sort of pleasure map to tell you which ones work best where. You can flip back to the hot-spots diagram on page 12 for reference. Some of the vibrator recommendations feature additional suggestions from my own line of sexual aids and devices. The Berman Center Intimate Accessories Collection was developed in response to my work with thousands of women over the years. After hearing so much feedback about what works and what doesn't, I was inspired to create a line of woman-inspired, woman-designed sexual aids and devices. All of the Berman Center products feature pleasing, ergonomic designs, quiet operation, and discreet packaging, accompanied by full instructions. Other models are featured elsewhere in this book. For information on the complete line of Berman Center Intimate Accessories, consult the Resource Guide at the end of this book.

NATURAL CONTOURS Designed by adult-film star and producer Candida Royalle, these crescent-shaped plastic vibrators have a pleasing, abstract shape, which makes them a discreet choice. They are great starter vibrators for women with no vibrator experience. They come in three different sizes based on the different sizes of women's pelvises. Since they are ergonomically curved, a *Natural Contours* vibrator slips easily over the pubic bone and is cradled in a woman's palm, allowing her to adjust the placement and pressure. They can be used to stimulate the clitoris and vulva, as well as other parts of the body. Each one has three different settings that can be used to vary the level of stimulation.

The *Natural Contours* vibrating cuffs are available in three sizes: Petite, which measures 4" in length and tapers from 1.5" to 1" in width; Superbe, which measures 4.75" in length and tapers from 2.5" to 1.25" in width; and Magnifique, which is 8" long and provides a stronger throb than the other two models. Too little power is a common complaint about the *Natural Contours* smaller models.

PROS: Good starter vibrator. Pleasant look, not obviously a vibrator. Small and convenient for travel.

CONS: Low power in smaller models. Can become rattly over time.

THE POCKET ROCKET Probably the most well-known of all vibrators, the *Pocket Rocket* definitely packs a punch in a small package. It looks like a pocket flashlight at first glance, measuring about 4" long by 1" wide. With just one speed, the *Pocket Rocket* delivers more intense stimulation than the *Natural Contours* line. The smaller tip makes the stimulation more concentrated on one area, which has its good and bad points. It helps to deliver a more powerful sensation, but does not cover as much area as other vibrators. Like *Natural Contours,* the *Pocket Rocket* can be used to stimulate nearly any part of the body. Try using it to stimulate the nipples, inner thighs, and abdomen. It is also excellent for use during intercourse to help a woman reach orgasm. By placing the *Pocket Rocket* between her and her partner, a woman receives the clitoral stimulation that makes an orgasm more likely.

The top of the *Pocket Rocket* has three metal balls, which help transmit the vibrations. It can be used uncovered or with one of several silicone covers. These covers completely change the type of stimulation you feel, which makes them a great way to mix it up. One cover has silicone nubs on top. Another covers the entire vibrator so it can be inserted vaginally. The *Pocket Rocket* also comes in a waterproof version for use in the bath or shower.

PROS: Good starter vibrator. Small, strong, and great for travel. Perfect for use with a partner during intercourse for clitoral stimulation.

CONS: Smaller surface area can be too restricting sometimes.

BERMAN CENTER OPTIONS:

Athena Waterproof Mini-Massager. A quieter version that includes four soft, silicone attachments and is also safe for use in water.

Maia Discreet Mini-Massager. A subtle and quiet vibrator that is great for stimulation on the go. It looks like a lipstick container, which makes it perfect for traveling with or carrying in your purse. Multispeed control gives you a range of sensation and it's still small enough to fit between you and your partner during intercourse to provide added clitoral stimulation. Can also be used alone for external stimulation, as well as in and around the vaginal opening.

X-COMMANDER (ARTIFICIAL INTELLIGENCE) This vibrator is similar to the *Pocket Rocket* but has a remote with many more possible settings. It also has three interchangeable bullets that are attached by wire to the remote, so you can experiment with different sizes (lengths and widths varying from 1" to 2"). In all, there are ten different settings, which alternate between constant vibration, pulsating vibration, or both. Stimulation can be gentle or quite intense, depending on what you choose. Men love this model, since the remote allows them to experiment with different types of stimulation and see your reaction. Not to mention we all know how much men like to take charge of the remote control!

A silicone ring attachment (that you can purchase at most erotica shops) adds even more possibilities for experimentation. The unique attachment covers the bullet with two different textures. One side features nubs and the other is covered in flexible cilia for a completely different sensation. The real standout is the rubber loop connected to it. When the bullet is looped onto a man's penis it helps to stimulate a woman's clitoris during intercourse. The man will feel vibrations, too. Couples who use *X-Commander* this way need to be careful about hard thrusting. I usually recommend that they rock back and forth instead. A woman can also attach the bullet to her hand, by putting her fingers through the loop, and stroke the shaft of her partner's penis or her own clitoris and labia.

PROS: Very versatile with lots of settings. Good for partner participation. Adjustable stimulation.

CONS: Small surface area. May seem complicated for beginners.

BERMAN CENTER OPTION:

Aurora Remote-Control Vibrator. Ergonomically designed and features a coated, nonslip grip for easy holding. Includes a silicone cover for different texture and for use during intercourse with your partner.

THE MAGIC WAND Lovingly endorsed for many years by the grandmother of masturbation, Betty Dodson, the Hitachi *Magic Wand* is a big vibrator that does a big job. It is great for women who are just starting out since it leaves little room for error. It is also recommended for women who have trouble reaching orgasm, since it is usually quick and effective to that end. This vibrator delivers intense stimulation whether it is used on the clitoris, vulva, or any other part of the body. Because it is often sold as a general massager, the *Magic Wand* can be easier to find than other models and is available at many department and home stores.

Measuring 12" long and 2.5" wide, the *Magic Wand* covers a larger area than the other models and provides intense stimulation with two different speeds. Women who find the vibration to be too strong can place a towel or washcloth over the head to soften the sensation (this works for almost any type of vibrator). Since the *Magic Wand* plugs into the wall, there are no worries about losing power or replacing batteries.

PROS: Great for women just starting out or experienced users. Quick and effective at bringing on orgasm. No concerns about battery replacement.

CONS: Large size is less convenient. Shape is more sexual than other models.

ACCUVIBE The *AccuVibe* is nearly identical to the *Magic Wand*. Like it, the *AccuVibe* offers lots of power, two speeds, and can double as a general massager. Some women prefer the *AccuVibe's* more contoured head, though both serve a similar purpose.

PROS: Great for women just starting out or experienced users. Quick and effective at bringing on orgasm. No concerns about battery replacement.

CONS: Large size is less convenient. Shape is more sexual than other models.

BERMAN CENTER OPTION:

Aphrodite Infrared Rechargeable Massager. The massaging head is flexible, so it moves with you. Infrared technology at the tip provides a heating sensation, with different settings. Includes three attachments made of soft silicone—two flat attachments can be used for different external sensations, while a cone-shaped attachment allows you to stimulate the area just inside and around the vaginal opening.

Insertable Vibrators

Longer vibrators that are designed to be inserted are often made of metal, rubber, silicone, or a new thermal plastic that mimics real skin in both its texture and ability to respond to heat. They can measure anywhere from 4" to 7" in length and from 1.5" to 2" in width. Most have attachments for added stimulation and versatility. There are some that stimulate the clitoris and vagina simultaneously to provide women with the penetration they often want and the clitoral stimulation they need to reach orgasm.

Here are some of my favorite vibrators designed primarily for internal stimulation.

VENUS WATERPROOF G-SPOT STIMULATOR, BERMAN CENTER INTIMATE ACCESSORIES COLLECTION Waterproof, sleek, and quiet, this vibrator is made of smooth silicone with strategically placed ridges for pleasure. Its streamlined shape does not have a very obvious or threatening look. The rounded tip can be used for G-spot stimulation, as well as deeper internal stimulation. Variable speeds allow you to adjust the level of vibration during use. Measures 6¼" long and 1½" wide.

PROS: Good starter vibrator for internal use. Safe for use in water. Made of silicone, which is durable and easy to care for.

CONS: May not be powerful enough for some women.

ADONIS G-SPOT AND CLITORAL STIMULATOR, BERMAN CENTER INTIMATE ACCESSORIES COLLECTION Made of an incredible, supple silicone that bends for flexibility, this vibrator features dual stimulation—it internally stimulates the G-spot, while providing clitoral stimulation at the same time. Two sources of vibration give you ultimate sensation. Finger grooves make certain the vibrator stays where you want it to. Soft pleasure dots, which rub against the clitoris, are also featured.

Remote control allows you to choose from three levels of intensity and four kinds of vibration for a world of possibilities. Measures 5½" long and 1½" wide.

PROS: Powerful double vibration. Provides external and internal stimulation simultaneously. Made of silicone, which is durable and easy to care for.

CONS: May be overwhelming for starters.

THE FLAMINGO VIBE This is another streamlined vibrator with elegant curves and a pleasing design that does not look overtly phallic. The slightly flared middle adds to the sensation and a curved end allows you to stimulate the G-spot. *The Flamingo Vibe* is powered by an impressive motor for strong vibrations and a feeling of fullness during use. Measures 6½" long and 1¼" wide.

PROS: Lots of power. Waterproof design. Hard plastic material for easy care.

CONS: May be too intense for starters.

THE RABBIT PEARL *The Rabbit Pearl* is the multitasker of vibrators. When inserted, it stimulates the vagina and the clitoris at the same time for a true sensory experience. Tumbling plastic pearls rotate in the middle of the vibrator for added sensation against the vaginal walls, while two rabbit ears flutter against the clitoris. For women who need both kinds of stimulation, the *Rabbit Pearl* may be their best bet for reaching orgasm. Measures 5" long and 1½" wide.

PROS: Simultaneous clitoral and vaginal stimulation. Adds novelty for experienced users.

CONS: May be too complicated for starters. Vinyl is porous and more difficult to keep clean.

Dildos

Whereas many vibrators can be used externally or internally, dildos are designed to be inserted. Technically, dildos are non-vibrating, though some have vibrating options that can be added. Dildos are often preferred by women who want a different kind of stimulation or do not find vibrators effective. They provide a feeling of fullness and internal stimulation that many vibrators can't or don't.

Dildos are available in three different basic materials: rubber, silicone, and a new thermal plastic that mimics real skin in both its texture and ability to respond to heat. Though less common, dildos are also available in glass, Plexiglas, and Lucite. Dildos come in many different shapes and sizes, from realistic penis-inspired designs to more streamlined models. Like vibrators, there is a wide range of variation in both length and diameter. Typically, dildos range from 4" to 7" long and from ¾" to 2" in diameter. If you are just starting out, I suggest trying something in the smaller range and experimenting with how that feels.

Some dildos are curved or made of flexible material, which allows the woman to adjust where it stimulates her internally. Many are designed to work the G-spot, which, for some women, can bring about intense orgasms. Dildos without vibrating components are always safe for use in the bath or shower. Many dildos can be used with a harness for hands-free stimulation and creative partner play. Some recommended models to try include:

JANE DOE 1 Designed by a women-owned company, the *Jane Doe 1* is a soft, lightly rippled dildo perfect for women with little to no sex toy experience. Unlike many models, it does not replicate a penis and many find this to be less threatening as a starter toy. Measures 5" long and 1¼" wide.

PROS: Good starter dildo. Made of silicone, which is durable and easy to care for.

CONS: May not feel substantial enough for some women.

SILK This line offers sleek, nonrealistic dildos in three different sizes. The *Silk* line of dildos is known for their feeling of fullness and smooth silicone construction. All three models are slightly curved to hit the spot—wherever that may be. *Silk 1* measures 4½" long and ⅞" wide; *Silk 2* measures 5½" long and 1¼" wide; *Silk 3* measures 7" long and 1½" wide.

PROS: Substantial feel. Slightly curved for versatility of use. Made of silicone, which is durable and easy to care for.

CONS: May be too firm for some women.

PEARL JELLY For women who like a realistic shape, the *Pearl Jelly* mimics a real penis in both design and size. It has the firmness of silicone, but is made of a jelly-like rubber, which works for women who prefer silicone-based lubricants. Measures 6" long and 1⅝" wide.

PROS: Realistic shape. A nonsilicone option.

CONS: Made of rubber, which is more difficult to keep clean.

Anal Toys

Many women find stimulation of the anus to be very pleasurable. This can include the area around it, as well as internally. Anal plugs and beads enhance these sensations. They are also something that men can enjoy, since the anus's proximity to the prostate makes it a highly sensitive area.

Anal plugs work in a similar way to dildos and vibrators. There are vibrating and nonvibrating options available, and they are designed to be inserted or used for external stimulation. Since the anus does not naturally lubricate itself, a generous amount of lubricant is necessary with any anal device. The plugs are generally 4" or 5" long and taper in width from 2" to ¾", not including the base, which is flared to prevent them from slipping inside. Some plugs are smooth, while others have very textured ribbing.

Anal beads resemble a beaded necklace and are used to stimulate the anus internally, by inserting and then slowly pulling them out. They can be used in the vagina, too, but be sure to clean them beforehand to avoid transferring any bacteria. Try the following:

SLIM JANE PLUG A smooth, streamlined shape makes this the perfect choice for women who are curious but inexperienced in anal stimulation. The *Slim Jane* resembles a slender cone and is made of a jelly-like rubber. Measures 5¾" long and 1" wide, with an extra large base.

PROS: Good starter anal toy.

CONS: Made of rubber, which is more difficult to keep clean.

SEVERIN PLUG The *Severin Plug* offers a different kind of stimulation with its gently rippled design. Available in two different sizes, it offers added sensations with its unique shape. Both models are 4" long and either 1¼" or 1½" wide.

PROS: Made of silicone, which is durable and easy to care for.

CONS: Ridges may not be enjoyed by all women.

BUBBLE BEADS One of many options in anal beads, these seamless plastic beads are on a long strand with a ring at the end for slowly pulling them out. The beads are made of jelly-like rubber and range from ¼" to 1" in diameter for all sorts of sensations.

PROS: Whimsical and different.

CONS: Made of rubber, which is more difficult to keep clean.

All sex toys should be washed well each time they are used. This will keep them free of bacteria and in good condition for as long as possible. Battery-operated or other electrical devices should not be submerged in water; try wiping them down with an antibacterial solution followed by a damp washcloth. Waterproof toys can be washed with mild soap and water.

Getting Creative

When it comes to erotic novelty items, if you can dream it, chances are you can find it. The following list is a mere drop in the bucket in terms of what is out there. All of the items are both useful and fun. They naturally complement any of the devices discussed earlier and are a great way to bring excitement and freshness back into a relationship all on their own. For now, the items are good for beginning self-exploration. In upcoming chapters, you'll learn how they can work for your relationship. The options that follow are some that the women I treat really enjoy.

To help you, I have also included a quiz that sorts through the options for you. The Passion Prescription Pad quiz, located in the Appendix, gives you specific recommendations to help eliminate uncertainty. These sexual prescriptions are distinctly tailored to help any woman reinvigorate her sex life. Check it out if you think you need some guidance in making the right choices.

Astraea Vibrating Panties with remote control, from the Berman Center Intimate Accessories Collection, offers a different take on the standard vibrating bullet. They do double duty as both underwear and vibrator. The panty's snug, lacy fit is available as a thong or brief, both black. The remote allows you to receive hands-free stimulation, which makes them perfect for when you want to have some fun at the next boring cocktail party you are attending together. And your partner will love having the remote control to surprise you when you are least expecting it.

Chocolate Body Paint by Kama Sutra comes with a soft brush and three different flavors—dark, milk, and white chocolate—to paint on the body. You can get creative with the designs, as well as how you and your partner remove them from one another. (Hint: The paint is edible.)

Honey Dust by Kama Sutra lets you and your partner tickle each other with a real feather duster while sprinkling a light, airy powder made of pure honey. The powder is edible, silky smooth, and tastes great. The feather duster feels amazing on bare skin and should be used to tease and delight.

Furry handcuffs like those from Fox Tails are lined with faux fur to make them comfortable any way you choose to use them. They fit both men and women and are a great way to bring some fantasy into the bedroom. Try them with a blindfold to put yourself completely in your partner's hands. Not only will it restore a sense of the unknown to sex, but you'll also notice your other senses go into high gear.

Flavored, colored, and textured condoms make having safe sex fun. Try LifeStyles flavored condoms during oral sex only, and try studded condoms during intercourse for a new sensation. These condoms add to the sensory experience of sex and make suggesting contraception more approachable.

How-to books are designed for both men and women and offer specific advice on how to please your partner or yourself. Some discuss techniques in great detail to create confidence when it comes to giving pleasure. Others suggest new positions or ways to increase variety. A wide range of subjects are available—so use your imagination if you are looking for some guidance. Several specific recommendations follow in the Appendix, as part of the Passion Prescription Pad quiz. The Resource Guide at the end of this book also lists some suggestions.

Videos are another great way to learn about technique, whether it's massage, self-stimulation, or ways to please your partner. The Sinclair Intimacy Institute puts out an excellent line of hands-on, educational videos for couples, on topics such as erotic massage and exploring fantasy. Erotic videos produced by and for women feature more developed story lines and softer sex than traditional pornographic movies. The videos skip graphic or disturbing sex scenes in favor of fantasy and plot. Many women find them appealing since the story lines create context for sexual arousal. The videos feature empowered female protagonists and actors with more realistic bodies. They also leave room for imagination, which is important in all of the movies that women love, erotic and otherwise. Female-friendly erotica is a great way to discover something new about what excites you. You may need to try a few before you find one you like. And remember, there's nothing shameful about exploring your curiosity with an erotic video. Candida Royalle is an ex-erotic film star turned producer who has a terrific line of female-friendly choices that many women enjoy. Try surprising your partner by buying one for the two of you—men often fantasize about watching erotic videos with their partners and this way you get to decide what you watch!

Sexual board games provide couples with a unique way to communicate and explore each other's minds and bodies. Most of the games work to create a conversation that brings a couple closer together. New things are discovered about each other and sensuality is emphasized. Board games are an excellent way to mend communication breakdowns and rediscover romance. Several specific recommendations follow in the Appendix, as part of the Passion Prescription Pad quiz.

AT LEAST FOR NOW, VIBRATORS and self-stimulation are as close as women can get to a magic little pill for great sex. I think it's refreshing that such a simple solution exists when everything else—our sex lives in particular—can, at times, seem so complicated. Though definitely not a cure-all, vibrators and self-stimulation are an excellent starting point for getting back on track and making sex what you want it to be. Whether mending an ailing relationship, getting the confidence to start a new one, or just learning more about yourself as a sexual being, square one is right here. Women who want more pleasure must begin with themselves.

I would venture to say that even if you are having problems in your relationship, or are upset about your lack of a significant other, rediscovering your sexuality will put a spring back in your step. By taking the initiative and bringing back pleasure, you gain a sense of confidence. And husbands, boyfriends, and future lovers can't help but notice that.

PRESCRIPTIONS FOR THE WEEK:
Week 2

✓ Fill out the Passion Prescription Pad (Appendix page 256) to figure out which sexual aids and devices will best suit your needs.

✓ Now go shopping! You can go to an erotica shop in your neighborhood or go online (see the Resource Guide). I suggest going shopping with your partner, but if that's too huge a step you can save that for later and just go by yourself for now.

✓ Try out your new toys by yourself first to get familiar with them; see how they work and how they'll best work on you. Then it's time to bring some of them into your sex play with your partner. Make sure he's read the Guy's Guide, and he'll be ready to explore with you.

✓ Start masturbating at least twice a week this week. Try to continue using your new vibrator(s) at least once a week over the course of the next nine weeks. The other time you can use your hands or a showerhead—whatever works for you. Now you can start exploring arousal and orgasm. You'll keep the blood flow going, get the plumbing cleaned up and ready to go, and you'll become a well-versed self-stimulator by the end!

✓ Try something new with your partner that you've been wanting to do but felt too embarrassed or anxious to do (for example, watching an erotic video or trying a new game). Have fun, keep it light, and laugh!

GUY'S GUIDE:
A Summary of Key Points for the Man in Your Life

1. Most women don't reach orgasm through intercourse alone. I know it is hard to believe, but it's true. And even when they do it's usually because of clitoral stimulation.

2. To make matters more complicated, it's not uncommon for women to find that they need more stimulation as they age or even during different life stages (earlier stages of pregnancy, while breast-feeding, and certainly as they age). This means more foreplay. One surefire way to get your partner to reach orgasm is by incorporating a vibrator into sex play. Don't be intimidated by this. If she needs a vibrator to reach orgasm during intercourse, she's in the majority, not the minority, and it's not a reflection on you.

3. Don't worry, your partner has already been briefed on the benefits of vibrators, and I can promise you no instrument is going to replace you . . . the warmth of your body, her connection to you, etc. In the studies I've done, women report that they don't feel their vibrators can possibly replace their partners. Instead they find that vibrators are a fun addition to sex with their significant others.

4. There are all sorts of sizes, shapes, and styles of vibrators. Many small models can be used during intercourse between you and your partner to provide her with clitoral stimulation.

5. I suggest you go shopping for sex toys with your partner. If you decide to surprise her with a new toy yourself, here's some advice. Bigger doesn't mean better, and she does not necessarily want something lifelike or with the most bells and whistles. The simpler the vibrator, the better. So start off slow.

CHAPTER THREE

The Physical Side of Sex

Is Your Body on Board?

■ SSSS ■

INCREDIBLY, WOMEN'S SEXUAL COMPLAINTS WERE once thought to be in their heads, while men's were attributed to physical causes. Women who were brave enough to seek help from their doctors for their sexual problems were most often told to relax, go home and have a glass of wine, or go for counseling. Fortunately, modern research continues to reveal that women's sexual problems are caused by a variety of factors—psychological and interpersonal, yes, but also hormonal, physiological, and anatomical. Though the "talking cure" has a valuable role, it is never going to be the only solution when it comes to what ails women sexually. In fact, many of the risk factors for sexual problems are the same for women as they are for men, including cardiovascular disease, endocrine disorders, and lifestyle choices such as smoking. The hormonal roller coasters of childbirth and menopause also make their own unique contributions to a woman's sexual health.

Taking your sexual pulse is truly a whole body experience. From a physiological standpoint, there are two essentials for great sex: balanced hormones and good blood flow (good pelvic floor muscles matter too, but we'll be getting to those later). All depend upon good health in general. While your sexual anatomy and response play the leading role, the rest of your body acts as the supporting cast. Many health conditions and medications that have nothing to do with sex can have a noticeable impact on your sex life nonetheless. Women must learn to recognize and treat the health challenges that crop up over the course of a lifetime to keep their sexual response functioning smoothly, too.

Before you begin, you should take the Berman Sexual Assessment located in the Appendix—an instrument I came up with in my first book, *For Women Only*. It will help you discover if your sexual function complaints are more physically, situationally, or emotionally based, and provide suggestions about directions to go in seeking treatment. Your options for maximizing and treating the physical barriers to sexual function are the focus of this chapter, while guidance for emotional and relationship stress follow in the following two chapters.

The Three Musketeers of Sex

Hormones play a vital role in your sexual response. Without them, not much would be happening in either your brain or your genitals. The sex hormones—estrogen, progesterone, and testosterone—affect sexual desire and arousal throughout the course of a woman's lifetime. Are you surprised to learn that women have testosterone, too? Testosterone is a fundamental source of sexual energy for women and men alike. Men have many times the level of testosterone that women do, which in large part explains their heightened sex drive. It also fuels their masculine characteristics, like facial and body hair and a deeper voice, which is why small quantities only are the rule for women.

The sex hormones are produced via a complex dance between your brain and your ovaries. Like all hormones, the sex hormones are chemical messengers that relay messages from one part of the body to another. During a woman's childbearing years, the brain's pituitary gland produces a hormone that signals the ovary to release an egg. As the follicle matures to cast out the monthly egg, two of the sex hormones—estrogen and progesterone—are produced. Both help prepare a woman's body for conception by thickening the lining of the uterus and regulating the menstrual cycle. Estrogen levels rise during the first two weeks of the cycle, called the follicular phase, while progesterone levels are highest during the final two weeks, called the luteal phase. If fertilization does not occur, the uterine lining is shed in a monthly period, and estrogen and progesterone levels both drop.

Estrogen and progesterone play a larger role than simply regulating the menstrual cycle. Estrogen helps keep the vagina lubricated and flexible, which is essential for comfortable sex. Estrogen also increases serotonin activity in the brain, which is associated with better mood, more energy, and improved memory. It works with other hormones and minerals to prevent bone loss and protects against heart disease by raising good (HDL) cholesterol. As a result, estrogen has both direct and indirect effects on your sex life. Your genitals benefit by staying supple and well-lubricated. Your body benefits by staying strong and healthy.

When your estrogen levels are too low, the vaginal tissues begin to thin and weaken and you may experience vaginal dryness. The most common result is painful sex. This is a time when your lubricant of choice comes in especially handy. Estrogen levels are typically at their lowest during perimenopause, and after menopause and childbirth, especially if you are breast-feeding. While estrogen levels will return to normal in women who have recently given birth after they stop breast-feeding, menopausal women undergo a permanent reduction when the ovaries stop functioning. Though the liver, kidneys, and adrenal glands continue to produce reduced amounts of estrogen, hormone replacement therapies (HRT) of either estrogen, progesterone, or both are often considered as a further antidote. For a complete discussion of HRT, keep reading!

Too much estrogen can be just as bad for your body *and* your sexual function. An estrogen surplus is associated with heavy periods, excessive PMS-like symptoms such as water retention, moodiness, and skin problems, and a heightened risk of reproductive cancers. Too much estrogen is often the result of too little progesterone. Progesterone works to balance the effects of estrogen on the body and to keep your system in hormonal harmony. When present in the correct ratio, progesterone ensures that estrogen helps the body, rather than harms it. Progesterone also has a relaxing effect on your body and your mind, so much so that too much progesterone can cause drowsiness, as well as memory and mood problems. When it comes to hormones, balance is the key.

Progesterone is strongly influenced by the hormone cortisol, which the body produces in response to stress. When you experience high levels of chronic stress, too much cortisol ends up circulating in your body, which in turn diminishes progesterone's effects. Estrogen then runs wild, throwing your body out of sync hormonally. Cortisol also hampers progesterone's protective effects on the adrenal system, which regulates the body's entire hormonal network. This is a perfect example of the circular relationship between body and mind. When you feel a high level of stress in your life, your body is affected. Over time, the changes to your body inevitably create problems that further stress your mind. For sexual function especially, and your overall health in general, the body and mind are intimately connected.

The final hormonal musketeer—and the one we now know is incredibly important for women's sex drives and sexual response—is testosterone. Like estrogen and progesterone, testosterone is produced by the ovaries and adrenal glands. It fuels a woman's sex drive, promotes a sense of well-being, and stimulates bone growth. Since testosterone relaxes the coronary arteries, it may reduce heart disease if present at appropriate levels. Testosterone peaks around the time of ovulation, which makes sense if you think in terms of evolution. More desire equals a greater likelihood that sex, and consequently conception, will take place, which is what sex was all about to begin with. Like the other sex hormones, testosterone declines as a woman approaches perimenopause and remains low thereafter. This can contribute to low libido and a feeling of low energy in general.

Testosterone can also decline in response to stress and depression. Men and women were previously thought to react with the same fight-or-flight response to stress. But recently, researchers have discovered that this may not be true for women at all. UCLA researcher Shelley E. Taylor has discovered a pattern she calls "tend-and-befriend," in which women respond to stressful conditions by protecting and nurturing their young (the "tend" response) and by seeking social contact and support from others, especially other women (the "befriend" response). Finally, an explanation for why we want to bond over a piece of chocolate cake with one of our girlfriends when we are upset! The difference is thought to be related to oxytocin, a hormone that plays an important role in childbirth and stimulates caretaking behaviors. Oxytocin causes a rise in sex hormone binding globulin (SHBG), which binds testosterone to the cells and makes it unavailable for things like libido, genital sensation, and general energy. Researchers think that oxytocin's effect, which is also secreted in response to stress in men, is canceled out by their higher levels of testosterone. Therefore, when men are faced with stress they are more likely to act out (the "fight" response) or want to be left alone (the "flight" response). The research is also important since it may help explain the drop in libido that is often seen after childbirth and while a woman is breast-feeding. The oxytocin secreted while breast-feeding may "turn off" testosterone, just as testosterone turns off oxytocin in men. More research into this exciting area is sure to educate us on how different even the most fundamental processes in women and men can be. Once thought to be the domain of men, testosterone is just as important for women and for their sexual function in particular.

Getting Tested

So what can you do to give your body some hormonal help? First, if you suspect there's a problem, it is important to get a full hormone workup done. This includes a blood test to assess your estrogen, progesterone, and testosterone levels. While most physicians routinely perform blood tests, some also perform a saliva test as a second measure of hormone levels. Saliva testing may offer a more accurate measure of bioavailable hormone levels, or the hormones that are not bound up in a woman's cells, and therefore available for her body to use. Sexual function, in particular, depends on this; however, controversy remains about the validity of saliva testing. Whichever test you choose, it's a good idea to get your hormonal profile done even if you are happy with your sex life. It gives you a baseline of your unique hormonal "fingerprint," since every woman's hormonal needs are so different. This comes in handy later if you start having problems so you know what to shoot for.

At the Berman Center, we do extensive hormonal testing that measures the level of five hormones: estrogen, progesterone, testosterone, dehydroepiandrosterone (DHEA), and cortisol. You've already learned how the first three affect your sexual function. You know that cortisol is a stress hormone that can powerfully affect your sex hormones. DHEA is part of the same family of hormones as testosterone, called androgens, and acts as a sort of precursor to it and also to estrogen. The testing allows us to get a baseline for functions that can be affected by hormone therapy. It also reveals if some other problem not related to sex hormones is causing your symptoms, such as diabetes or thyroid disorder. We typically measure the following when a woman comes to our center: total cholesterol, liver function, glucose, thyroid stimulating hormone (TSH), sex hormone binding globulin (SHBG), and free and total testosterone. It's important to have an index of cholesterol levels and liver function, since testosterone therapy can raise cholesterol and compromise liver function at higher dosages. Knowing the baseline levels allows us to monitor both and make sure no adverse side effects are occurring.

Of course, not all women require testosterone therapy. Some do well with just estrogen or a combination of estrogen and progesterone. It all depends on what your tests reveal, what your symptoms are, and whether or not you still have your uterus. There is controversy swirling around when to give testosterone therapy and what level is considered too low. Your free and total testosterone levels are both important for determining whether you need testosterone replacement. Normal values for free testosterone are normally 3 to 8.5 picograms per milliliter (pg/mL) for premenopausal women and 3 to 6.7 pg/mL for postmenopausal women. Determining total testosterone levels is the real area of controversy, since many physicians consider a wider range of testosterone levels to be normal. There are women whose physicians believe the lowest acceptable level for total testosterone is 20 nanograms per deciliter (ng/dL) and therefore won't treat them with testosterone. There are other doctors who think anything below 40 ng/dL for total testosterone is grounds for replacement. So the same woman with the same symptoms might receive testosterone replacement from one physician and not from another. Instead of being treated hormonally, these women are told they should seek counseling to figure out why they don't feel good, why they don't respond sexually or want to have sex. If women find themselves in this gray zone of between 20 and 40 ng/dL of total testosterone, they may need to become their own advocates. Start questioning results, be aware of the controversy and get a second opinion if you think you could benefit from testosterone replacement.

Depending on what the tests reveal, you have several options for dealing with a hormonal imbalance. The trick, however, is finding a physician who will give proper credence to your test results and symptoms, and then prescribe an appropriate regimen. This can be either an endocrinologist or gynecologist, since both are skilled in hormones. Some resources for finding a physician are listed in the Resource Guide. While I can't guarantee the quality of each and every physician, I can confirm they are all interested in women's sexual health and are getting educated about it. It's always important to approach your physician with complaints about your sexual response that are as specific as possible. This may include inadequate lubrication, low genital sensation, and low sexual desire. Depending upon your blood test results, there are several hormonal options for tackling any or all of these problems. They include pills (oral), creams, and gels that are applied either to the skin or directly to the vagina, and also patches and sublingual lozenges. I often recommend that women try topical options because they can be compounded to your specific needs and work on the spot, so to speak, which means the hormones do not circulate throughout your body to the degree that they would if taken orally. For this reason, any potential risks are theoretically lower than with traditional HRT therapy. Also, if there are any adverse symptoms you can stop immediately. More information on these alternatives follows in the next section, but first, a discussion about the recent maelstrom over HRT.

The Real Deal on HRT

As women approach menopause, many begin to notice striking changes to their libido and their sexual function, such as vaginal dryness and decreased orgasm quality. Sometimes the changes are apparent even earlier, in the late thirties or early forties, when she is in perimenopause. The changes result from reduced levels of estrogen, progesterone, and testosterone as the ovaries begin slowing down production. Hormone replacement therapy (HRT) can help with sexual side effects and other common symptoms, like hot flashes, insomnia, and mood disturbances. There has been a lot of controversy recently about HRT. The decision by the National Institute of Health to halt two phases of the Women's Health Initiative (WHI) study is, understandably, making many women nervous. The WHI studied the effect of long-term hormone therapy on more than 27,000 healthy, postmenopausal women ages fifty to seventy-nine. Researchers found that an increased risk of stroke, heart disease, and breast cancer for women taking estrogen and progesterone HRT, and an increased risk of stroke for women taking estrogen-only HRT, were too dangerous to allow the study to continue. As a result, women and physicians all over America swiftly abandoned hormone therapy.

While women definitely should *not* be putting their health in jeopardy by choosing hormone therapy indiscriminately, I feel that the risks of the WHI study have been overblown to the point of sensationalism. The real numbers tell a different story. For women on estrogen-only HRT, eight more of every 10,000 experienced stroke than those not on hormones. For women on combination (estrogen and progesterone) HRT, eight more of every 10,000 developed breast cancer. Even if it is true, do eight more women *possibly* suffering from a devastating illness like stroke or breast cancer mean everyone else should throw in the towel on hormones? The women studied in the WHI were older and, on average, had gone through menopause many years earlier with no hormonal treatments. They may have had pre-existing health conditions that put them at higher risk for developing these illnesses.

Or, the shock of estrogen to their systems after having gone so many years without it also could have skewed the results. The bottom line is that every woman must discuss the pros and cons of the issue, based on her personal history, with her physician. It feels wrong to throw such a huge population of women into crisis, not to mention their loved ones, when so many of them were not affected.

The North American Menopause Society agrees. They released an advisory panel report that reviewed the WHI and other relevant studies. They concluded that the risks found by the WHI should be taken seriously for now but that more trials are needed to fully understand the risks and benefits of hormone therapy. The report suggested that different types of hormones and dosages would likely lead to different outcomes. It also cautioned against generalizing the findings of the WHI to all women, since study participants were older and not presenting with any menopausal symptoms. The report also pointed out that the increased risk of stroke found in the WHI study has not been replicated by any other large trial.

The risks of HRT can be minimized by using patches or creams, rather than pills. Delivering hormones through the skin means the hormones are not metabolized by the body and do not pass through the liver, which may help to reduce risk. It also allows for a lower dosage to be used, since the hormones do not get broken down by the body before entering the bloodstream, which further reduces risk and side effects. Bio-identical hormone therapy provides similar benefits. If you're not sure what bio-identical hormones are, they're a natural alternative to the synthetic hormones that most women are prescribed for menopause management. Bio-identical hormones are derived from a variety of plant or animal sources and are chemically identical to the hormones produced by a woman's body. Since the hormones are natural, the body does not respond to them as a foreign substance. Bio-identical hormones are customized, in contrast to the one-size-fits-all approach of pharmaceutical brands of HRT. Every woman is different and needs a hormone cocktail that is best suited to her. Again, women interested in bio-identical hormone therapy will have to look for a physician with expertise in it. Some resources follow at the end of the book.

Bio-identical hormones can be compounded in capsules, sublingual lozenges, or topical and vaginal creams and gels. Testosterone can also be added for libido problems. Best of all, bio-identical hormones can be monitored and adjusted over time to get symptom relief at the lowest possible dosage. For all of these reasons, they may be a safer alternative than what was used in the WHI study and the hormones that most menopausal women currently take. Under the guidance of your physician, compounding pharmacies will create customized hormone prescriptions that regular pharmacies can't. To find a compounding pharmacy in your area, consult the Resource Guide.

Alternatives

As I mentioned earlier, there are many options for treating specific complaints about your sexual function, aside from systemic HRT. These may be good alternatives for women who are experiencing vaginal dryness or poor genital sensation as a result of low hormone levels. In fact, lubrication is the easiest facet of your sexual response to improve. Being well-lubricated is essential to enjoyable sex. A lack of adequate lubrication can lead to vaginal dryness, burning, and soreness, both during sex and after it. If your body is not producing enough of it, an endless array of water- and silicone-based lubricants exists. Flip back to Chapter 2 if you need some suggestions. If inadequate lubrication is the result of low estrogen levels, estrogen replacement can often do the trick. Two prescription options—Estring and Vagifem—improve vaginal lubrication and also help with urinary health. Both allow the estrogen to be delivered locally to the vagina and not absorbed into the rest of the body, reducing side effects. Estring is a flexible ring that is inserted into the vagina, where it remains for three months. It provides a consistent level of estradiol, a type of estrogen, to the genitals. Results are usually seen within two to three weeks. When properly inserted, the ring usually cannot be felt by you in general (or your partner during intercourse). The ring is removed by hooking your finger through it and gently pulling it out, at which time a new ring is inserted. Vagifem is a tablet that's inserted with a tampon-like applicator and dissolves in the vagina. It is inserted once a day for two weeks and twice a week thereafter to maintain its effects. There are also estrogen creams available, which are applied inside the vagina every day; however, many women prefer the convenience and tidiness that the ring and tablet offer them.

If it's not lubrication that's causing you problems, but a lack of genital sensation during sexual activity or intercourse, topical testosterone treatments can help. Targeted testosterone products seem to be the next big thing if you look at the pharmaceutical industry. Testosterone cream is already available by prescription for men, and many physicians prescribe it off-label for women. The most common dose is a 2 percent cream, which when applied to the clitoris and inner labia every other day, improves sensation in the genitals. Women usually respond wonderfully to this type of treatment, though it's important to take care in the amount used. Too much testosterone can cause hair growth at the site of application and an enlarged clitoris and labia. This is true for any form of testosterone therapy. Other potential side effects of testosterone, topical or otherwise, include weight gain, increased facial hair and high cholesterol. However, these side effects can be tempered by the right dosages given under the care of an informed physician.

Certain types of testosterone therapy help not only with sensation, but also with low sexual desire. Some new options on the horizon for women include a testosterone patch from Procter & Gamble, called Intrinsa, and a testosterone spray from Vivus. The Intrinsa patch delivers testosterone transdermally (through the skin), which may be safer and more effective than other forms of testosterone replacement. Since testosterone enters the bloodstream at a gradual, continuous rate, a steady level is maintained. The patch is transparent and measures about the size of an egg. It is worn discreetly on the abdomen. The exciting thing about Intrinsa is that it not only improves clitoral sensitivity and vaginal lubrication, but also boosts libido. In clinical trials women wearing the Intrinsa patch experienced a statistically significant boost in sexual desire and frequency of sexual activity. While experts forecasted a fast track to FDA approval based on these results, Procter & Gamble suffered a setback when they were told that more studies were needed to determine long-term safety. They are currently conducting such tests and if they can prove long-term safety, Intrinsa will be the *first* prescription medication available for the treatment of women's sexual dysfunction. With Viagra coming up on its ten-year anniversary in the not too distant future, I'd say it's about time! Another option, a topical testosterone spray from Vivus, also looks promising. It has been shown in clinical trials to significantly improve women's sex drives when compared with a placebo. More clinical trials are currently under way. There are also several gels being developed and tested. Stay tuned for results on these and other testosterone therapies for women in the years to come.

While exciting, it's important to remember that testosterone will revive sexual desire only in women who suffer from low testosterone to begin with. If you're unhappy with your partner or yourself, no drug can cure that. Working out those issues with therapy and good communication, which is coming up in Chapters 4 and 5, is always best.

Beyond Hormones

If hormones are the messengers of sex, then blood vessels are the cars they drive in. The blood vessels are your body's pathway to sexual arousal. The genitals are made up of a dense network of blood vessels and nerve endings, which ultimately are connected to all other blood vessels in the body. When sexually excited, the blood vessels swell to create a feeling of fullness throughout the genitals. All of the genital structures expand, which contributes to your partner's sexual pleasure and also to yours. For this reason, the markers of arousal—lubrication, swelling, and heightened sensation—all depend on a healthy body. Increased blood flow makes things tighter for him and more sensitive for you, especially as the clitoris expands internally and wraps around the vagina. The swollen blood vessels also allow the vagina to become slippery and well-lubricated. With the increased blood flow that occurs with sexual arousal, a transudate of fluid is released from the blood vessels lining the walls of the vagina and combines with mucus from the cervix to create lubrication.

To put it mildly, blood vessels matter. Poor blood flow can affect almost every aspect of your sexual response. For starters, there are several medications and health conditions that can interfere, such as high blood pressure, diabetes, and others you may not even suspect. Pelvic trauma from past surgery or childbirth can also affect blood flow by damaging key blood vessels. Consult the next section for a full list of potential risks and what you can do to manage them. It's important to treat these conditions for your general health, as well as to minimize the impact they may be having on your sexual function.

How can you determine if something more serious is preventing your blood flow from being what it should be? The best method for evaluating your pelvic blood flow is ultrasound technology. At the Berman Center in Chicago, we give women an ultrasound as part of a comprehensive examination of their genital function. A separate machine assesses their vaginal and clitoral sensitivity to temperature and vibration. Such tests allow us to identify if poor blood flow is at the root of a woman's sexual complaints or if there is a loss of sensation independent of blood flow.

We also examine the genitals for structural soundness. Aging, childbirth, and menopause can all transform the sexual anatomy and affect its ability to function as it was intended to. The women I see at my center are evaluated on a variety of levels—from their sexual history and current relationship quality to physical measures of genital response and structure—to give us the whole picture of their sexual health. There really is no better way to understand exactly what is shaping a woman's sex life emotionally *and* physically.

As mentioned earlier, it can be difficult to find a doctor who is willing or able to perform these tests. Sometimes women find that when they approach their primary-care physician or even their ob-gyns with a sexual complaint, they are met with quick-fix solutions or given a referral to a therapist. I've met many women who have been offered a prescription for Valium or Prozac without any sort of physical or mental assessment of what is actually going on, beyond the standard examination. Many doctors are simply used to prescribing a pill or referring a patient to therapy. They are not trained during medical school or postgraduate training to talk about sex and are not always informed about the latest technology and treatments that are available for sexual function complaints. Women deserve the time and attention it takes to treat a sexual complaint properly. Finding a doctor who understands the complexity of a woman's sexual makeup is essential.

While your state of mind and relationship quality matter, it's equally important that your body is able to respond sexually. Sometimes, a largely physical problem can be part of what's keeping you from a satisfying sex life. If left untreated, the problem will no doubt begin to have emotional consequences on your relationship. Physical treatments are not always the only answer, but they can often be *part* of the answer.

Get Your Blood Flow Moving

Fortunately, many options exist for getting your genital blood flow moving again and for helping with sensation and lubrication. The little blue pill that has done wonders for men's sex lives can help women in certain cases, too. I am talking about Viagra, ladies. Viagra works for women's bodies the same way it does for men's. It relaxes blood vessels in the genital area to increase blood flow and, in the process, enhance sensations and lubrication. For women who want a better physical response and feel at ease in their relationship—meaning there are no current major conflicts or unresolved issues from the past—Viagra, Cialis, and Levitra can offer a whole new world sexually.

Now, you wouldn't know this if you looked at the current research on women and Viagra. Several studies have reported that Viagra fails at inspiring women sexually. There are two problems with these studies. One is that the benchmark has been set so high by men's success with Viagra, that anything less is seen as a failure. Viagra works in 90 percent of men with erectile dysfunction—literally a magic little pill. Unfortunately for women, the situation is a bit more complex. There will never be one pill or treatment that works for every woman. Whereas a man's sexual dysfunction most often comes down to a physically based problem, in my clinical experience that's only true in about one-third of women's complaints. A woman's sexuality is bound up in her emotions, body image, and relationship satisfaction, as well as her physical response. Many sexual issues are better treated with therapy or with a combination of medication and therapy. Which brings me to the second problem with the women and Viagra studies: They failed to separate women with sexual problems that were emotionally based from those with purely physical problems.

Some researchers and I did just that. We helped to carry out a multicenter study for Pfizer, the makers of Viagra, in which women were screened extensively to make sure no emotional factors were at work, things like past trauma, abuse, or current relationship troubles. We also made sure the women had no hormonal imbalances, which affect sexual response all on their own. What *did* the women in our study have? A healthy desire for sex in the context of a happy relationship, with a desire to improve how their body performed while "in the moment." We found that among these women, 82 percent of those who took Viagra were more pleased with lubrication and sensation during sexual activity than before they started taking it. They also reported significant improvements in orgasm ability, enjoyment during intercourse, and overall sexual satisfaction when compared with women who took a placebo. Viagra helps bring back the sensation in women who want it and are not struggling with past or present relationship issues. Though it won't help every woman, it's nice to know the option exists.

Viagra is best taken on an empty stomach about one hour before you plan to have sex. And remember, foreplay is still necessary! The pill simply primes your body for arousal—you still need to *want* to have sex in the first place and to put in the effort once you start having it. Viagra gives you about a four-hour window of opportunity. If you feel like that's too limiting, or want to eat before you get busy, newer options like Cialis and Levitra work similarly to Viagra; however, Levitra gives you an eight- to ten-hour window for sexual activity and Cialis gives you a twenty-four- to thirty-six-hour window. Cialis is not affected by food intake and Levitra is affected only by fatty foods. All of the drugs have similar side effects, including headache, facial flushing, and nasal congestion. None should be taken with any medications containing nitrates, since the combination could cause a dangerous drop in blood pressure.

Another prescription option for improving blood flow to your genital area is the Eros clitoral therapy device (CTD). The Eros-CTD is the first device of its kind. Developed by UroMetrics, it works by creating a gentle suction on the clitoris and surrounding tissue. This actually mimics oral sex to increase blood flow to the clitoris. Since we know how important both the clitoris and good blood flow are to sexual satisfaction, the Eros-CTD is designed to get the job done. And the benefits don't stop there. The device helps not only with sexual arousal, but may also prevent the collagen buildup in the arteries leading to the clitoris that comes with age. Sexually arousing and antiaging—what could be more perfect? How about a nonprescription alternative? The Berman Center Intimate Accessories Collection offers a similar device, the *Selene* Vibrating Clitoral Pump. It provides many of the same benefits, with a suction that draws blood flow to the clitoral area. You can use it before or during intercourse to increase stimulation and arousal or while you are self-stimulating.

The sexual health company, Vivus, has found promising results for yet another topical spray called Alista. Though still in clinical trials, Alista has been shown to significantly increase sexual arousal and decrease feelings of anxiety in women with low arousal. The spray is applied topically to the genitals through dose-controlled technology. Alista contains the drug alprostadil, which is thought to increase blood flow to genital tissues. Vivus hopes to have the product ready for FDA approval sometime in 2006.

If you're not looking to go to the doctor just yet, there are some excellent nonprescription alternatives for heightening your body's sexual response. You have learned about the many benefits of vibrators, which enhance sexual response in the women who use them. Vibrator use improves sexual desire, arousal, and orgasm ability during solo and partner sex. Plus, they add novelty to the same old bedroom routine, which can do wonders of its own. Another device, called *Slightest Touch,* delivers mild electrical currents to stimulate your sexual nerve pathway. Before you get scared, the device works by delivering barely noticeable stimulation through electrode pads attached to the inner parts of the ankles. It's designed to bring you to a state of maximum arousal. Many women find that it relaxes them, while also awakening their pelvic nerve endings. By heightening the body's sexual readiness, the makers of the device claim it helps to make orgasms more likely and more intense. Women with certain health conditions or who take various prescription medications should not use the device, so be sure to consult the manual before trying it out. *Slightest Touch* has not been tested in clinical trials, so it is supported by anecdotal, not scientific, evidence. The theory is that the stimulation is targeting the tibial nerve, which is connected to the region of the spine that corresponds with genital sensation.

Clinical trials have also begun for the *Orgasmatron,* a medical device originally designed to treat bladder problems and pelvic pain (a technique known as InterStim Therapy) by Medtronic. A doctor by the name of Stuart Meloy was using InterStim Therapy and began to notice that his female patients were reporting orgasm as a side effect of their treatment! Knowing a good thing when he saw one, he quickly patented the device to treat sexual dysfunction. He is currently recruiting women for clinical trials to determine if the *Orgasmatron* holds scientific promise for the treatment of women's sexual dysfunction. However, the device requires that tiny electrodes be implanted in the spine and a battery pack just under the skin of the buttocks, so it will be interesting to see how far women will go for the "big O."

And don't forget about Zestra oil. This all-natural, botanical oil is applied to the genitals before foreplay and works to create a tingling sensation. In clinical trials, Zestra was proven to enhance sexual desire, arousal, and orgasm ability. It also works superbly as a lubricant. Zestra is available without a prescription, since it is made of herbal botanicals.

Whether prescription or nonprescription, the choices are there for you to get creative and reawaken your sexual response. However, this brings up an important point. It's essential to make sense of all the options you are confronted with—especially herbal remedies. We will explore this in more detail in Chapter 10, but just because a product is herbal and natural, doesn't necessarily mean it is safe. Any herbal product could interact with other medical conditions or medications you are taking. Also, if it's not regulated by the FDA you can't be sure that what the company claims actually is true. For such claims to be valid, they must be demonstrated in clinical trials. Keep this in mind when exploring new treatments and devices that may not be FDA-approved.

The Body's Roadblocks to Great Sex

You've learned about the importance of blood flow and hormones for good lubrication and genital sensation during sex. Because sexual arousal depends on these physical responses, which in turn depend on a healthy body, you can see the connection between your general health and sexual health. Many health conditions can impact your body's sexual response. There are also other challenges the body can pose to a satisfying sex life, beyond blood flow and hormones.

Most obvious is any change to your sexual anatomy. When your genital function is disrupted because of childbirth, menopause, or any of a number of gynecological conditions and surgeries, your sexual response is invariably affected. The degree to which this is true depends on your particular situation and, often, the health of your pelvic floor. As you will learn in Chapter 6, your pelvic floor is a network of muscles, ligaments, and other tissues that keep your pelvic organs in their proper place—including the vagina, rectum, uterus, and bladder. If this support network is weakened, one or more of the organs can change positions in what is known as pelvic floor prolapse. Prolapse comes from the Latin root "to fall," which is exactly what happens to your internal organs. Like a domino effect, one organ falls and displaces one or more other organs. The result can be a feeling of pelvic pressure or heaviness (specifically in the vagina or rectum), urinary incontinence, and constipation. Pain and discomfort during sex are also a common result of pelvic floor prolapse.

Virtually anything that tears or weakens your pelvic floor muscles can cause pelvic floor prolapse. Childbirth, menopause, and aging are all risk factors. Though pregnancy and childbirth do not cause pelvic floor prolapse for all women, they do for many—especially in the case of multiple vaginal deliveries or difficult labors. Heavy pushing during delivery, pressure from the baby on the internal organs during pregnancy, *and* delivery can exact a strong cost from a woman's sexual anatomy. So can an episiotomy, in which the perineum intentionally is cut to allow the baby to emerge from the vagina. Sometimes it can take years for the symptoms of pelvic floor damage to emerge. Declining estrogen levels in the time leading up to and after menopause further compromise your pelvic floor's soundness. A lack of estrogen weakens the pelvic floor tissues, making prolapse more likely. While some weakening of the pelvic floor is normal, there are steps you can take to keep yours in good shape. Maintaining a strong pelvic floor should be a lifelong activity with lifelong benefits. They are essential to your sexual health routine! In Chapter 6, you will learn everything you need to know about Kegel and pelvic floor exercises. Also, for menopausal women, combining the exercises with a good hormonal regimen can offer great results.

Other gynecological conditions that can interfere with your sexual response include endometriosis, uterine fibroids, interstitial cystitis, and polycystic ovary syndrome. Endometriosis occurs when the tissue that normally lines the uterus ends up in other parts of the body. How the tissues escape from the uterus is not clear. Endometriosis puts the reproductive anatomy at risk by promoting the development of scar tissue in the Fallopian tubes, ovaries, and anywhere else the endometrial cells implant themselves in the body. In addition to infertility, this can cause chronic pain in the pelvis and lower back, heavy painful periods, and pain during or after sex. Fibroids are benign tumors that develop in the uterus. Their size can vary from quite small, even microscopic, to quite large. Not all women with fibroids have symptoms, but those who do often complain of pelvic pressure, heavy painful periods, frequent urination, and pain during sex. Interstitial cystitis is a chronic bladder condition characterized by a frequent urgent need to urinate and abdominal, vaginal, and rectal pain. In my experience, I have found women with interstitial cystitis also have problems with sexual arousal and orgasm ability. As with endometriosis and fibroids, the precise cause of interstitial cystitis is not known. Polycystic ovary syndrome (PCOS) occurs when the ovaries become enlarged and have several fluid-filled sacs, or cysts. PCOS is the leading cause of infertility and the most common reproductive syndrome in women of childbearing age. The symptoms of PCOS can vary widely. Many women experience acne, growth of body and facial hair, and male-pattern baldness. This may be the result of increased testosterone. Infrequent or no menstrual periods are another common symptom, as is pelvic pain. The cause of PCOS is unknown.

All of these conditions are most often diagnosed with an ultrasound or MRI of the area. Treatments vary depending on the severity of symptoms and whether a woman plans to have children. In mild cases, pain medication is all that's recommended. When the symptoms are more distressing, everything from hormone suppression to surgery may be suggested. Each carries with it a unique set of risks and benefits for both sexual and general health.

All gynecological conditions challenge women's sexual well-being. They add stress by causing pain and interfering with normal reproductive processes like ovulation, menstruation, and becoming pregnant. In addition, many of the surgical options for treating them put women at further risk for compromised sexual function. The medical field still does not know where all of the important nerves and blood vessels are situated in a woman's pelvis. As a result, many are inadvertently damaged during pelvic surgeries, which can pose a real problem for sexual response. Severed nerves and blood vessels compromise lubrication, sensation, and feelings of fullness in the genital area when you're aroused. Pelvic surgery for any gynecological condition should always be a last resort. Fortunately, new and improved surgical alternatives are being developed as both science and technology move forward. Laparoscopic surgery for many gynecological conditions is often an excellent alternative, since it is less invasive and therefore may be less damaging to nerves and blood vessels than traditional surgery. Laparoscopic techniques make use of a tiny camera that allows the physician to see inside the area being operated on, without having to cut it open. The result is less recovery time, less risk of infection, and virtually no physical scars. Laparoscopic treatments have been developed for everything from hysterectomy to the treatment of ovarian cysts.

A great less invasive option is uterine embolization, useful for the treatment of fibroids. Your physician injects small particles of plastic called polyvinyl alcohol (PVA) into the uterine artery. This blocks the blood supply to the fibroids, causing them to shrink. Though some women experience a loss of sensation or uterine contractions during orgasm, the technique is being refined so that vaginal branches of the uterine artery are spared. However, the fact remains that nonsurgical alternatives like hormone therapy or suppression, and less invasive laparoscopic options should always be explored first. Even if hysterectomy is determined to be the best choice, the uterus and/or ovaries can often be removed laparoscopically or vaginally, instead of through an incision in the abdomen, to increase your chances of reducing long-term side effects.

A hysterectomy, in particular, can pose significant hazards to your sex life. Hysterectomy is the second most common pelvic operation in women, after C-section. More than 600,000 are performed each year. While there are certainly cases where it's the best option—as in any sort of malignancy—hysterectomy should be considered as one in a range of possible treatments for conditions like prolapse, endometriosis, and fibroids. It's a serious choice that should be carefully considered. If possible, it may be beneficial for a woman to keep her cervix. Since the cervix is surrounded by a large number of nerves and blood vessels, sparing it maintains a significant source of arousal. Women who experience internal orgasms might particularly benefit, since contraction of the cervix is partly involved in this type of orgasm. Women who have had uterine cancer are not candidates for keeping the cervix, since the likelihood of cancer developing in cervical cells is too great.

Hysterectomy can be a double whammy when the ovaries are removed since it affects both blood flow and hormones. Because the ovaries produce most of the body's estrogen and about half of its testosterone, removing them sends a woman's body into a hormonal free fall. The resulting surgical menopause can bring on the symptoms of menopause with alarming intensity. Hot flashes, insomnia, and mood changes are often more severe than in women who go through menopause gradually. Sexual side effects include thinning vaginal tissues, lack of lubrication, and decreased genital sensation. The situation is made worse by the potential for damaged blood vessels and nerve endings cut during the surgery, which further disrupt the body's ability to become aroused. Sexual desire often plummets due to both physical and hormonal changes.

Maintaining the ovaries can help preserve a woman's sexual response. However, physicians are often cautious about leaving a woman's ovaries in cases of cancer. The reality is that the risk of ovarian cancer is incredibly small across a woman's lifetime—about 1.4 percent, or a one-in-seventy chance. Though risks must be considered on an individual basis, preserving the ovaries can help keep the body in sync hormonally, which has benefits for general and sexual well-being. However, it is common for the ovaries to atrophy, limiting their production of hormones.

As with any health decision, each and every woman must make the choice for herself. Hysterectomy is not always bad, especially when it's performed for the right reasons. Who wants to have sex when in pain or consumed with worry over a health condition? Many women benefit physically, as well as emotionally. Less pelvic pain, bleeding, and other gynecologic problems caused by the original condition are a welcomed improvement. Feeling free of such physical impairments often has a positive effect on sexual well-being and quality of life. We should just make sure we're not resorting to hysterectomy by default when so many other options are available.

Is Your Medicine Cabinet Getting in the Way?

Many medications can have sexual side effects that are worse than those created by the health condition itself. For example, antidepressants, birth control pills, and even antihistamines can all affect arousal, desire, and orgasm, independent of the conditions they are designed to treat. It is important to review all of the medications you are currently taking. Sometimes modifications can be made to the dosage, or another option can be substituted to lessen side effects. At the very least, you should understand how the drugs you take may be affecting your sex life so that other options—like vibrators, lubricants, and other interventions—can be put to good use.

Use the chart on pages 64 to 66 to determine if a particular medication may be causing your body to get its sexual signals crossed. Then talk with your physician about tailoring your dose or substituting another medication. I've listed the most common sexual problem caused by each medication, but every woman's situation will differ. Don't assume that just because you're taking one of them that you will have a problem with your sexual response. Likewise, keep in mind that a sexual problem could be stemming from a medication you never even suspected.

General Health

How about other health concerns? Heart disease and high cholesterol both result from the buildup of plaque inside the body's arteries. Over time, the buildup narrows the arteries and restricts blood flow to vital organs. The result can be a heart attack or stroke, if enough blood is not reaching the heart or brain. The same buildup can diminish blood flow to the genitals. And you know what that gets you—less sexual arousal. Too little blood flow to the

Drug	Common Types	Sexual Side Effects	Suggestions
Birth control pills	Ortho-Novum Ortho Cyclen Yasmin	Low sexual desire may result from reduced testosterone production and increased production of the sex hormone binding globulin (SHBG), which reduces circulating levels of testosterone.	Try NuvaRing, which is not processed through the liver and therefore does not increase levels of the sex hormone binding globulin, which decreases testosterone. Try a low-dose pill (such as Loestrin, Alesse, or Mircette), which may have fewer sexual side effects and other side effects like water retention, breast tenderness, and weight gain.
Antihistamines	Nonprescription: Sudafed Benadryl Claritin Prescription: Allegra Zyrtec	Vaginal dryness can result. Certain types cause drowsiness, which can affect sexual desire.	Try a nasal spray, such as Flonase, that does not circulate throughout the body and may reduce sexual side effects.
Antidepressants	Tricyclics: Anafranil Elavil Sinequan Tofranil Pamelor	Tricyclic options often have sexual side effects, in addition to other unpleasant symptoms like fatigue, constipation, and dizziness. SSRIs eliminate many of	Try Wellbutrin, which may have a low incidence of sexual side effects and weight gain that others may cause. Try Cymbalta, which may have

Drug	Common Types	Sexual Side Effects	Suggestions
Antidepressants (*continued*)	SSRIs: Prozac Zoloft Paxil Luvox MAOIs: Marplan Nardil Parnate	these symptoms, but still have a high rate of sexual side effects, like low libido and delayed or a total lack of orgasm. MAOIs are often prescribed when other choices do not work, since they have a higher risk of side effects, sexual and otherwise.	low sexual side effects and also may help with chronic pain. Investigate alternative therapies, such as vitamin B supplements and regular cardiovascular activity, which may help with some symptoms of depression.
Antihypertensives	Diuretics ACE inhibitors Beta-blockers Calcium channel blockers Angiotensin receptor blockers	Low libido and impaired sexual arousal can occur because of reduced blood flow.	Try calcium channel blockers, angiotensin receptor blockers, or ACE inhibitors, which have less effect on sexual function. Experiment with different types of drugs, since many options exist. Reduce weight, eat right, and exercise.
Anticancer	Nolvadex Megestrol	Certain types that affect the ovaries reduce the amount of hormones produced, causing vaginal dryness and discomfort and depression.	Investigate immune-boosting therapies as a complement or alternative, such as fish oil supplements and a plant-based diet.

Drug	Common Types	Sexual Side Effects	Suggestions
Sedatives	Xanax Valium	May cause a loss of sexual desire and problems with arousal.	Try to temper long-term use, which increases risk of sexual side effects. Investigate alternative therapies, such as yoga and other relaxation techniques.

pelvis can also lead to thickening of the vaginal walls and smooth muscle tissue of the clitoris. Thicker tissue means it's more difficult for the substance released by swollen genital blood vessels to make it to the surface for good lubrication. High blood pressure has also been found to damage the body's blood vessels and make them more prone to the buildup of fat. So in addition to eating right and exercising for your heart's health, it's important for your sexual function, too. Tips on treating your body right follow in Chapter 6. It's an integral part of your general *and* sexual health.

Diabetes is another seemingly unrelated health condition that can have an effect on your sexual response. This endocrine disorder is a result of either too little insulin or the body's inability to use insulin, which can lead to high levels of glucose in the blood. Over time, high blood sugar can damage nerves that are important for blood flow. Some women experience a complication of diabetes called neuropathy, or nerve damage, that can reduce sensation and vaginal lubrication. Pain during sexual activity is then more likely and problems with orgasm may also occur. In addition to using a lubricant, women with diabetes benefit from exploring new sexual techniques. Positions and stimulation that worked before may have to be modified. Incorporating a vibrator into sex can be a great solution, since it helps overcome any nerve damage that might be affecting sexual function. Diabetes also predisposes women to yeast and urinary tract infections, since too much sugar can lead to the overgrowth of bacteria in the body—including in the vagina and urethra. High blood glucose can sap your energy, leading to fatigue and less interest in sex. For all of these reasons, maintaining appropriate blood sugar levels over the long term is essential. Women who are still in their childbearing years should monitor how their glucose levels may change across the monthly menstrual cycle. More insulin when glucose levels are higher may help reduce the likelihood of a yeast or urinary tract infection and boost energy, sexually and otherwise.

Other endocrine disorders that affect the thyroid and adrenal glands can disrupt your body's sexual response. Underactive thyroid, or hypothyroidism, is especially common in women. The thyroid affects almost every organ, tissue, and cell in the body. In addition to weight gain, feelings of fatigue, dry skin, and irregular menstrual cycles, low thyroid can also cause low sex drive. Hypothyroidism is sometimes referred to as a silent disease because early symptoms are often so mild that women fail to realize anything is wrong. Many women with low thyroid feel understandably out of control about their weight gain even before being diagnosed. Women who feel self-conscious about weight gain are relieved when they discover low thyroid is the culprit and that medication can help normalize it. Synthetic hormones to replace those not being adequately produced by the thyroid usually alleviate many of the symptoms, including low libido. They also help regulate appetite and body weight, which indirectly benefits your sex life by restoring a sense of confidence in your body. Alternative treatments include avoiding certain types of foods, including cabbage, peaches, radishes, soybeans, peanuts, and spinach, which can interfere with the production of thyroid hormones. The Shoulder Stand yoga position done once a day for at least twenty minutes is also believed to improve thyroid function. In it, you rest your body weight on your shoulders while lying with your torso and legs suspended in the air. Using a wall to support yourself is usually helpful.

For women with cancer, sexual function is affected in a variety of ways. Cancer and its treatments can disrupt the physical aspects of a woman's sexual function, as well as her psychological well-being. Body image and relationship quality are just two of the issues affected by cancer. They often stem from the treatment as much as from the illness itself. Treatments for cancer vary depending on the type and degree of cancer present. In the case of reproductive and colorectal cancers, pelvic surgery is common. As you've learned, pelvic surgery impacts a woman's ability to reach orgasm, contributes to pain and loss of vaginal elasticity, and decreases lubrication and sensation. Chemotherapy and radiation treatments take a further toll on sexual function, putting a woman's body into menopause. Although there may be a focus on survival as the foremost concern, women rightfully wonder about how to reestablish their sex lives once they have adjusted to a cancer diagnosis and determined a course of treatment. Sex is an important part of life, including for women who are battling or have survived cancer.

Communication about sex is always important, especially when there has been a life-altering change like cancer. Women and their partners should work together to plan sexual activity at times of the day when pain is lowest—for example, when pain medication is at its peak or when fatigue is at its lowest. Women might want to instruct their partner on how to use the "teasing touch." Most women like a lighter touch, and this can be arousing and stimulating. Sexual positioning can also be important for comfort and reduction of pain. And don't forget about VENIS—the pleasurable sexual activities that can lead to satisfying sexual experiences and do not have to include vaginal intercourse (see Chapter 8 for a complete discussion of VENIS). Women can also make use of the pharmacological and non-pharmacological options discussed earlier in the chapter to enhance arousal, lubrication, and sensation. Even though hormonal interventions can be tricky for women who have hormone-sensitive cancers, there are some options for these women that can be considered. For example, Estring and Vagifem are minimally absorbed into the bloodstream and help with lubrication. Most oncologists are comfortable using these products with their patients. DHEA is a precursor to testosterone and may be appropriate for women with certain types of cancers. Group therapy experiences with other women can provide a substantial amount of support. Women should also involve their partners in therapeutic approaches. When it comes down to it, communication and flexibility of sexual expression are the best way of understanding the difficulties that come with cancer and to find solutions together.

Finally, there are lifestyle choices that can affect the body's ability to respond sexually. Smoking and drinking too much alcohol impair sexual function in more ways than one. Smoking reduces blood flow to genitals (as well as the heart and extremities). It also decreases estrogen levels and HDL, or good cholesterol. As a result, chronic smoking poses risks to both your general and your sexual health. Kicking the habit is one of the best gifts a woman can give to her body. Alcohol is another substance that can harm sexual function. Though an aphrodisiac in smaller quantities, too much alcohol diminishes sexual response. Women who've been over-served often find that they have in-adequate lubrication, decreased sensation, and a more difficult time reaching orgasm. They may also find that too much alcohol consumed by a partner brings its own performance issues to the table, like difficulty achieving or maintaining an erection. Keep it moderate if you want to keep your sex life healthy!

SEX KEEPS YOU CONNECTED TO your body, and a healthy body keeps you connected to sex. It's a circular relationship that takes work, but the benefits are well worth it. Making sure your hormones are in balance is a lifelong ac-tivity. So is ensuring good blood flow. Though the standards we hold our bod-ies to may change with age, staying healthy should be a lasting priority.

It's also good to know there are tangible medical options for taking charge of your sex life. You can mend your mind, nurture your relationship, and con-tour your body, but sometimes you just need a physical boost to your sexual re-sponse that comes with a targeted treatment. Take advantage of what's out there—you've earned it! And hopefully there are many more options for women to come. More tools in your arsenal to make your sex life *everything* you want it to be.

PRESCRIPTIONS FOR THE WEEK:
Week 3

✓ How are your sexual desire, sexual arousal, sensitivity, and response? Are you able to achieve orgasm? It is time to assess your sexual situation and the physical factors that may be affecting you. If you think you may have a sexual function complaint, take the Berman Sexual Assessment (Appendix, starting on page 252) to get a sense of what your next steps should be.

✓ Go through your medicine cabinet. Are you taking any of the medications listed in this chapter that may be affecting your sexual health? If so, are there other options you can consider? Make an appointment to discuss the possibilities with your physician this week.

✓ Get your hormones tested! I recommend that every woman have her hormone levels tested in her early thirties for a baseline test. So whether you are having symptoms of unregulated hormones or you have no complaints at all, make an appointment to get your blood tested this week and ask for the tests that are covered starting on page 48.

✓ Don't forget! You are supposed to keep the genital blood flowing by masturbating twice a week—either with one of the new toys you bought last week or with your hands.

GUY'S GUIDE:
A Summary of Key Points for the Man in Your Life

1. A woman's sexual response can be diminished by her physical health. In fact, many of the risk factors for women's sexual problems are the same as they are for men. Take note! Cardiovascular disease, endocrine disorders, and lifestyle choices such as smoking can all affect your sexual function. Women face added challenges from the hormonal roller coasters of childbirth and menopause.

2. Testosterone is a fundamental source of sexual energy for both women and men, though men have many times the level of testosterone that women do, which, in large part, explains their heightened sex drives. Too little testosterone is a common physical cause of low libido in women and men. Especially after childbirth and while breast-feeding, a hormone called oxytocin is secreted, which may turn off testosterone in women.

3. If you suspect there's a problem, it is important for your partner to get a full hormonal workup done. This includes testing her estrogen, progesterone, and testosterone levels.

4. Blood flow is another important aspect of sexual function, for both women and men. Poor blood flow can affect almost every aspect of a woman's sexual response, especially sensation and lubrication. Along with other treatments, the little blue pill that has done wonders for men's sex lives, Viagra, can help women in certain cases, too.

5. A weak pelvic floor can impair a woman's orgasm ability. Childbirth, menopause, and aging all weaken the pelvic floor. Though many women never experience any problems, multiple vaginal deliveries or difficult labors are two of the most common risk factors.

6. A hysterectomy can also pose significant hazards to a woman's sex life. Hysterectomy can be like a double whammy, since when the ovaries are removed, a woman's body is sent into a hormonal free fall. Surgical hysterectomy can also damage blood flow to her sexual organs.

7. Smoking and drinking too much alcohol impair sexual function in more ways than one.

8. Antidepressants, birth control pills, and even antihistamines can all affect arousal, desire, and orgasm, independent of the conditions they are designed to treat.

9. Women can begin experiencing symptoms of menopause, technically called perimenopause, as early as their late thirties. As women approach menopause, many begin to notice striking changes in their libido and their sexual function, such as vaginal dryness and decreased orgasm quality. Hormone therapy and other options can help.

10. If your partner is unhappy with herself or you, however, no drug or medical treatment can cure that. Working out those issues with therapy and good communication is always best.

CHAPTER FOUR

Fix Your Mind

■⟨⟨⟨⟨■

It's important to have a healthy relationship with yourself before you try to make the most of your relationship with anyone else. Since the brain is the largest sexual organ, how you feel about yourself has a significant impact on your sex life. Self-doubt, insecurity, and regret are natural emotions that every woman struggles with to one degree or another. However, they are also intimacy spoilers. By working on the negative voices of the past (and often the present), *you* make your life the way you want it to be.

When it comes down to it, you are responsible for your happiness, both inside and outside the bedroom. Taking responsibility for your life makes you the master of your own destiny. Your sex life naturally benefits. So while the quality of your relationship is important, first you must get yourself where you want to be. Becoming one-half of a great couple comes after!

The Building Blocks

The voices of the past can be difficult to silence. Our parents do it, our lovers do it—they say and do things that stick with us for a lifetime—often without even meaning to. Stopping the past from seeping into the present is essential to your general happiness and to your sexual satisfaction in particular. There is no easy solution, but the desire to change is half the battle.

If the prevailing theme of this chapter is to nurture who you are, this simply takes it one step further. Destroying the negative voices of your past is the key to remodeling the way you think about yourself and your sex life. Even the most deeply ingrained patterns can be changed. At first it takes conscious effort to substitute old, more comfortable ways of thinking with new ways. Over time, changing the way you think becomes more automatic. New patterns replace old. You retrain your brain with mental exercises, just as you retrain your body with physical ones. It is a gradual process.

The most fundamental building blocks of every woman's sexuality are the early messages and experiences in her life. As children, and even as young adults, it is baffling when we are confronted with criticisms and reprimands about parts of ourselves we never questioned. Many years often pass before we are able to look objectively at how they shaped us. Negative messages about sex and about ourselves, which invariably affect us sexually, come in all different guises. It may be that you were told sex was shameful by a parent or that your response was inadequate by a partner. You may have had some type of trauma or abuse in your past. Body image is a source of anxiety for virtually every woman at one time or another. Silence can be a powerful force, too. If you watched your parents coexist without intimacy or physical affection, that sends a strong message without words. If you felt left out of the dating scene when you were younger, you may carry that with you even after you've found someone who loves you. It is all of these messages, models, and experiences that can prevent us from reaching our potential, sexual and otherwise.

Your choice comes into play when you decide what to do about these voices. Nothing will ever change the past, but you *can* choose how you respond to it. Some patterns will take more work to break out of; others may fade away as soon as you become aware of them. The goal is to write yourself a new script. Whether your rewrite takes a week or several years will depend on your circumstances. What's certain is that it is one of the most important efforts you can undertake. Looking at the past and taking charge of the present means you are growing as a woman. What else is there?

Building a New Foundation

Lesson number one for getting out of the past and into the present is "Stop Worrying!" For women, this can seem like learning not to breathe since our powers of analysis and tendency to obsess are near and dear to our hearts. Worry is a way of controlling the unknown. If you're like most women, you spend so much time wondering if the roof will need to be repaired, if your child will succeed in life, if your backside will look like a dinner plate by the time you are middle-aged, and endless other what-ifs, that you often forget to enjoy yourself in the meantime. There are also deeper worries that can plague you. Will you repeat mistakes your parents made? Will your partner leave you for someone younger, more attractive, smarter? The benefit of choosing not to worry is that you focus your attention on solutions, instead of on problems. While you can't be completely unrealistic and expect to never worry again, you can turn the worry flood into a worry trickle. Resist old ways of thinking. There may have been people or experiences in your life that made you feel like catastrophe was always around the next corner. Remember, worry does nothing but make you feel worse about possibilities that might not ever happen. It consumes energy that could be better spent living your life.

A good exercise is to think about all of the worries in your past that have come and gone. Most likely, the majority of them never came true. Each time you find yourself worrying, ask yourself what the solution is. Choose either to focus on the solution or move on. You can also put your worries aside for the moment and come back to them later. I used to do an exercise when my son was very ill that I found works well for me and many of the women I treat. At night when you are lying in bed and find yourself obsessing about the millions of things you are worrying about, imagine yourself in a garden with a huge tree—it's your worry tree. Imagine hanging all of your worries on the tree. The tree will hold them for you and keep them until you are ready to think about them again. Sometimes visualizing yourself letting go of the worries, even for a little while, really helps. Over time, you will find that you are less likely to worry and more likely to feel confident about handling life's peaks and valleys.

Getting a grip on worry also prevents it from poisoning your intimate relationships. Healthy intimacy depends on trust. When you spend your time worrying about everything that could go wrong with your relationship, you begin to erode that trust. While it can be difficult if your trust was violated in the past, taking a leap of faith is the only way to move beyond it. When you force yourself to see your relationship as a fresh opportunity, you stop reacting to the past and start focusing on the present. Sometimes your partner needs a little help in this department, too, and in the next chapter you will learn about the two-way street that intimacy is. But by making a concerted effort to stop worrying in your own life, you do your part. It also prevents many of your worries from becoming a reality. If you are constantly voicing your insecurities to your partner about your appearance or his attraction to you, it puts ideas in his head that might not have ever occurred to him otherwise! There is no need to let your partner in on every little flaw you think you have. Not to mention that the more confident and secure you seem, the more attractive you are to your partner. He doesn't want a needy, insecure girlfriend or wife—he wants to see you as desirable and attractive. Likewise, too much worrying about your partner's inadequacies can also mar your potential for intimacy. Instead of adding to a mental laundry list of annoyances, shortcomings, and criticisms, try to remind yourself what made you fall in love with him. Keep a present state of mind about your partner's good qualities. In fact, each time you feel a negative thought, counteract it with a positive one. You're more likely to keep yourself from getting in a mental rut.

Next is "Just Say No," or as I also like to call it, "Stop the Guilt." You need to make yourself a priority. Doing what makes you happy is not selfish; it is absolutely necessary to maintain your energy levels. Don't let other people pressure you into doing things you don't want to—be they mothers, friends, children, or partners. Every woman has a finite energy supply. You need to make sure all of it isn't being used up by your responsibilities. Between personal and professional obligations, most women feel stretched thin. Chronic stress affects women differently from the way it does men. Stress may make men want to have *more* sex, since it activates the fight-or-flight response, which can increase testosterone production. I know; it's not fair. Women, however, go into the tend-and-befriend mode we discussed in the previous chapter, which sets off a hormonal chain reaction that leaves women less physiologically primed for sex, in addition to feeling emotionally exhausted from daily life.

You can make small choices to help stop the feeling that life is bulldozing you. First and foremost, do what's important to you instead of worrying about others' expectations and opinions. Women are often driven to perfection in their desire to please and think they have to do everything to the fullest. Don't be afraid to take some shortcuts. Buy cookies at the grocery store for the next bake sale. Enlist some help with cleaning, or accept that the dishes can wait until tomorrow. Make time for activities that don't require anything of you but pleasure. Whether it's a night out with your partner, or coffee with the girls, take some time to get away from taking care of others. Enjoy yourself with the people you care about—life is not all about errands!

Often women will tell me that their lives have gotten so busy with kids, work, and family obligations that their friendships have all but disappeared. It's important to maintain your own woman-to-woman relationships away from motherhood or the men in your life. Think back to the times you used to spend with your girlfriends, before you had all of your current obligations. It's a great energy booster, fabulous support system, and an extremely effective stress reliever. Spending time chatting and laughing with other women is one of the best things we can do for our mental health. If you've lost track of your friends, make an effort to reconnect. Take the reins and plan a girls' night out with three or four women you'd like to reconnect with (or hang out with for the first time). You can also join a book club or take a class in a subject that interests you. It can even be a kids-oriented class that provides you with an opportunity to meet other women. Just make sure the time you spend involves some kid-free time, as well. Don't be shy. Most women will jump at the chance to spend time with the girls, if you take the initiative.

Another essential part of women's lives that gets eaten up by hectic daily schedules is sleep. Though it seems obvious, make sure you sleep! Sleep has become the sex of our modern, fast-paced world. It can be difficult to find the time, but getting enough sleep has a domino effect on the rest of your life and on sex in particular. Too little sleep affects hormone levels, which throws everything out of whack. Your mood drops, you don't have the energy to exercise, you can't concentrate, you may even eat more—not exactly the ideal environment for sexual desire or your emotional well-being to thrive. If you can't get enough sleep at night, try working in a nap during the day. Research has found that as little as a ten-minute nap can restore alertness, mood, and mental performance. Having a brief nap in the afternoon can help keep you going during sleep-deprived times. Finding the time to enjoy yourself will help you recharge, too. For the next week, take two hours to do only what you enjoy doing. Whether it's for one hour twice a week, or several smaller breaks, indulge yourself whichever way feels best. This means no calls, e-mails, chores, or orders from anybody else!

Last but not least is "Take Responsibility for Your Happiness." Changing your life begins with changing yourself. Even if you can't control the circumstances or people in your life, you can choose how you respond to them. Untangling yourself from self-defeating ways of thinking makes you realize you can change your perception. And when you think before you act, you naturally change the tempo of your life. Focus on the fact that you always have a choice. It's only when we feel like we have no choice that depression and anxiety set in as a result of our sense of helplessness. If you go right in to a fear reaction, your choices immediately seem limited to fighting, fleeing, or simply freezing. If you hold onto your sense of choice, you focus on your spirit and your mind in order to find new solutions and you're much happier as a result. When you have a sense of personal power, you feel power over your fate and over avoiding feelings of helplessness and hopelessness. The bottom line is that life always creates stresses and challenges—it's your attitude in facing them that makes the difference.

When you are faced with a new challenge, focus on your strengths. While our initial tendency is often to focus on our weaknesses, it only reinforces our fears. When you focus on your strengths and reinforce your awareness of them every day, you feel much safer. In particular, avoiding the three P's when faced with a new challenge can really help. They are permanence (thinking the problem will last forever), personalization (thinking that all problems are your fault), and pervasiveness (thinking that one problem extends to every situation). Think about what you are going to do *about* the problem, instead of seeing yourself as the victim. Falling into the trap that bad things always happen to you, that you can't fix this, and that you need someone else to rescue you is not productive. This is not someone else's problem or someone else's fault; it's your life. Sometimes you have to dig deep and get creative about how to solve problems. Honing your skills of appreciation can help, too. Research has shown that it's impossible to feel appreciation and fear at the same time. Finding a way to feel love and appreciation for whomever or whatever is troubling you will help soothe you, create a sense of hope, and make everything look not as bad. Finding a sense of agency about your own happiness primes you to make your life everything you want it to be. You learn that no person or situation makes you happy. You make yourself happy and then move on to improving other aspects of your life.

Finding Your Inner Goddess

What would you think if you could look at yourself through another's eyes? If you're like most women, you would probably relentlessly compare yourself—with other women, societal ideals, and maybe even past versions of yourself. In fact, all too many of us make a lucrative career out of comparison shopping each and every day of our lives. It's time to get a new skill set and become a professional at loving *you*. Unconditional love is not just for partners, friends, and children. It's most important for yourself.

When it comes to sex, women are especially quick to criticize themselves. They worry that they are not responding enough in bed, that they are not meeting their partners' expectations, or that they need to be different from their usual selves in countless other ways. Sometimes women can become so overwhelmed with self-doubt that they begin to ignore their sex lives completely. The truth is that sexual satisfaction flows from an uninhibited, confident mind-set. This means not only quieting the voices of the past, but also tuning out daily distractions and stress. Every sexual experience should be a new opportunity to explore your body, your relationship, and the moment.

Feeling good about sex starts long before you enter the bedroom (setting the stage just before sex is important, too, but we'll get to that in Chapter 8). Getting rid of negative emotional clutter is essential to getting yourself in a positive sexual mind-set. Instead of sizing yourself up, both inside and outside the bedroom, putting energy into what you *like* about yourself gets you out of comparison paralysis. It takes practice, but you just might realize that the woman you've always wanted to be was there all along. When you do, the right sexual mind-set is just around the corner.

Confidence: It Does Your Body Good

Finding ways to create a sense of confidence in all areas of your life naturally spills over into your sex life. Confidence in your body is especially important. It is also notoriously thorny for most women. Did you know that nearly 80 percent of women are dissatisfied with their appearance and more than 45 percent of women are on a diet at any given time? In fact, many women spend a lifetime jumping from one diet to another in hopes of waking up one day with the body they've always wanted—or maybe, the body they once had. Yes, it's important to eat well, exercise, and make sure you are keeping the physical attraction alive between you and your partner, but none of us is perfect, and you must ultimately learn to accept and even love your body, flaws and all.

We all want to look like Jennifer Aniston. Who wouldn't? But when 9.9 out of 10 women don't, we should start asking ourselves why we hold onto the idea that we *should*. We stopped believing in Santa Claus when we found out he didn't exist, but somehow women walk around every day thinking they need to match up to something just as imaginary. Aside from staggeringly rare genetics, we also do not have access to the personal trainers, nutritionists, makeup artists, and wardrobe consultants that help celebrities like Jennifer Aniston look the way they do. Not to mention the money, rest, and relaxation that comes with being an A-list movie star! Comparing yourself with someone who has those types of resources sets you up for automatic disappointment. Unfortunately for women, we are bombarded by the media on a daily basis with images of perfect women with perfect bodies and perfect everything else, which leaves too many of us with a bad case of the body blues.

Making the most of what you have is the task at hand. It's finding that fine line between self-improvement and self-acceptance about your physical appearance that can be most difficult. There are all sorts of tips coming up in Chapter 6 for getting your body in shape; however, this is about your mental fitness. Changing the way you think about your body is as important as the effort you put into the way it looks. When you feel a case of the body blues coming on, refer back to this section to snap yourself out of it.

First and foremost, change your visual scenery as much as you are able to. Throw away your fashion and celebrity magazines. Put up pictures of yourself that make you feel happy—whether it's the way you look, what you're doing, or who you're with in the pictures. Choose artwork that celebrates different female shapes or is abstract. Limit the amount of time you spend watching television or movies, which are populated with completely unrealistic women *and* men. Make your world look like you! When you give in to the temptation to buy a bad magazine or two, remember that magazines are a business like any other. Of course they are going to tell you about the many makeup products, skin care products, and diets you need to take part in; that's their strategy for getting you to keep reading. The more inadequate you feel, the more magazines you will buy to improve yourself. In fact, thinking about the motive behind the message is a good strategy for all media. Advertisements, movies, and television shows all dangle the carrot for one good reason: to get your money in one form or another.

When you turn your attention away from the ideals that are scattered across our cultural landscape, you begin to regain a sense of what's real. This is the perfect setting in which to begin rediscovering some body confidence. Just as you explored your genitals, it's important to do the same with the rest of your body. Face yourself, ladies! If you run around pretending like you do not exist below the neck because you don't look at your body in a mirror, you are never going to discover what you *like* about your body. I know it sounds intimidating, but looking at yourself naked is essential to body confidence. Plus, it helps with getting over your inhibitions about other people seeing you naked. Set aside a time when you know you will be alone for an hour. I suggest showering or taking a bath beforehand, since you will already be naked and you can do things to relax while in the shower. Put some effort into your scenery. Light a few candles and turn on your favorite music. Do what makes you feel happy and comfortable. While showering or bathing, relish in the moment. Enjoy the water as it washes over your face and moves down your body. Take care as you wash each body part, feeling your contours.

Once out of the shower, towel yourself off as you stand in front of the mirror. This is a great time to indulge in a luxurious new body lotion or oil. Apply the lotion slowly to each part of your body, while looking at yourself in the mirror. What do you like? What do you wish were different? Sometimes it's helpful to speak out loud as you move from one area of your body to another. Maybe it's your thighs you don't like, or your stomach. But are your arms toned? Or possibly you've always had great, shapely legs or beautiful eyes. Touch each part as you speak about it. Pay attention to areas you might not think of as sexy, like your neck, hands, and feet, even your eyes and ears. Contemplate the amazing functions your body is capable of—all of your internal systems working in harmony to keep you alive, the fact that your reproductive organs function. Your body is so much more than its appearance. Focus on the miracle of it, your human body, and the experiences it has been through. From pregnancy and childbirth to sex with your partner to running at the gym, your body is an impressive structure in which to experience life.

Once you are dressed, look at how your clothes might make you feel differently about your body. Clothing is a creative way of celebrating and enhancing your uniqueness. It can change your shape or express your personality. No matter if you think your hips are too big or your breasts too small, your clothing is a reflection of how you choose to present yourself to the world. Did you know that the average American woman is 5'4", weighs 145 pounds, and wears a size 12, while the average model is 5'11", weighs 117 pounds, and wears a size 2? Don't think that you have to look a certain way to wear the clothes you love. Your body is a source of pride, to be dressed and decorated as you see fit.

It's important to keep up an enduring sense of connection to your body. Participate in activities that make you feel good. You don't have to go to a gym to do this. Take a walk, or dance around the room when you're alone. Do anything that gives you a sense of awareness and appreciation of your body. Even just breathing deeply while sitting at your desk or carpooling the kids can make you feel connected. Breathe in slowly, paying attention as the air moves down your torso and your stomach expands. Feel your body collapse inward as you exhale out. Focus on other activities that put your body to use: Your reflexes are quick as you navigate down a busy street, your hands are powerful as you prepare a nourishing dinner, your body is in a womb-like state while you are snuggled up on the couch watching the evening news. All of these sensations are your body.

Lose Your Inhibitions

Working on how you think about your body primes you to move beyond your inhibitions. When you realize you are a beautiful woman, and celebrate what makes you an individual, you unlock your own natural sexiness. Pushing the limits of your sensuality is the logical next step in getting in touch with the vixen inside.

To say that most women have grown up with a conflicted attitude about sex is an understatement. When young, we are warned to protect our honor, guard our virginity as if it were an endangered species, and not give away our "milk" for free. All along the message is very clear: Good girls don't have sex for sex's sake. And while that message runs through our heads and bodies, we are confronted with images of sex at virtually every turn. Women shampoo their hair with orgasmic bliss, half of America gets flashed at the Super Bowl, and even preteen girls become inadvertent billboards with words like "juicy" stamped across their behinds. Somehow, women are also expected to be confident, sexual sirens once they *finally* do have sex.

It's no joke that women can feel like they're stuck between a rock and a hard place when it comes to sex. And the solution, once again, is to turn away from the messages, expectations, and ideals and to find the true voice of desire from within. You must discard the subtle (and not-so-subtle) messages about your sexuality and start with a clean slate. Sex is good. It feels good, does good things for your body, and is a natural part of life. Remember, your sexuality is one of the most fundamental instincts you have! Far from feeling ashamed, you should enjoy the gift that your sexuality is. It offers a way of connecting to yourself and to those you choose to share it with that is completely unique.

I know, easier said than done. If you've spent years masturbating under the covers or placing your partner's pleasure at a higher priority than yours because you're embarrassed to ask for what you want, old habits can be hard to break. But they can be changed. Since women experience sex in their minds as much as in their bodies, changing your thought patterns can be a potent catalyst. First, it's crucial to stop the negative sexual messages that play over and over again in your mind. To do this, make a list of your important sexual experiences. From the earliest you can remember to losing your virginity to your current relationship—write them down so you begin remembering the details. Next, think about how you felt about each of them, what you liked, what you felt insecure about. This can be both sexually and otherwise. Think about how you changed from one experience to the next. Maybe you felt timid about being naked in your early experiences or maybe you didn't have your first orgasm until much later. The idea is to get a mental picture of your sexual journey so far. Make notes as you do it. Write what you enjoyed about each experience and anything you didn't. The good part about looking at the past is that fewer memories stick with you as time passes, but the ones that do remain for a reason.

Once you've made your list, add any messages about sex you received during your childhood. Outside of your first sexual experiences and relationships, early messages from authority figures such as parents and teachers have an enormous impact on your sexual development. What you accomplish in writing all of this down is a sexual narrative. It's important to have a story that makes sense of your sexual development, even if there are still many more chapters to come. Looking back can help you understand feelings and possibly even patterns that you might not have recognized before. You should also be able to pick out the negative beliefs you carry with you, such as "I am ashamed of my body" or "I was told I would be disrespected if I had sex." Write these down on a separate piece of paper. Then take the piece of paper, fold it up, and put it to rest. This can mean in the bottom of your jewelry box or with a stack of old letters. It is symbolic and represents you casting off your most common sexual insecurities.

Of course there has to be something to replace them! Since you've already begun embracing your body, it's a natural continuation to keep gently pushing yourself. Try walking around naked in stilettos. Vamp it up—head held high, shoulders back, and buttocks out. Talk yourself into feeling sexy. And I mean really do it. Stop finding excuses, or feeling embarrassed or silly. You have every right to feel like the sexual being you are. In addition to getting more comfortable with yourself naked, make sure you dress the part, too. Lingerie and clothing choices help you feel sexy. Do little things to remind you of your sensual side, like wearing a bright red bra and panties underneath your work suit or showing some cleavage for no good reason at all! You don't have to conform to any ideal; you just have to do what makes you feel sexy. Keeping a confident sexual energy going on a daily basis keeps you in the right mind-set.

In fact, forcing yourself to think about sex does wonders in itself. After all, the more you think about sex . . . the more you think about sex! Part of getting rid of your inhibitions means allowing yourself to entertain your most outrageous sexual thoughts. I'm talking about fantasy, ladies. While we can choose what we express in our behavior, our minds often take us in unexpected directions. Fantasy should be used to indulge these wanderings. Maybe you have a crush on someone forbidden or someone you would never become involved with in your real life. You may pass a stranger on the street and find yourself thinking about him *or her* for the rest of the day. The object of your fantasy can be anybody, even someone you have simply made up in your head. Indulge yourself and quiet any judging internal voices. If nothing else, your fantasies are merely an escape from reality that allows you to exercise your imagination. At their best, fantasies provide inspiration for pushing the boundaries in your real sex life.

Ultimately, let your mind wander and see what you come up with. The nicest thing about fantasies is that they are all normal. Since you are not necessarily going to act them out, there is no limit on what you can indulge in your mind. You might even try keeping a fantasy journal, in which you write about your most explicit sexual daydreams. Just keep it somewhere private if you don't want your partner reading it! Once again, you are working on making sex a regular celebrated resident of your mind. Instead of suppressing your sexual thoughts, you are actively bringing them to life. Thinking, writing, and even talking about them is the best way to do it (for more on when to share fantasies with your partner, see the following chapter).

If you need a little inspiration, I've got some ideas to get you started. Maybe you want to be seduced, even ravaged or dominated. Many women who feel in complete control of their real lives and have no interest in being forced to do anything, find this type of fantasy surprisingly arousing. Especially for women who spend all of their time and effort caring for the people around them, the idea of sitting back as the object of desire to be romanced and pleasured is quite exciting. Imagine you are on a deserted beach, when a handsome stranger or someone you have a secret crush on happens to find you there. He slowly begins to seduce you, rubbing and kissing you in all the right ways. He's pushing you into the sand as he devours you. You resist as he begins undressing you, but then you realize you like the thrill of what he's doing to you. You can taste the salt and sand as he kisses you. The water from the tide is making both of you slippery and wet. You are turned on even more by the fact that he's taking advantage of you. He wants you and takes you for his own pleasure.

Or maybe it's a handyman who comes over to fix something in your house. You feel the sparks fly from the moment you answer the door. As he's working, you go upstairs to use the bathroom. You are surprised to find him standing outside when you come out. He carries you into your bedroom without asking and takes off your clothes before you know what's happening. He tells you how much he loves your body, and how you smell and feel. As he gets you more aroused, you want him, too. But he won't take his clothes off as you grab at them. He holds your hands above your head with one hand and satisfies you with the other. He is completely focused on your pleasure.

Or maybe you are the one who wants to be in charge in your fantasies. Imagine you are a wild seductress who pursues sexual gratification without limitations or expectations. You are in control. For women who are more meek or submissive in their regular lives, it can be stimulating to imagine taking the reins sexually. Maybe you are an exotic dancer, wearing nothing but a thong as you seduce a roomful of men. All eyes are on you as you confidently dance around the stage, caressing your breasts and tousling your hair. You step down from the stage to take a wildly attractive man into the back room to have sex. After removing his pants, you use him for your satisfaction. Maybe you are an exhibitionist, enjoying it all the more that his friends are watching as you take advantage of him. Or maybe you are inflicting pain, getting pleasure out of embarrassing him and watching him suffer. You are in total control and focused only on your needs.

Maybe you are into something really forbidden—something that goes against all of your real-life values. You might have a strong attraction to your child's teacher, whom you've always found both charming and attractive. Maybe he's even married. You decide to pay him a visit one day when no one else is around to discuss a problem you are having with your child. Like always, he is attentive and motions for you to sit down on the couch in his office. You begin speaking and find yourself staring deeply into his eyes. He pays so much attention to you and seems to understand you so perfectly that you wonder why your husband can't be like him. Before you know it you are crying and holding your face in your hands. He comforts you, putting his arm around your shoulder and allowing your head to rest on his chest. Without thinking, you look up and begin kissing him. He resists, but then begins kissing you back. You are in a frenzy, grabbing each other's clothes and kissing violently. He does not even undress you, but lifts up your skirt and unbuttons his pants and you have sex right there on the couch. It is over quickly, but you feel satisfied and comforted. You both stand up and rearrange your clothes, sharing one last intimate gaze. You grab his hand, knowing this will never happen or be spoken of again. You leave his office and head home to make your family dinner, the glow of your tryst still on you when your husband walks in the door from work.

For the more timid, you can also be a fantasy voyeur. Imagine watching someone else dominate, be victimized, seduced, or do any sexual act you envision. Maybe you are in a bar having a drink and you notice people going through a doorway that leads downstairs. You follow and realize it is a sex club. You have always wanted to watch other people have sex, and this is the perfect opportunity. As you stand in the back among the foreign crowd, you feel excited but nervous. You can't believe that everyone around you is there for the same purpose. All of a sudden the lights dim and a statuesque woman walks onto the stage wearing nothing but stiletto heels and a black lace bra and panties. She is beautiful, without a hint of hesitation in her eyes. You feel as if she is looking directly at you. A man emerges and stands behind her. He's rubbing his hands up and down her body—over her breasts, down her torso, and between her thighs. The woman looks straight ahead at the crowd and is getting turned on by everyone looking back at her. The couple turns to face each other and begins kissing and rhythmically moving their bodies against each other. The air is thick with sensuality and tension. You and an attractive stranger exchange a quick glance, knowing that both of you are getting aroused. The man and woman begin undressing each other. Again, you feel like she's staring right at you as he caresses her—now completely naked. He throws her onto a red velvet bed that's on the stage. He climbs on top of her, and they begin having sex, moving and moaning in symphony. You love what you're seeing. You keep locking eyes with the stranger. It feels dangerous, but you are excited and want to see him afterward.

Voyeuristic fantasies are great for women who enjoy the intensity of a sexual scene without having to take part in it. You might imagine being up close and personal, watching two people have sex, or maybe you are observing a threesome from a one-way mirror or even under the bed. This way you can enjoy the titillation of watching what you may not have the courage to act out, even in your imagination. You are letting yourself get creative sexually in a way that is totally safe, both mentally and physically. You can take risks and be someone you would never have the nerve to be in real life. There is no judgment in fantasies!

Fantasy also allows you to take charge of your sexual pleasure. Put to good use along with masturbation and vibrators, orgasms are your own gift to yourself. By acting as if you deserve pleasure and taking the initiative to get it, you do not leave your sexuality at anybody else's discretion. Of course, it's important to teach your partner how to pleasure you, too (and tips for that are coming up later in Chapter 8); however, exploring yourself inside and out is an essential part of overcoming inhibition.

If none of the fantasies mentioned strike a chord for you, try this simple format for brainstorming your own. Write down a setting that you find provocative or comforting—it could be anything from a luxurious bath to a coworker's office to somewhere totally imaginary, like a chic hotel in Paris or an exclusive celebrity-only party. Next, describe the role you envision yourself taking. Are you hidden in the background? Are you the center of attention? Maybe you are sitting with a group of people or observing others. Write down what you are wearing and what you feel like. Let your imagination take over. You're confident or timid, a siren or an undiscovered treasure. Describing your role and appearance should help shape the fantasy. If you're the one in charge, what will you do to the others? Or what will they watch you do? If you are a coy, or even unwilling, participant in your fantasy, what is someone else going to do to you? Your fantasy can be as lurid or conservative as you want it to be. You're the boss.

Get In Touch with Your Sensual Side

At this point, you should be well on your way to discovering your sensual side. But lasting sensuality is not simply about learning to appreciate your body and creatively overcomeing inhibitions; it's about making the sensory experience a part of your everyday life. Getting in touch with your senses immerses you in the moment. When you practice doing it outside the bedroom, it becomes more automatic once inside it.

In fact, finding ways to enjoy the smells, sounds, and textures of your daily routine reinvigorates you completely. We use so few of our senses as we race through the activities of the day. Take a minute to stop and smell the roses, literally. Look around at your neighborhood's homes, trees, and flowers. Walk past a bakery and inhale the delicious smells. Spend your lunch break outside to rev up your senses and prevent dullness from seeping in. Take a walk instead of the bus or train on your way home, or choose a stop that is a bit farther away than the one you would normally take. If you're a stay-at-home mom, take your kids to the park so you can get outside. You are their best guide in helping them tune into their senses, too. Touching, cuddling, and nuzzling prime your child's senses from an early age. In fact, we all begin as sensual beings, but get farther away from touch and other primal urges as we mature. It's important to restore the connection to our senses. Getting in touch with your world helps, since it energizes you with sunlight, fresh air, and a change of scenery. It gets you in the moment by engaging all of your senses. In Chapter 9, you will also learn about using food to spark the senses—both for you and your partner.

When you resist gliding through life on automatic pilot, your sex life naturally benefits. It's vital to notice the world around you and how you respond to it. Once you get into a mind-set that is focused on your perceptions and sensations, it is a small leap to getting into the sexual moment. The more work you put into tuning up your senses, the more sensual you become. Enjoy the pleasure of being touched, how it feels against your skin. The tingling sensation in your genitals brings that part of your body to life. Close your eyes to immerse yourself completely in what you are feeling. There is nothing else that matters for this moment.

In the following chapter, you'll learn about making sex with your partner a full-blown sensory experience. For now, you need to start practicing in your daily life *and* when you are masturbating. Make it a point to masturbate at least twice in the next week. Anytime you feel your mind wandering or analyzing, refocus your attention. Let your senses guide you, instead of your thoughts. Each and every sexual experience, whether by yourself or with someone else, is about the moment. Let it define itself by letting yourself go.

Reaching Out for Help

There are times when more help is needed than you can provide yourself. Taking steps to understand your past is not always easy, especially in the case of trauma or abuse. The objective perspective of a trained therapist can help guide you toward healing. There are six primary challenges that can affect a woman's sex life, which I refer to as emotional daggers. Since I've addressed each of them at length in my past books, I have listed just the common symptoms below. If you think any of them describe you, or if you have two or more symptoms of one of them, it is important to seek the help of a licensed therapist. There are also many excellent resources, such as books and support groups, if you are interested in learning more. Consult the Resource Guide at the end of this book for specific suggestions.

DEPRESSION

Persistent sad, anxious, or empty mood

Feelings of hopelessness, pessimism

Feelings of guilt, worthlessness, helplessness

Loss of interest or pleasure in hobbies and activities that were once enjoyed, including sex

Decreased energy, fatigue, being "slowed down"

Difficulty concentrating, remembering, making decisions

Insomnia, early-morning awakening, or oversleeping

Appetite and/or weight loss or overeating and weight gain

Thoughts of death or suicide

Restlessness, irritability

Persistent physical symptoms that do not respond to treatment, such as headaches, digestive disorders, and chronic pain

ANXIETY

Persistent restlessness or feeling on edge

Chronic exaggerated worry

Irritability

Difficulty concentrating

Being easily fatigued

Muscle tension

Difficulty falling or staying asleep, or unsatisfying sleep

Pounding heart

Shortness of breath

Feeling faint or dizzy

STRESS

Nervousness or anxiety

Sadness or depression

Forgetfulness

Indecisiveness

Insomnia

Negative thoughts

Back pain or muscle tension

Headaches

Indigestion or bowel disturbances

Hives or skin rashes

Grinding of the teeth

ADDICTION

Inability to function without substances (alcohol, drugs, pills, etc.)

Experiencing unpleasant symptoms when you don't use substances

Needing more of the substances to experience the same effect

Secretive behavior surrounding substance consumption

Stealing or borrowing money to purchase substances

Withdrawal from friends and relatives

Neglecting responsibilities at work or home

EATING DISORDERS

Recurrent episodes of binge eating

Recurrent inappropriate behavior to prevent weight gain, such as fasting, vomiting, excessive exercise, or using laxatives, diuretics, or enemas

Obsessive thoughts about body shape and weight

Resistance to maintaining body weight at or above a minimally normal weight for age and height

Intense fear of gaining weight or becoming fat

Infrequent or absent menstrual periods

TRAUMA AND ABUSE

Experiencing any of the following in either the past or present warrants the attention of a therapist. All can be committed by parents, relatives, lovers, friends, coworkers, and strangers.

Sexual abuse (inappropriate or unwanted touching, oral sex, or intercourse; date rape; verbal taunting; watching sexual acts against your will)

Physical abuse (non-accidental injury or restraint that may or may not leave physical marks)

Emotional abuse (criticism, humiliation, isolation, threats of abandonment, threats of harm, or invasion of personal space that persist[ed] despite your distress; altering your feelings, needs, and behavior because you fear[ed] the response of another)

In many cases, two or three months of therapy is enough to start working your way out of a problem. Since it will depend on the particulars of your situation, there is no concrete time frame. A problem that has been present for as long as you can remember is different from one that has developed all of a sudden. Especially for sexual abuse or other kinds of emotional or physical trauma, the circumstances will play a large role in determining the right course of treatment. A woman who was sexually abused on a long-term basis by someone she was close to has different needs from a woman who was fondled once by a neighbor's relative. What's important is that every woman knows help is available. Depending on the nature of your situation and what you hope to get out of it, you can be in therapy for as long or as short as you like.

It's essential to find a therapist you connect with, just like with any other relationship. A good fit will allow you to take the emotional risks that are fundamental to productive therapy. Sometimes this means trying out more than one therapist. Many therapists are willing to do a trial session, in which you meet for half the length of a regular session for half the cost. It offers you the opportunity to meet in person and discover if you have a good rapport or not. Even if a therapist is well-qualified and has excellent credentials, there is nothing wrong with rejecting him or her because the right fit is not there. Feeling comfortable is most important. That being said, it is still important to make sure the therapist you choose is properly qualified. A qualified therapist usually has one of four degrees: a Ph.D. (doctor of philosophy in some psychological field), Psy.D. (doctor of psychology), M.F.T. (master of marriage and family therapy), or M.S.W. (master of social work). All of these mean the therapist has gone through an accredited program to earn his or her counseling degree. Therapists with Ph.D. and Psy.D. degrees have had the most academic training, usually four or more years. Therapists with M.F.T. and M.S.W. degrees have typically gone through two years of academic training. Ideally if the therapist is an M.S.W. he or she has focused on clinical social work. A master of social work can have many different focuses and the clinical social work background provides excellent clinical and academic training for therapists.

In addition to academic training, therapists must be licensed to practice. While academic experience is important, the clinical work experience the therapist has had is most crucial. No matter what their degree, all therapists should have a minimum of two years of clinical experience, in addition to their academic work. Each state has different requirements for licensure; some states require several years of experience before they will grant a license, while others require almost none. If you are unsure about a therapist's credentials, ask to see his or her degree and state license. Ask about past experience. Also, you can usually trust that therapists who are part of one or more established insurance plans have a fair amount of experience, since health care companies have more stringent requirements.

I am often asked about the difference between general therapy and sex therapy. Though it's a fine line, I recommend general therapy when a problem primarily affects nonsexual parts of a woman's life and sex therapy when some aspect of her sex life is the source of the problem or concern. A general therapist can help if you are having symptoms of any of the six emotional daggers discussed earlier, which may be affecting your performance at work or your relationship with partners, family, friends, or children, or any of a number of other situations. However, for problems that are compromising your sex life or capacity for intimacy, a sex therapist is best. General therapists often do not have experience dealing with sexual problems and sometimes may not be comfortable discussing them. You want to make sure you are able to open up to the person you are seeing without feeling self-conscious. A good sex therapist should always have experience in general therapy, too. When I said it was a fine line between sex therapy and general therapy, I meant that sex is never just about sex—there are always many issues at work, so it's important for a sex therapist to be well versed in matters other than sex. The best resource for finding a certified sex therapist is the American Association of Sex Educators, Counselors, and Therapists at www.aasect.org. While all of these therapists have had extensive experience dealing with sexuality and sexually related concerns, not all of the therapists listed are necessarily licensed by their state and do not necessarily have experience in general therapy.

<hr/>

You can see why good sex is as much about your mind as it is your body. Like a wise investment, the more you put in, the more you get back in the long run. Nurturing your emotional well-being allows everything else to fall into place. From feeling good about your body to getting the nerve to get creative, your sex life begins to take on a life of its own.

Putting energy into your relationship with yourself provides the added benefit of keeping you dynamic. Quieting the voices of the past allows you to grow in places far beyond the bedroom. When you change, your life changes, and it's exciting to know that you can shape your reality. Whether single or in a relationship, luck favors the fearless. Keep working to be everything you can be.

PRESCRIPTIONS FOR THE WEEK:
Week 4

Instead of suppressing your sexual thoughts, you are actively bringing them to life. Thinking, writing, and even talking about them is the best way to do it.

✓ Change your visual scenery as much as you can. Throw away your fashion and celebrity magazines. Put up pictures of yourself that make you feel happy—whether it's the way you look, what you're doing, or whom you're with in the pictures.

✓ I know it sounds intimidating, but looking at yourself naked is essential to body confidence. Follow the instructions on pages 80 and 81 and give it a shot!

✓ Try one of the sensory exercises like the one starting on page 81. Put some effort into your scenery. Light a few candles and turn on your favorite music. Do what makes you feel happy and comfortable. While showering or bathing, relish in the moment. Enjoy the water as it washes over your face and moves down your body.

✓ Try a new kind of movement—walking, dancing, etc. You may even want to try dancing around naked—either by yourself or with your partner.

✓ Start a sexual journal this week. You may have one at home, or you can go to any bookstore and pick out a journal that appeals to you. Keep a log of your sexual thoughts, insecurities, hopes, challenges, and successes. You'll find that if you put some effort in, you'll be able to look back on your journey over the next six weeks and feel not only quite proud of yourself, but also learn a lot about yourself along the way.

✔ You should be able to pick out the negative beliefs you carry with you, such as "I am ashamed of my body" or "I was told I would be disrespected if I had sex." Write these down on a separate piece of paper. Then take the piece of paper, fold it up, and put it to rest. This can mean in the bottom of your jewelry box or simply burn it. It is symbolic and represents you casting off your most common sexual insecurities.

✔ Feed your fantasy life—spend at least ten minutes a day this week thinking about sex—you'll find it escalates from there.

✔ Make a list of everything you are supposed to do this week (not on this week's prescriptions, but in general). Now put them in order of priority and then cross off as many as you can . . . if you can actually cross off half of a very long list you're doing great, but that can be a tall order. Accept the fact that there'll always be a rolling to-do list, and you can put things off to make room for yourself. Try to make this a habit whenever you are feeling overwhelmed by your to-do list.

✔ Call a girlfriend this week and make a date to get together. If there's no one you can think of, your homework is to reach out to a new friend—perhaps another mother at your kid's school or a woman you know at work—and invite her out to coffee.

✔ Over the next five weeks, take two hours each week to do only what you enjoy doing. Whether it's for one hour twice during the week, or several smaller breaks, indulge yourself whichever way feels best. This means no calls, e-mails, chores, or orders from anybody else!

✔ If you have two or more symptoms listed on the Emotional Daggers List in this chapter, get in touch with a therapist and make an appointment this week!

✔ Don't forget to make a point to masturbate at least twice in the next week!

GUY'S GUIDE:
A Summary of Key Points for the
Man in Your Life

1. When it comes down to it, every person is responsible for his or her own happiness, both inside and outside the bedroom. Taking responsibility for your life makes you the master of your own destiny. Your sex life naturally benefits. So while the quality of your relationship is important, first you must get yourself where you want to be. Becoming one-half of a great couple comes after!

2. Since women experience sex in their minds as much as in their bodies, changing thought patterns can be an especially potent catalyst for positive change in the bedroom.

3. The building blocks of a woman's sexuality are the early messages and experiences in her life (as are yours). Past negative messages about sex have a powerful effect on her sexuality—even today. It may be that she was told sex was shameful by a parent or that her response was inadequate by a former partner. Silence can be powerful, too. If she watched her parents coexist without intimacy or physical affection that sends a strong message without words. Body image is a source of anxiety for virtually every woman at one time or another.

4. Chronic stress affects women differently from the way it does men. Stress may actually make men want to have *more* sex, since it activates the fight-or-flight response, which can increase testosterone production. When women get stressed, their bodies release the hormone oxytocin, which ultimately leads to less free testosterone circulating in her body. Less testosterone often means less interest in sex.

5. Every woman has a finite energy supply. Doing what makes her happy is not selfish; it is absolutely necessary to maintain her energy levels. Help her out with some of her responsibilities and burdens, and you'll see her libido perk up.

6. Often, women will tell me that their lives have gotten so busy with kids, work, and family obligations that their friendships have all but disappeared. Encourage her to connect with friends and engage in activities that make her feel like a woman, not just a mother, or girlfriend, or wife. The more connected she is to herself as a woman, the sexier she will feel.

7. Beware of sleep deprivation in the woman in your life! Sleep has become the sex of our modern, fast-paced world. While it can be difficult to find the time, getting enough sleep has a domino effect on the rest of her life and on sex in particular. Too little sleep affects hormone levels, which throws everything out of whack. Her mood drops, she won't have the energy to exercise, she won't be able to concentrate, she may eat more—not exactly the ideal environment for sexual desire or her emotional well-being to thrive.

8. There are six primary challenges that can affect a woman's sex life, which I refer to as emotional daggers: depression, anxiety, stress, addiction, eating disorders, and trauma and abuse. If you suspect your partner is suffering from any of these, make sure you support her in getting the help she needs.

9. I am often asked about the difference between general therapy and sex therapy. Though it's a fine line, I recommend general therapy when a problem primarily affects nonsexual parts of a woman's life and sex therapy when some aspect of her sex life is the source of the problem or concern. General therapists often do not have experience dealing with sexual problems and sometimes may not be comfortable discussing them. You want to make sure you are able to open up to the person you are seeing without feeling self-conscious. A good sex therapist should always have experience in general therapy, too.

CHAPTER FIVE

Fix Your Relationship

■〉〉〉〉■

REMEMBER THE TINGLY FEELING YOU had when you first met your mate? You would think all day about seeing him at night. Your stomach did tiny flips as you gave each other a kiss, a touch. During sex, you felt as if you might melt into each other's bodies and never want to separate. Flash to the present: You enjoy the deep affection you and your partner share, but the fires of your initial passion have become more of a slow burn. Maybe kids, career, or simple boredom have taken their toll. While much of truly sensational sex is a fleeting biochemical moment during every new relationship's infatuation stage, there is no reason to resign yourself to sexual dreariness. If you've found yourself asking, "How soon will it be over?," or "Not tonight again!," your relationship is probably due for a tune-up.

Finding ways to keep the sparks flying between you and your partner takes work both inside and outside the bedroom. It can be the hardest thing in the world to open yourself up completely to another, but it is also the most rewarding. Intimacy is what this chapter is all about. As a couple, you must learn to talk to each other even when the subject is unpleasant. The best relationships are built on trust and vulnerability. If you work to make those what they should be, the sex often follows more naturally. Sometimes, however, the sex can help get you back there. Communicating about your wishes and fantasies, as well as your expectations, is a window into your potential as a couple.

Why Sex Matters

Far and away, the most important building block to a woman's sexual desire is the quality of her relationship. When sex is working in a relationship it's an important but not necessarily a central part of what's working. When sex isn't working, it takes on a life of its own and becomes a big white elephant in the room with the couple. As you probably know from your own experience, feeling emotionally close to your partner often inspires you to want to be sexual with him. For your partner it is the opposite—if he's like most men, he usually needs sex in order to feel emotionally close to you.

You can see how a cycle of sex and intimacy develops. If a woman feels close to her partner, she is more likely to be sexual. The sexual activity then fosters even more intimacy in the relationship, making her primed for yet more sex. The reverse is also true. A woman who feels disconnected from her partner is less likely to feel sexual desire for him. He then doesn't have the means to feel that closeness to her and becomes emotionally disconnected. And guess what? The more emotionally disconnected he is, the less she wants to have sex with him. The different ways men and women approach sex can sometimes create a fundamental breakdown. He's not giving you the emotion, and you're not giving him the motion, and many couples know that things can quickly spiral out of control.

In order for sex to be successful in a relationship, women and men must work to understand what the other one needs. When a woman does not feel valued by her partner—whether by the time he spends with her, the compliments he pays her, or countless other relationship deal breakers—she begins to lose interest in sex. When the sex starts to go, his care and attention often does, too. For their part, men need to understand that they must give their partners attention on a regular basis that is not seen as purely sexual. Often, men do not realize that what goes on outside of the bedroom is as important as what goes on inside of it when it comes to sex. Though there are those couples who can fight like cats and dogs and still have great sex, it is more the exception than the rule. Or, it is the type of passionate relationship that is thrilling, but burns too brightly to ever really last. As a rule, couples must work on feeling connected as a team in all areas of their lives. Your job is to ask for what you want and need in the relationship to keep the sexual fire burning in the long term. Sometimes, men simply need to have it spelled out for them.

In fact, asking for what you need outside of the bedroom helps double your pleasure later. First, it works to recharge your sexual battery by sharing with your partner and giving him the opportunity to show he cares. Second, it helps you to quiet your mind. Unlike men, women often have a hard time focusing on the sexual act. The less that's bugging or distracting you, the more likely you are to enjoy yourself in the moment. A sense of intimacy and connection are a woman's real erogenous zones. Making your relationship what you want it to be puts both in the palm of your hand.

The Way We Were

Sex is the fiber of your relationship. It is the act that distinguishes you from roommates and offers a way of revealing yourselves to each other that is uniquely yours. At its best, sex is a channel for communication and connection between you and your partner. At its worst, sex is a chore that begins to feel like a mere echo of the pleasure you once shared. In addition to the newness of sex when you first met, emotions ran high as you explored and luxuriated in each other. As real life inevitably intrudes on your relationship, it's essential to find ways to tune back into those early days when everything was exciting. More often than not, men and women find that they have different sex drives once the dust has settled. Compromise is the key. Both partners need to feel satisfied with what's going on in the bedroom. There is no normal amount of sex, just as there is no repertoire of activities that is going to work for every couple, every time. The key is making it work for the two of you.

That said, I believe that barring illness, emotional struggles, or relationship chaos, you should never go more than two weeks without sex. In fact, to reverse the cycle of feeling like your partner doesn't pay you enough attention anymore and him feeling like you never want sex, *just try having sex with him*! This can be a hard lesson to learn for many women. Giving of our bodies seems unfair—especially when we aren't feeling fabulous about our relationship. We tend to withhold sex when we're angry, especially if we know it's what he really wants. However, by trying to raise the white flag and giving him a little action, you'll find that you'll likely jump-start your connection to each other. Sex is one of the main vehicles by which men feel close to you. By giving him that physical connection, he'll be inspired to be more intimate in other ways. Have you ever noticed how close and connected you feel after sex? Usually he's more affectionate and in a better mood, sometimes for days after.

When women notice this they balk at how simple men are and how "all they want is sex." What I think women miss is that sex is not just about physical release for men (though they enjoy that too!). It's the way in which they feel connected and close to their partners. It's the glue that makes them feel bonded and part of the relationship. Without it they often drift, feeling rejected, unattractive, and disconnected. It's no wonder a little sex makes them feel so much better about the relationship. Instead of feeling frustrated that you are somehow giving in, why not see it as a loving act? As a way to connect with him in his "language of love." As soon as you start communicating with him in his language, I guarantee he'll be much more willing and able to communicate with you in yours.

Reconnecting can feel insurmountable at times, especially after the sex has all but disappeared. Couples fall into a dance with each other that is wrought with frustration and miscommunication. They often struggle with lower thresholds for anger at each other, feel emotionally distant, and are less likely to show each other any physical affection any more. Women will say that they aren't willing to reach out to hug or hold their partner's hand because he might think she's initiating something and she will have to reject him again. He stops reaching out to her because every time he touches her she thinks he's initiating sex and cringes. Even the most natural parts of their physical and emotional intimacy can start to feel awkward and strained.

Breaking the stalemate with your partner is much easier than you think. Just give him some action! This maxim applies not only when you may be feeling frustrated with your partner, but also when you are exhausted. When you've worked all day and bathed and fed the kids, and he turns to you for sex at 10 P.M., you're thinking *yeah right*. However, if you start kissing and let yourself get into it, you might find that you end up enjoying yourself. You are still at extreme risk for a mercy fake—women feel pressure to fake orgasm with their partners for every reason under the sun. Whether he's trying so hard that you feel it's the most merciful thing to do, you're worried about hurting his feelings, or you just want to get things over with as soon as possible, the mercy fake is the worst kind of anti-communication. I know that it's often a time management technique so you can get to sleep. However, part of communicating effectively is telling your partner when orgasm is simply not going to happen. You can still enjoy the sensations and intimacy of sex without reaching orgasm (don't worry, he'll hear that from me too in his Guy's Guide at the end of this chapter). Your partner should accept this and feel reassured that it has nothing to do with him. As you will learn in Chapter 8, a woman's capacity for orgasm is not the sure thing that it is for men. It also is not always the measure of good sex. The female orgasm is determined by her physical response, how she is feeling about herself that day, how she is feeling about her partner, whether the kids made it to school on time, his technique and lasting power, and sometimes even world hunger and the alignment of the moon and stars! Orgasms can be tough to come by on a regular basis for many women, especially during intercourse. Accepting this is half the battle toward having a satisfying sex life. While it is often an alien concept to men, for whom orgasm is the ultimate goal, it's a reality that *both* of you need to understand.

Having realistic expectations of what sex should be is an essential ingredient of long-term satisfaction. Sex changes from day to day, as well as over the course of a relationship. Men especially need to learn that the one magic formula they are always utilizing is not always going to work every time. As your body and life change, so does what works and what doesn't work sexually. Staying flexible keeps you dynamic as a couple.

Getting Back in Touch with Your Passion

You should, however, make good use of the past for inspiration. Getting back in touch with what made you click when you first met can help reinvigorate your desire. Think about what made you fall in love with your partner and gently remind him. Instead of making him feel guilty by telling him how much you miss reading the Sunday papers together in bed, or the way he used to kiss you, try taking the initiative yourself. Surprise him by plugging the kids into cartoons, bringing him breakfast in bed, and reading the papers together. Tell him how much you are enjoying yourself. Or the next time you have a chance, reach out, grab him, and kiss him like you used to, then whisper in his ear how much kissing turns you on. In fact, all couples need to remember kissing. It is one of the most sensual acts, often associated with many wonderful memories of your early days together. Make it a point to give each other at least one good kiss a day. Not a peck, but a real wet kiss, and try to make it last ten seconds if you can! The kids may get embarrassed, but it's good for them to see their parents' affection for each other. You can also try writing your partner a letter about what it felt like when you first fell for him. Describe how your body felt and what you were thinking. Tell him the many hopes you had for your potential together as a couple. Or just say it to him in person.

Another way of tuning into the past is by remembering the two A's: appearance and appreciation. First, appearance. When we get settled in a relationship, our nesting instincts set in along with our comfort level and it's not uncommon for us to get a little lazy about our appearance. We trade in our sexy dresses for sweats and a scrunchie in our unbrushed hair throughout the weekend. Between caring for kids, the house, and ourselves, who has time to coif? But very often, our complacency with our appearance is encouraged by our partner's dwindling positive feedback. You think, he never notices when I dress differently or shave my legs. Why should I bother? Well, the bottom line is that you should bother. Putting effort into your appearance not only makes you feel attractive but also shows your partner you still care. Think back to the mental energy you would put into deciding what outfit to wear, how to do your hair, and what makeup would make you look your sexiest when getting ready to see him. Men are visual creatures and looks do matter. Your appearance is always going to be an important part of your partner's attraction to you. As you learned in the last chapter, taking pride in your appearance is an important part of who you are.

Next is appreciation. Remember when the littlest act on his part could find you gushing with appreciation and adoration? He probably does, too. A large part of his relationship satisfaction comes from feeling effective and good at being your partner. Try making it a point to tell him how much you appreciate how hard he works, that he mows the lawn, or even that he threw his socks into the hamper. Let him know the next time he says something to make you feel good or he's done something that makes him a great dad. Sometimes it's nice to make him feel appreciated for no good reason at all, so just tell him how handsome he is or how nice he looks. He's more likely to do nice things for you if he feels like you notice them.

Now, don't think your partner completely gets off the hook here. Like I said earlier, men need to make the right effort outside the bedroom to get what they want inside it. He needs to give you the same kind of feedback when you've made a special effort to look good or when you have picked up the house. He also must realize that just because you're a committed couple, it doesn't mean he should think he gets sex with no work! While you have the two A's of appearance and appreciation, he's got two A's himself: appearance and attention. Men have to worry about attractiveness, too. Taking care of your appearance and staying active is an investment both partners should make. Then there is attention. Men get lazy about the effort they think they need to put into sex as a relationship gets comfortable. Your job is to remind him of the romantic or helpful efforts he used to undertake to impress you. While it's never going to be like it used to be, he can do little things to show you he's thinking about you. Surprising you with flowers from the grocery store, calling you or e-mailing you during the day to let you know he's thinking about you, or making sure he comes home from work when he says he's going to are just some of the ways he can show his attention to you. Foreplay begins long before you enter the bedroom. While in the past it may have been drawn-out romantic dinners and entire days spent lounging around alone together, now it comes in the form of helping out around the house or with the kids so you can recharge your batteries, take a nap, or maybe even take a leisurely bath! If you let him know that a little attention will go a long way toward getting you in the mood later, he may be more receptive.

It's also important for both of you to pay attention to simple logistics. Working on logistics allows you to be more available when the opportunity for sex arises. Make your bedroom a safe and sex-friendly haven. It should be free of clutter and distraction, such as bills, work, and pets. It's also a good idea to get rid of the television and computer if you can stand it. Your bed should be used for two things—sleeping and having sex. If you don't have the television on when in bed, you're much more likely to tune into the person lying next to you. And to make sure no interruptions occur, get a lock on your bedroom door if you have children or others living with you. Feeling like you have total privacy for just the two of you is essential. Nothing is going to happen to the kids and doors can unlock as quickly as they are locked if you are needed. It's also important to set aside time to be intimate. Communicate with your partner about when in the day you like to have sex. Many women feel their most sexual in the morning, when they are relaxed and have been sleeping next to their partner all night. Even if he likes it at night, he will be happy to oblige you with some morning nookie if you simply ask. Setting the alarm a half hour early one day a week gives you the time. You can also try showering together in the morning, before anyone else is awake.

Using Body Language to Your Advantage

Saying what you want and expressing your appreciation are great, but a little body language can help you communicate with your partner nonverbally. It's also great for getting a read on his state of mind when he isn't talking. The eyes in particular can make a million intimations without needing to say a word. Our eyes say a lot about how much or how little we are interested in someone else. Though it's subtle, the pupils dilate in response to attraction. When you want to convey interest, linger a little longer when you catch your partner's eye. While you are sitting at the dinner table surrounded by kids throwing food and fighting with each other, take a deep breath and try to catch his eye. When he looks at you keep eye contact. Focus on how attractive you find him or how much you love him and try to communicate that message through your eyes. You can do it across the dinner table or across the room, and he'll know what you're thinking.

Body language works in the same way. How can you convey a sense of interest or pick up on when he's trying to capture your interest, aside from eye contact? Interest is indicated by turning your body toward a person, often mimicking their position or posture. When you're excited about someone, your posture perks up, head tilts, and you hold each other's gaze briefly. Many times, one or both of you also adjust your hair or clothing—as if to say you care about what the other thinks. Continued interest comes across with regular smiles and eye contact, and keeping an open posture. Gently touching yourself or other objects also shows interest. Mirroring your partner's body language is a great way to open yourself up to him, without saying anything. He may not even notice what you are doing exactly but it will feel good, like the early days in your relationship when you were doing it all totally unconsciously.

But what are some signs that he may be bored or uninterested? The most obvious is unalert eyes or a blank stare. Holding his head in his hand, tapping his leg or foot, or drumming his fingertips all may mean he's restless with what's going on at that moment. If you're worried about your partner's sincerity, there are some telltale signs for that, too. Someone who is being sincere has his feet firmly planted in the ground, arms relaxed, with palms open and up when gesturing. The head is usually slightly tilted and the body conveys a sense of openness. His posture is neither defensive nor closed off, since he is not deceiving or stretching the truth.

The idea is to work on your communication with each other in all ways. Sexual or otherwise, problems do not magically solve themselves. It's important to work to keep the lines of communication open, as the health of your relationship is essential to the health of your sex life. In addition to riding the ebb and flow of your relationship, remember what made you think you were each other's one and only, too.

Spicing It Up

There's a reason committed, married women often have better sex than single women—they feel connected and safe with their partners. Three-dimensional emotional sex is always better than sex in which that feeling of kinship is missing. You just have to put a little more effort in to keep the spark alive and maintain your partner's interest. When you feel like your sex life is a drag, take a moment to look back with relief on your single days when you were trying to attract a mate and riding the roller coaster of dating. Then, get creative!

Revving up your sex life is an endeavor that takes you both inside and outside the bedroom. Changing your routine restores novelty to your relationship. Tying the knot does not mean that you should stop tying each other up! *If* that's what tickles your fancy. There are usually two sexual problems a couple runs into as their relationship progresses: They either do the same routine every time they get into bed and it works, but is less than exciting, or they do the same routine despite one or both person's changing needs. In both cases, the solution is to create a mood of exploration in your relationship.

In Chapter 8, you will learn all about the different positions and techniques that can help make good sex great. This is a prelude to that, in which you and your partner get yourselves in the right mind-set. Getting creative does not necessarily mean that you have to do sexual acrobatics and become someone you are not. In fact, operating under a sense of pressure to be kinkier than you are is the worst thing for your sex life. Rather, it's about getting in touch with some of your deeper desires and gently pushing yourself to move beyond the same old routine. Just as you began learning to relish in your senses as a woman in the previous chapter, now it's time to apply that to your relationship. There are endless opportunities both inside and outside the bedroom for boosting your sensual power as a couple.

Slow Down

The first step toward changing your routine happens inside the bedroom. Whether you're satisfied but not thrilled or the sex has stopped working completely, slowing down can help heighten your senses. The technique is known as sensate focus. It helps you and your partner find out how the other likes to be touched and reveals new sources of pleasure for you. The goal is not arousal, but exploration and connection. You should set aside forty minutes when you will be relaxed and not pressed for time. If the kids or others in the house are an issue, make sure you have at least a couple of hours alone so you won't feel rushed. Comfortable surroundings are another essential. Whether it's your bedroom or a hotel room, make some effort with ambience. Soften the lighting, play a little music you both like, make sure your bed is soft and cozy and that the room is warm. Depending on what you prefer, you can begin sensate focus with your clothes on or off. If you're going to feel more comfortable with clothes on, do it that way in the beginning. Ideally, sensate focus should be done over the course of four different occasions; however, if that is not realistic, you can work through each phase in one sitting. Each stage is about forty minutes, so if you are going to do it all at once, you may want to shorten each stage to twenty minutes or so and linger longer on the stages you especially like. But you will still need at least a couple of hours, if not longer.

The Guy's Guide at the end of this chapter will help you lay the foundation for this, but if you are worried about your partner being resistant, tell him that you want to try something new. Emphasize that it will just be for a little while to help you get closer to each other. You will be focusing on maximizing all of your senses to improve your sexual response—both separately and as a couple. He's more likely to get on board if he knows what you are working toward.

The first stage consists of touching and stroking the nonsexual parts of the body—in other words, the breasts and genitals are off limits! Only one person gets touched at a time and no talking is allowed at this stage, so you can focus on the physical sensations. Each of you should have twenty minutes in which your body is being explored and twenty minutes in which you are exploring the other person's. The purpose of this kind of touching is to give you a heightened awareness of your body's sensations. As you lie on the bed, think about how it feels when your partner strokes your face or your arms. How about when you touch his neck or chest? Both of you should be completely focused on the contours and textures of touching and being touched.

In the second stage, you expand to sensual touching, but without intent of sexual arousal (if that's possible). Spend another twenty minutes each, giving and receiving touch. During this stage it's good to place your hand on top of your partner's and indicate when something feels especially good by stopping his hand or applying more pressure. He should do the same. There should still be no talking as you stroke each other's bodies.

In the third stage, the clothes need to come off if they are not already. Begin mutual touching, or touching each other at the same time now. Instead of focusing your attention only on what it felt like to be touched or to do the touching, you are now incorporating the sensations of both at the same time. Look at the genitals and notice where the different parts are. Get to know them as well as every other part of each other's body. Your bodies should be making contact, including the genitals, but no intercourse! In particular, you should explore rubbing your vulva against your partner's penis without any penetration. Use your hands to stimulate each other's genitals, while still focusing on the rest of the body, too. Pay attention to the way your bodies respond—his erection, your lubrication, other changes and sensations. But remember to refrain from intercourse. By keeping focused on the sensations, instead of on performing sexually, you change how you are interacting sexually. Refraining from intercourse also allows you to explore without any anxiety or expectations about what comes next.

After you have explored mutual touching for twenty minutes, the final stage involves what's called non-demand intercourse. This means that your partner enters you with his penis and you simply hold it inside. Though it may be difficult at this point, try to resist thrusting so both of you can focus on the sensations of him inside of you. If you feel like it's too hot, have your partner withdraw and go back to touching each other's bodies elsewhere. You will probably find that you are overcome with desire for each other! Often, all it takes is a little slowing down to crank up the heat again. Whether you want to finish with intercourse or some other activity like oral sex or mutual masturbation is for you to decide as a couple. Just remember this activity for times when you feel as though you're in a sexual rut. Getting in touch with your senses again and slowing everything down will help make you feel like new again. Temporarily taking intercourse out of the picture rekindles a sense of passion and anticipation into sex. More tips on this also follow in Chapter 8.

Another less involved way of heightening the sensual experience is to take turns blindfolding each other. Letting your partner blindfold you puts you completely in his hands. It can feel thrilling to have no idea what's coming next, as long as you trust him, of course. Taking away your sight also boosts your other senses. Touch might feel more titillating, taste more profound, and even the sounds of getting it on with your partner more of a turn-on. A blindfold is the perfect opportunity to make use of other sensory props, such as ice cubes, candle wax, and vibrators, if that's your thing. You can also blindfold each other at the same time and see what it's like to interact sexually while both of you have your senses heightened. You can even take turns and tie each other up, experimenting with one person being in control of the other.

Add a Dash of Novelty

As long as it's something that can involve your partner, you should make it a point to dig deep into the desires of your psyche. Encourage him to do the same. A good fantasy life is some of the surest fuel there is for your sex life. And while you should let your mind wander to the outer edges, you should always practice discretion in what you choose to share with your partner. A fantasy about someone else is the prime no-no. Revealing a fantasy that will make your partner feel insecure does just that. If you don't think it's something you can incorporate him into, keep it to yourself for your own stimulation. Tell him the same rule applies for his fantasies. However, opening up to each other about appropriate fantasies is an incredible way to spice things up. There is no obligation to act on them, if either of you feels uncomfortable. Simply talking about them can be great foreplay and also give you a window into each other's longings.

Get together with your partner to create a fantasy of your own. This should be fun—a way to expand your sexual horizons and have a laugh, if nothing else. The goal is to meld together both of your desires into a shared fantasy. If you need a warm-up, flip back to page 85 in the previous chapter to get your creative juices flowing. You might even want to read the fantasies out loud to each other. Next, write down a few of your favorite sexual wishes or talk them out if that works better for you. What turns you on? What would you like to see your partner doing or him you? Maybe there is an activity you have always fantasized about but never shared. Keep in mind the rules about making sure your partner is included in the fantasy, but otherwise, let yourselves get a little down and dirty! It could be that you have sex while other people watch, or maybe the two of you are spying on a sexual scene. Your partner may have a schoolgirl fantasy that you never knew about. Or maybe you will finally admit to him that you like the idea of two men at once. Remember, it is fantasy and no one says it is something you have to do in real life. It is simply a way to get the sexual energy flowing—in your minds and between you and your partner.

If you do want to act them out, don't let the confines of the bedroom limit you. It can be really exciting to act as if you don't know each other in public places. You can pretend like you are strangers or that you are having an affair with each other. Try meeting at clandestine places, like a bar or hotel. You can pick each other up, pretending as though you've never met. You might drop by your husband's office dressed like a maid and have sex with him on his desk. Or he could follow you into a single-occupancy bathroom when you're out to dinner and have a passionate quickie. The level of risk and experimentation is going to differ for every couple. The guiding principle is that it should always be fun for both people involved. Props can help you get inside an alternate reality while in the bedroom. Like a man in uniform? Get your partner a suit from the secondhand store and tell him what you want him to do to you. Maybe he used to love strippers back in the day? If you're comfortable, do a striptease for him with music and all until you're wearing nothing but the skimpiest lingerie you could find. There are even health clubs that offer strip aerobics classes now, if you need a little practice!

Doing something dangerous outside the bedroom that has nothing to do with sex can also stimulate your attraction. It's a combination of the adrenaline rush and your brain flooding with dopamine. Skydiving, bungee jumping, even high-stakes gambling, if you can afford it (and don't tend toward gambling addiction), all work to push your limits. Anthropologist Helen Fisher points out that the chemical reaction let loose by doing new activities is similar to the one responsible for the lust and elation experienced at the beginning of a new relationship. So get out there! At the very least, you should explore at least one new activity together as a couple every year. Activities that use your bodies are highly recommended, such as dance lessons, yoga, or massage classes. But really any new activity will work. From cooking classes to tennis to getting season tickets, the idea is to learn something new together. Spicing up your relationship means keeping it interesting both inside and outside the bedroom.

It Takes Two

Like everything in life, our intimate relationships are a subtle negotiation. They are a balance between passion and practicality, between getting and giving. Making your relationship work means juggling your needs and wants with your partner's. There has to be a clear understanding of what each person is capable of giving to the other. By approaching life as a team, you make a pact that you will compromise along the way, while also reaping the benefits of each other's strengths. When you start out in love, the road ahead looks smooth. Both of you are filled with idealism about linking up for the journey of life. But as the bumps in the road inevitably come, it's the couples who find a way to keep moving together who weather the rough patches. The moment one person begins to break away and the other does not reach out to retrieve him or her, the partnership is at great risk.

A loving relationship has to be an ongoing negotiation. It is not a battle for control or a one-way street, in which one partner is getting his or her needs met while the other is not. Having a real relationship with each other is among the most difficult tasks there is. It means you are looking at yourself honestly, while trying to join with another. A good relationship is one in which both members learn to give in to the other at times, despite what they may want as individuals. Maybe there will be certain areas you compromise in and others your partner does. When asking for help or anything else from your partner, it's important that it is not entirely on your terms. If you want more help with housework, for instance, make sure you accept what he is able to give. Cleaning the kitchen again because you don't like the way he did it will only make him feel inadequate and much less likely to clean it again in the future. Let him put his own unique stamp on things. Likewise, you should not feel like you're the one doing all of the giving. If he's gone five nights a week because of work, basketball with the guys, and other solitary interests, there is nothing unreasonable about asking him to set aside some time for you. In fact, it can be the perfect opportunity to take up that new hobby or activity together, as discussed earlier. If you approach him with concrete suggestions, instead of complaints, he is more likely to be responsive.

It's always better to speak to your partner in specifics, instead of overwhelming him with emotions and complaints. The second men feel like you are nagging them, they shut down. Most will either stop listening or do whatever they think it takes to placate you. Neither is good for your relationship. When he stops listening, your communication begins to break down. When he does something just to shut you up (literally), he will likely begin to harbor resentment as time goes on. By taking the initiative to approach him with constructive concerns and a focus on solutions, you greatly enhance your chances of coming to a mutual resolution. If you feel you're doing more than your fair share of housework, approach him with a positive attitude and a list of the daily and weekly chores that you can agree to divide up. If he has a habit you don't like, such as heading straight for the television when he gets home at night, frame it that you would like to enjoy more time with him after work and plan something fun for the two of you to do together. If he needs some time alone when he first gets home, make a TV-date for later in the night. The idea is to approach every situation with a solution in mind. Staying constructive means you remain two people on the same team, instead of two people at each other's throats.

Fight to Love, Not to Win

Every couple fights. It's the way you choose to fight that makes the difference. Fighting to win, instead of to resolve what you are fighting about, is the biggest mistake couples can make. It is also the most common—especially when in the midst of a passionate argument. If you can take a step back and make the conscious decision not to let the argument escalate, you will likely see some changes in how you and your partner fight. When you lead by example you are in a much better position to ask for the same changes from him.

Obviously, you are never going to agree on everything; however, there are some tried-and-true methods that make sure your fighting is productive, instead of destructive. Most important is to avoid the buildup of anger, resentment, or any other negative thoughts about your partner. This leaves you with one of two options—either bring it up or let it go. Your partner is not a mind reader. If something is bugging you, and even if you have discussed the very same habit or behavior before, you must bring it to his attention. Not giving him the opportunity to discuss the problem keeps you in a vicious cycle of resentment and misunderstanding. Likewise, if you do decide to keep quiet and forgo a confrontation, you must not hold a grudge! Adding to your list of what drives you crazy about your partner does nothing but get you deeper and deeper into the victim role. You are in control of your happiness. Make it clear what kind of treatment you expect, and let your partner know when you feel a line has been crossed.

If your partner is stonewalling and unwilling to discuss a problem, walk away temporarily. Pleading with him to talk to you when he doesn't want to is a losing game. Try approaching him later, preferably within a few hours, to set up a time to discuss it. This technique should also be used for fights that have spun out of control. When one or both of you is going for the jugular—and you know where that is—make the decision to walk away and cool off. Your partner may be furious at the time, but you are already in dangerous territory when your fighting starts escalating toward verbal attacks. Some signs of destructive fighting include bringing up the past when it is not relevant, saying things simply to hurt the other person, bringing up third parties like his mother or your best friend, and any sort of name-calling.

Good conflict resolution is the bedrock of your relationship. It allows you to get your point across, as opposed to just backing down to avoid a fight, and gives you and your partner the opportunity to find new areas of growth. The trick is not to let your emotions get the best of you. In addition to walking away, you can also break through the fighting cycle by agreeing to repeat each other's feelings before you respond. This changes the tempo of the argument. It helps prevent those impulsive, hurtful statements from flying out of your mouths and it also confirms that you are really listening to each other and have heard correctly. Too often during conflict we react based on what we think we hear, instead of what was actually said. When you must repeat what the other person just said, the intensity is automatically reduced. Each of you takes turns speaking. You must look at your partner as he explains what he's feeling, without rolling your eyes or interrupting. When he's finished, you respond, "I understand that this (fill-in) is how you feel. This is how I feel." It also helps to start your sentences with "I" instead of "you." Explain how you feel, instead of accusing him of making you feel that way. Instead of saying "You are so inconsiderate," say "When I think you aren't listening to me, I feel hurt and ignored." Fighting fair means you don't blame the other person or make accusations.

The point is that fighting should always be about what's best for your relationship, instead of what's best for you as an individual. Getting wrapped up in who's right and who's wrong will start to fracture you as a couple. Like sex, it's about working out the kinks so that both people are satisfied. Where you get into trouble is when one person expresses his or her emotions and the other either ignores him or her or tries to talk him or her out of it. Every person deserves to be validated. It should be important enough to your relationship for both of you to put aside your opinions and open yourself up to what the other one has to say. Your relationship is not a contest. It should be your safe haven.

Reaching Out for Help

Sometimes there are problems that go beyond the day-to-day spats and disagreements. Getting past the anger can be tough. Whether because of a larger disconnect between you and your partner or an unpleasant part of your past that keeps rearing its ugly head, working it out often requires the help of a third party.

Here are some other signs that there could be more serious problems brewing in your relationship.

❑ You would describe your relationship as more like roommates than lovers.

❑ You feel incapable of effectively communicating with each other.

❑ You keep having the same fight over and over again, with no resolution.

❑ One or both of you is easier to anger; the other person's little habits more bothersome than in the past.

❑ One or both of you is less affectionate, either inside or outside the bedroom.

❑ One or both of you is having feelings for someone else.

There are endless factors that can be at work to cause any of the above. While they are not covered extensively within the scope of this book, therapy should be considered if you really feel like you are at an impasse in your relationship.

Women often ask me how they should know when they have a real sexual problem or if the sexual challenges they face are really normal variations in a healthy relationship. I always say that on some level the couple knows. But there are some clues. Maybe it's the frequency of sexual activity that has declined or the quality of it. For men and women, when our partner doesn't want sex, we automatically blame ourselves instead of considering that there may be a problem with him or her. Every couple also goes through natural ebbs and flows in their sex life. The amount and quality of sex you are having will always vary, both from one couple to another and from one stage of life to the next. Times of high stress, recent childbirth, and sometimes for no apparent reason at all can each cause sex to slip into the background of your relationship—temporarily. A problem arises when there has been a disruption to your sex life for six months or more consistently. This means no periods in which sex worked, such as on vacation or after you had a fun night out. However, when sex is good under those special circumstances only, it should be a warning about what might be missing in your relationship. Whether it's reducing stress or spending more time together as a couple, you should identify what needs to be changed. Just don't panic unless you're seeing a real lack of sexual synchrony for six months or longer.

His Sexual Function

As you learned in Chapter 3, sexual dysfunction in women can be the result of hormones, stress, poor blood flow, and even certain medications, in addition to emotional issues or relationship conflict. All inhibit your ability to respond sexually, as well as your desire for sex. What about for men? In addition to premature ejaculation and erectile dysfunction, men can also suffer from low libido. At least one in five men has low sexual desire, which may come as a surprise since it's talked about so rarely. Most men feel a sense of pressure to want sex all the time—and definitely more than their wives or girlfriends want it. And yet, men's and women's libidos may be more similar than we think. Men can experience a waning sex drive for the same reasons women do: imbalanced hormones, health problems, aging, depression, and stress. They can also lose interest in sex when their relationship is not going smoothly. If you're worried about your partner's libido, pay attention to what's going on in your relationship. All of the things we've been talking about in this chapter can influence his sex drive, as well as yours.

Low testosterone is the most common physical culprit when a man finds his sex drive is lower than it used to be. In addition to fueling the male sex drive, testosterone increases muscle mass, decreases fat, helps makes bones stronger, and enhances mood. Usually, testosterone begins declining after age thirty. While some men never notice a difference, each year more than four million men experience andropause, the male equivalent of menopause, in which testosterone levels drop sharply. Fortunately, many options exist for restoring testosterone. FDA-approved prescription gels, creams, and patches provide many of the physical and psychological benefits of natural testosterone. Some popular options include gels like AndroGel and Testim, patches like Androderm and Testoderm, and a dissolvable tablet called Striant. More important than any medication, however, is that men and women realize low sexual desire happens to men. Instead of feeling embarrassed or alone, talking about it gives you the opportunity to focus on how you can solve it together. The main thing is to talk about it and acknowledge it, in addition to seeing a doctor to get to the bottom of any physical causes. Research has shown that if you support him and go with him, then he's much more likely to get help and benefit from it.

It's important to be delicate about any sexual function issue your partner is having. Try not to make a big deal about it at the time if he loses his erection or ejaculates too early. If it is happening consistently, try bringing it up outside the bedroom as something you'd like to work on together. Both early ejaculation and erectile dysfunction (ED) will affect virtually every man at one time or another during his life. Premature ejaculation is a recurrent problem for about one-third of men. Chronic erectile dysfunction affects about 5 percent of men in their forties and 15 to 25 percent of men age sixty-five and older. Early ejaculation is a more subjective problem to define. Whereas for some couples three minutes of thrusting after penetration is adequate, for others (and probably most women) it is not. Early ejaculation depends on what works for you as a couple. Some couples accept that he comes first during intercourse and then continue with other stimulation so she is satisfied. In addition to manual or oral techniques, some men with a short refractory period (the time until he can get another full erection) are able to last longer and satisfy their partner through intercourse the second time around. As long as you keep up the foreplay while he's getting his erection back, you make good use of a woman's less finite arousal pattern by going for a second round.

If early ejaculation is a problem, it helps if your partner focuses on tuning into his body. Breathing deeply during sex can sometimes help control the arousal and tension that lead to early ejaculation. He can also practice the Stop and Start Method, developed by Masters and Johnson. He should begin by masturbating alone, bringing himself close to orgasm and stopping. After relaxing, he should continue bringing himself closer and closer to orgasm until he can't hold it any longer. Doing this several times by himself without distraction will help him learn where his point of no return is. He can also try it with an erotic video to simulate a real sexual encounter, once he has practiced a bit. When he's ready, the two of you should engage in sexual activity that stops short of intercourse. As he approaches the point of orgasm from manual, oral, or other stimulation, he should signal you to stop. You should practice this a few times before attempting intercourse. When you decide to try intercourse, have him on bottom and you on top. This way he's more relaxed, and you can control the degree of penetration. Patience and relaxation are the keys to making this technique work. Even if he reaches orgasm early a couple of times, keep trying. Another method you can try is the Squeeze Method, in which either you or your partner squeezes the base of his penis to reduce his erection at the same point the Stop and Start technique would be used. A similar process applies—he should do it on his own first, and then practice it together. Another option is the SSRI family of antidepressants, such as Prozac and Zoloft; some men just take them several hours before sexual activity. They inhibit arousal, which makes it easier for him to control ejaculation; however, keep in mind they have other side effects.

Whereas early ejaculation is more common in younger men, ED increases in incidence with age. It is marked by the repeated inability to get or keep an erection firm enough for sexual intercourse. Far from an inevitable part of aging, ED is a highly treatable problem that most often has physical causes. Disease, medications, and anything else that interferes with blood flow is the common culprit for ED. Fortunately, there are many options for treating it. Viagra, Levitra, and Cialis all work to relax the smooth muscle of the penis and increase blood flow. Refer back to pages 55 to 57 in Chapter 3 for a complete discussion of their differences and any contraindications. There are also infections, vacuum devices, and surgical alternatives for treating erectile dysfunction. Encourage your partner to investigate the pros and cons of each with his physician. Ultimately, he's lucky that he has so many options at his disposal.

The Role of Couples Therapy

While it's essential to sort out the physical from the emotional when it comes to sexual dysfunction, they are often interconnected. Embarrassment or anxiety about performance during sex often creates problems in other areas of the relationship. It's important to investigate with your physician any physical causes that may be at work, as well as to explore the emotional issues that have cropped up as a result, or were there to begin with, with a couples or sex therapist. The therapist will also help you work through stress and other non-physical causes that may be at work.

Most often, one member of the couple is more interested in therapy than the other. And it is not always the woman, though that is the stereotype. Whatever the nature of the problem, getting to the root of it is essential. Many couples go through a period of conflict about sex and then become complacent about it. They resign themselves to the idea that they can be good parents, friends, and roommates, and that sex is not important. Many ask, why rock the boat if it works for them? My answer is that without passion, a relationship is very vulnerable. The fiber that ties you together becomes thin, and any stress in the relationship, whether it's death, illness, or economic crisis, can permanently rupture it. It is not uncommon that at some point one of you will start an affair or find that when the kids are grown, you simply want to walk away and start again because you miss having passion in your life. Sex is a crucial part of your connection to each other, and when it's missing, the relationship is fundamentally tenuous.

Getting a reluctant partner to go to therapy can be daunting. Some men see therapy of any kind as a touchy-feely activity that can't really help. They're worried they are going to have to get too personal or they are too embarrassed to admit they need a third party's help with their relationship. The best approach to take is one in which you focus on yourself. Emphasize that you want him to come to therapy so you can feel better about your body or more sexually adventurous. It will help take away his fear that he will be targeted as the bad guy by you and the therapist. If he's still reluctant, ask him to try it out for a few sessions with no commitment. That gives you the opportunity to go as a couple for a few sessions and take it from there. It also makes him feel less boxed in. It may even be helpful to meet the therapist first to make sure you think your partner will like him or her. If he's really reluctant, you might get only one shot, so you want to make sure the odds are in your favor. As I said in the previous chapter, it's OK to interview the therapist first to make sure you are going to have a good rapport. That is normal practice, and any therapist should be open to it.

If he absolutely refuses, you can go by yourself and get tips from the therapist about how to encourage him to participate. However, a flat-out refusal on his part to work on your relationship with a third party can also be a warning sign about your future together. It shows he is not willing to compromise, especially if you've given him the option of just trying out a few sessions with no commitment.

As with individual therapy, make sure the therapist you choose is someone both of you can relate to. Sometimes, men are more apt to go to a male therapist because they feel they'll be better understood. However, sometimes they want to see a woman because they fear they will be too embarrassed to admit their sexual shortcomings to another guy. It's important to get your partner's take on who he would be more comfortable with. Ideally you want to choose a couples therapist with solid sex therapy experience. It's rare that relationship dynamics are not reverberating in the bedroom and vice versa. In sex therapy, the therapist essentially takes over a couple's sex life to rebuild it from the ground up. Intercourse is temporarily eliminated so that couples can learn how to communicate in a new way about sex. New rules and concrete techniques are introduced by the therapist, which the couple practices at home and then discusses at each session. All the while, the therapist and couple explore how a particular sexual problem is affecting the rest of their relationship. If you or your partner are not interested in sex therapy, however, a couples therapist can help with conflict resolution, infidelity, issues with money or kids, or when one person wants out of the relationship and the other does not. Couples therapy helps you learn better skills for communicating and understanding your partner's perspective, which are helpful in resolving a stalemate. Just beware that many couples therapists are not equipped to deal with sex, should the issue come up. Knowing your therapist's credentials is important for making sure he or she can meet your particular needs as a couple.

RELATIONSHIPS CAN BE COMPLICATED, but they can also be incredibly rewarding. They are the inspiration for, and beneficiary of, our sexual energy toward each other. You take the good with the bad and hope that you are building toward something greater. Every relationship teaches us something new about ourselves. Whether in the past or in the present, they open up a part of us that may not have been apparent before. By making the right choices in your relationship, having the right attitude, and giving as much of yourself as you can, you have the solace that you are doing your best. Your partner will likely be inspired by your example.

Love especially requires continual work and patience. For the long term at least, love is not a sentiment that magically keeps growing. You must nurture it, be gentle with it, and also be serious in order to keep it thriving. It's a delicate balance between having fun and doing the hard work that's needed. Love is the subject of great movies, great books, and great speculation for one simple reason: It's what we're all after. Make the most of yours.

PRESCRIPTIONS FOR THE WEEK:
Week 5

✓ If you haven't already done so, it's time to stop the sexual stalemate. Barring illness or extreme relationship conflict, reach out and touch your partner—sexually, that is. Try to have sex with your partner once this week. You'll notice the negative spiral in your relationship will start to unwind.

✓ Have a staring contest with your partner. Set a timer for three minutes and during this time really look at each other. Don't stare blankly at each other or past each other, but look into each other's eyes. Look at each other's faces and really see each other. Three minutes may feel like a long time, but it's a great way to reconnect and see each other again.

✓ Take a moment to really look at your partner's hands. Run your fingers over the fingers and fingernails; touch the fingers, fingernails, and wrists. Try to memorize the hand so that you could pick it out in a crowd. Notice its strength and how slender or soft it is.

✓ After you've explored each other's hands, try it on the rest of the body. Take turns. Lie naked in front of him on your back or stomach (you can even close your eyes if you are self-conscious). You should lie there quietly while your partner explores your body with his eyes and hands, then you do the same, with the intention to learn totally about each other's bodies. Touch between the toes, the inner thighs, every inch of each other. Notice the differing texture of the skin and the way your partner responds to your touch. Don't miss any part and include the genitals if you are willing. The goal is not to arouse each other but simply to explore. So the touch should be sensual, but the only intention is exploration. Look at the genitals and notice where the different parts are. Get to know them as well as every other part of each other's bodies. When you are finished with one side, turn over and do the same thing on the other side. Take as long as you each need (at least twenty minutes for each of you) and no talking! Do this at least once this week.

✓ Once you've taken turns, you can explore each other's bodies simultaneously. Take a bath or shower together first if you want and after you have spent some time just looking at each other, you can start touching ... give equal attention to all parts of the body ... don't linger too long on one spot. Once again the goal is not arousal but exploration and connection. Touch from each other's faces down to the toes. There should be no orgasm, no intercourse, and no talking. Do this at least once this week as well.

✓ Try to send a loving message to your partner with your eyes this week. Whether it's in the middle of a chaotic dinner with the kids or while you are out at a cocktail party, catch his eye and imagine sending him loving thoughts about how attractive you think he is, how sexy you think he is, and how much you care about him— all with your eyes. See if you get a reaction, either in the form of a blush covering his face, a reciprocal look, or an increase in affection.

✓ Don't forget! Masturbate at least twice a week, keep writing about your experiences in your sexual journal, and be sure to take two hours this week, whether it's with friends or by yourself, but with no work or home demands and no errands.

GUY'S GUIDE:
A Summary of Key Points for the Man in Your Life

1. Finding ways to keep the sparks flying between you and your partner takes work both inside and outside the bedroom. It can be the hardest thing in the world to open yourself up completely to another, but it is also the most rewarding. It's important to know that once you've been together for a while, and especially if you have kids, spontaneity goes out the window. But that doesn't mean you can't keep spicing things up!

2. When sex is working in a relationship it's an important but not necessarily a central part of what's working. When sex isn't working, it takes on a life of its own and becomes a big white elephant in the room with the couple.

3. Far and away, the most important ingredient of a woman's sexual desire is the quality of her relationship. For most women, feeling emotionally close to her partner often inspires her to want to be sexual with him. For many men it is the opposite. He usually needs sex in order to feel emotionally close to his partner. The different ways men and women approach sex can sometimes create a fundamental breakdown. While she should try to reach out more to you sexually, it's crucial that you try to make more of an emotional connection with her as well.

4. It's really helpful to try to give your woman some physical and emotional attention that is not seen as purely sexual. This means holding her hand, cuddling her, and complimenting her with no sexual expectations! Often, men do not understand that what goes on outside of the bedroom is as important as what goes on inside of it when it comes to sex.

5. Also, put some effort into the two A's: appearance and attention. Just as you want her to, take care of yourself physically and make her attraction to you a priority. Also, don't get lazy about the effort you think you have to put into sex. Foreplay begins long before you enter the bedroom. Remember the early days of your relationship when you were courting her. Surprise her with flowers, call her, or e-mail her during the day to let her know you're thinking about her, or make sure you come home from work when you say you're going to. A little attention will go a long way toward getting her in the mood later.

6. A woman's capacity for orgasm is not the sure thing that it is for men. It will vary from day to day, depending on what's going on in her personal life *and* your relationship: things like how she is feeling about herself, if she is stressed out, and so on. Your technique and staying power also matter—and the same moves are not going to work every time. Accepting that orgasm is not always going to happen for her is half the battle toward a satisfying sex life. It's one big way that men and women are very different sexually.

7. Continually work on your communication with each other in all ways. Sexual or otherwise, problems do not magically solve themselves. It's important to work to keep the lines of communication open, as the health of your relationship is essential to the health of your sex life. In addition to riding the ebb and flow of your relationship, remember what made you think you were each other's one and only.

8. Keeping the spark alive does not necessarily mean that you have to do sexual acrobatics and become someone you are not. Get in touch with some of your deeper desires and gently push yourself to move beyond the same old routine. There are endless opportunities both inside and outside the bedroom for boosting your sensual power as a couple.

9. Fantasy is a great way to turn up the heat. Just be careful that the fantasies you share with each other allow the other person to be included. You can talk about them to explore your desires and then decide if you want to act them out. For fantasies you keep to yourself, the good news is that they are all normal. Since you are not necessarily going to act them out, there is no limit on what you can indulge in in your mind and use to fuel your sexual response.

10. Get together with your partner to create a fantasy of your own. This should be fun—a way to expand your sexual horizons and have a laugh, if nothing else. If you need a warm-up, flip back to page 85 in the previous chapter to get your creative juices flowing. You might even want to read the fantasies out loud to each other. Next, write down a few of your favorite sexual wishes, or talk them out if that works better for you. What turns you on? What would you like to see your partner doing or her you? The goal is to meld together both of your desires into a shared fantasy.

11. Men can suffer from sexual dysfunction, too, and it's nothing to be embarrassed about. Talk about it with your partner and investigate treatments together—there are many out there. Both early ejaculation and erectile dysfunction (ED) will affect virtually every man at one time or another during his life. Low sexual desire affects at least one in five men, and low testosterone is the most common physical cause.

12. Don't be afraid to get help for your relationship, either. Some men see therapy of any kind as a touchy-feely activity that can't really help. They're worried they are going to have to get too personal or they are too embarrassed to admit they need a third party's help with their relationship. A flat-out refusal on your part to work on your relationship with a third party is unfair. It shows you may not be willing to compromise. If your partner feels strongly about it, try going to just three sessions to give it a try and see what you think. At least you will have made the effort!

13. Most important, fighting to win instead of to resolve what you are fighting about is the biggest mistake couples can make. It is also the most common. Try to let go of the competition in your fights and concentrate on trying to resolve it or make peace.

CHAPTER SIX

Sexercise

Love Your Body and He Will Too

■\\\\\■

GOOD SEX IS SIMILAR TO GOOD exercise. You get all hot and sweaty. You become more aware of your body's potential. Everything feels alive. It makes sense that the two go hand-in-hand. Finding a routine that works and making it a daily part of your life is one of the best decisions you can make—for your sex life and for your health. Exercise reminds you that you are a physical being. The sensations of a body in motion bring to life your muscles, heart, and mind. Up first is a muscle group that you may not think much about but that really matters for your sex life! They're your pelvic floor muscles and they are often neglected by even the most regular of exercisers. The benefits of working them are tangible for your sexual health.

Exercise also gives you a reality check. While your partner may still love you if you've got a few extra inches on your body, he won't necessarily *lust* you. It can be a hard truth to swallow, but for your sex life the way you look is as important as the way you act. In addition to fueling your sexual response, exercise can help arouse your partner's interest, too. No one expects you to look like a supermodel. It's about looking like the best version of you!

Your Sex Muscles

The pelvic floor muscles are the backbone of your sexual response. They support all of your pelvic organs, including the bladder, rectum, and uterus, as well as the vagina. The pelvic floor muscles serve as a sort of hammock, extending from your pubic bone to the bottom of your spine. As shown in Figure 5, the bladder, rectum, and upper vaginal opening all pass through your pelvic floor. If there ever were a muscle essential for your sexual function, this is it.

Keeping the pelvic floor strong and sturdy, however, does not happen naturally from regular exercise. In fact, women who spend major time and effort strengthening their abdominals put themselves at risk if they are not also strengthening their pelvic floor. Strong abdominal muscles can bear down on the weaker pelvic floor muscles, compromising their ability to remain supportive. It is crucial to make sure you are keeping your sex muscles as fit as your other muscles. You shouldn't be surprised by now to learn that the benefits are for both your general and sexual health.

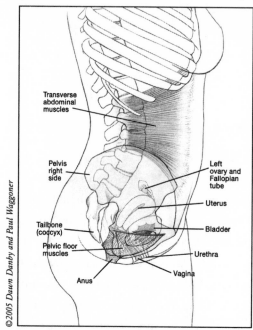

Transverse abdominal muscles

Pelvis right side

Left ovary and Fallopian tube

Uterus

Tailbone (coccyx)

Pelvic floor muscles

Bladder

Urethra

Vagina

Anus

©2005 Dawn Danby and Paul Waggoner

Fig. 5. Pelvic Floor and Transverse Abdominal Muscles

In terms of general health, your pelvic floor gives you control over urinary and bowel functions. It works by squeezing when you cough, sneeze, or to prevent leakage when you just don't want to go to the bathroom, including urine leakage during sex. A strong pelvic floor makes sex sensational in general. Improved blood circulation to the genitals and increased vaginal tone and lubrication are just some of the rewards. Like any kind of muscle, working your pelvic floor muscles brings them to life. Vaginal tone and response improves. Your arousal is heightened during sex. Orgasm ability and intensity also improve dramatically, since your beefed-up pelvic floor muscles are primed to contract more powerfully—the enhanced blood flow and lubrication don't hurt either. I have worked with many women who reported muffled or nonexistent orgasm. Once they strengthened their pelvic floor muscles and learned how to use them, orgasm returned and became more intense. A strong pelvic floor also tightens the vaginal opening, which heightens sensation for both you and your partner by adding friction during penetration and thrusting.

Strengthening the Pelvic Floor

OK, you say, so how do you make the most of these renowned pelvic floor muscles? The place to begin is with Kegel exercises. Named for the man who identified them in 1948, Dr. Arnold Kegel, these exercises are a daily must for every woman's sexual fitness routine. Done right, they usher in all of the benefits already mentioned. The key to Kegels is targeting the right muscles. Internally, the Kegel muscles are in the shape of a figure-8, which wraps around the vagina and the anus. They are the same muscles you use to stop the flow of urine midstream. If you have to try this to identify them it's fine, but don't exercise your Kegels this way on a regular basis. It can affect your ability to empty your bladder and potentially make you more prone to urinary tract infections. Another technique for locating your Kegels is to insert a finger into your vagina and tighten the muscles around it. Check to make sure you are not engaging any other muscles, such as your abdomen, inner thighs, or buttocks. A biofeedback device, called *Myself* Kegel Trainer, by a company called Des-Chutes Medical, can also help you locate and strengthen your Kegels. A tampon-size probe is inserted into the vagina and the machine lets you know if the right muscles are being targeted and how long to flex them for.

When you feel confident that you've found your Kegels, find a place to sit or lie down. Begin by making sure you have an empty bladder. Next, tighten the Kegel muscles and hold for ten seconds. Then relax them for ten seconds. These exercises work your slow muscle fibers—the ones that are responsible for long-term strength. It is also important to work the fast muscle fibers, the ones that react to sudden stresses like laughing, coughing, and sneezing. To work them, squeeze your pelvic floor muscles for one second, then release for one second. Basically, you are squeezing and releasing, squeezing and releasing in rapid succession.

Try to do a set of slow exercises, followed by a set of fast exercises. Start slowly, working your way up to more repetitions. This week, begin by doing five slow exercises, in which you tighten for ten seconds and release for ten seconds, followed by five quick exercises, in which you tighten and release at one-second intervals. Do them at a set time each day, so it's something that becomes a regular part of your routine. The best thing about Kegels is that no one has to know you're doing them. As you become more comfortable, you can do Kegels in the car, during an especially long meeting at work, or even when you exercise. Put those famed female multitasking skills to good use! Gradually, you should try to work your way up to a set of ten slow and ten fast Kegel exercises. You can repeat the set up to three times per day.

Another great way to do your Kegels is with one of two pelvic exercisers, Isis and Juno, from the Berman Center Intimate Accessories Collection. I developed these unique Kegel exercisers to offer women more options for keeping the pelvic floor healthy. Both are made of a smooth Lucite and could be mistaken for unique paperweights! You can use water-, oil-, or silicone-based lubricants with either of them. The beginning pelvic exerciser, Isis, has a streamlined shape with a nub in the middle. It's designed to be inserted into the vagina as far as you are comfortable with so the vaginal muscles can squeeze and release around it. With some practice, you can try it while standing up, using your vaginal muscles to hold it in place.

Isis is also excellent for women who struggle with pain during intercourse (dyspareunia) or involuntary vaginal spasms (vaginismus) when penetration is attempted. The Isis allows you to address the dyspareunia or vaginismus by working toward gradually inserting something into the vagina at your own pace and comfort level, while focusing on keeping your muscles relaxed. The practice of Kegel exercises helps with dyspareunia and vaginismus, too, since they allow you to develop a sense of control over when your vaginal muscles tighten and relax.

The weighted pelvic exerciser, Juno, is great for more intense strengthening. It contains a series of weighted balls inside the Lucite, which gradually increase in size and give this exerciser a rippled appearance. Beginners can start with the small end. Insert it while standing up and support the other end gently with the palm of your hand. Eventually, work your way up to where you can hold it inside your vagina without the support of your hand. Then try the larger end of the exerciser, initially supporting it with your hand. The ultimate goal is to hold this part inside your vagina while standing with no extra support. The Isis and the Juno can also be used for pleasure. They provide internal stimulation when you stimulate your clitoris manually or with a vibrator. The Juno especially offers great sensation due to its rippled shape.

Depending on the frequency of Kegel exercises you do, results are generally seen within four to six weeks, while significant changes start showing up after about three months. Keeping up a regular routine is essential. Incorporating Kegels into your daily life is the surest way to guarantee the health of this important—and often overlooked—part of your sexual anatomy. You can also put Kegels to good use during intercourse by tightening and releasing them around your partner's penis. This increases the friction for both of you, enhancing arousal.

Another essential part of your pelvic floor, which gets even less attention than your Kegels, is your transverse abdominals. If you refer back to Figure 5 on page 128, you can see them as well. The transverse abdominals are the deepest layer of abdominal muscles in your body that run like a band around your entire torso. They encase the front and back of the pelvis. The transverse abdominals' main job is to compress your abdomen (two words: flat stomach!). They are integral to posture, back support, and core strength, as well as pelvic floor strength. Learning to engage the transverse abdominals along with the Kegels gives you the full range of pelvic floor strength and motion. Both increase your chances of having a strong and healthy pelvic floor throughout your entire life. See page 134 to learn an easy, effective *Pelvic Push-up* routine that puts your Kegels and transverse abdominals to work for your sex life. It's one of the best health routines you can do for your sexual anatomy.

Sometimes, however, Kegel and transverse abdominal exercises are not enough for repairing a weakened pelvic floor. Every woman experiences a certain degree of pelvic floor weakening as she ages—especially if she has been pregnant, had multiple vaginal births, or gone through a traumatic or prolonged labor. Some women never experience any symptoms; however, many others do, including women who have never given birth, since the pelvic floor weakens naturally as a function of age. Pregnancy and vaginal childbirth, however, pose the greatest risk to a woman's pelvic floor strength. Pregnancy weakens the pelvic floor because of the pressure a growing fetus places on all the pelvic organs, which in turn stresses the pelvic floor. Vaginal childbirth can be particularly damaging, since long periods of pushing and stretching of the pelvic floor muscles compromise their ability to be supportive afterward. The pudendal nerve, which controls sensation and muscle contraction of the vaginal opening, can also be injured when the perineum is cut during an episiotomy to allow passage of a baby. The perineum is a common area permanently stretched by vaginal childbirth.

Losing control of your bladder when you cough or laugh is a natural side effect of giving birth or growing older. However, it's a natural side effect you can do something about. In addition to the risk factors of age, pregnancy, and childbirth, factors such as smoking, obesity, chronic disease, and too much caffeine can place you at increased risk for incontinence. Working to reduce your risk in each of these areas reduces your likelihood of developing incontinence. Healthier habits can also improve incontinence if it's already happening. Regular Kegel exercises are your best bet for mild or moderate incontinence. However, if pelvic floor prolapse has occurred, in which an organ drops out of place due to a lack of pelvic floor support, more intensive intervention is needed. Since when one organ falls it affects all other organs around it, many symptoms can result, including a feeling of heaviness or fullness in the pelvis, pain in the pelvis, pain during sex, bowel incontinence, or constipation. Some women describe feeling as though their internal organs are going to fall out of their vaginas. While Kegels are still useful for bladder control and preventing the problem from getting worse, other medical treatment is usually necessary.

Treatment options for pelvic floor prolapse or severe urinary incontinence include biofeedback, electrical stimulation, medication, and surgery. Biofeedback is used in conjunction with Kegel exercises to provide you with visual feedback of how your pelvic floor muscles are working. It helps you to recognize better—and consequently control—their function. Electrical stimulation passes a mild electrical current to the muscles surrounding the bladder through a small vaginal or anal probe or an electrode placed on the perineum. The electrical currents simultaneously stimulate the pelvic floor muscles while relaxing the bladder muscles. There are also many new medications on the market for the treatment of incontinence, which you can investigate with your physician. Surgical options for incontinence include injections of collagen and a new synthetic material into the urethra, as well as placement of a sling or hammock inside the pelvis to support the bladder. Many types of pelvic floor prolapse are treated similarly. Given the risks of any type of pelvic surgery, it's important to make sure you have exhausted every possible option before you consider it. A good gynecological physical therapist can evaluate the health of your pelvic floor and help you isolate and strengthen the muscles that are key to maintaining bladder control and sexual function. Very often good physical therapy and strengthening of the pelvic floor can prevent the need for surgery.

The Special Benefits of Yoga

Yoga provides the ideal opportunity for you to get in touch with your pelvic floor muscles. It also restores you, which is a necessary complement to traditional exercise routines. When it comes to sexual fitness, your mind space is as important as your physical shape. Traditional exercise revs you up and primes you for great sex. Yoga takes it one step further to focus more exclusively on the mind-body connection and therefore generates bigger and better benefits to your sex life. You've started retraining the way you think about yourself—learning to focus on the positive and embrace your individuality. The practice of yoga is a natural continuation of that. Yoga helps quiet mental chatter and self-judgment, which are distractions from enjoyable sex. Through meditation and learned powers of concentration, it offers an excellent way for reconnecting the mental and the physical. Yoga delivers you to the moment.

Women often get intimidated by yoga. We envision perfectly serene instructors who can sit in a full split for hours on end while meditating peacefully. Yoga seems inaccessible and ethereal; however, this is an image that popular magazines and trendy celebrities have in large part created. In reality, yoga is about taking your time, finding your comfort zone, and gradually changing the way your body moves and responds. What most women find when they try their first yoga class is a comfortable, accepting environment. Beginner classes especially have people at a range of different skill levels participating.

I often recommend yoga to women who are highly stressed or have too many things on their plate. Any kind of exercise helps, but when you go for a run or ride a bike, you often find yourself making to-do lists in your head or thinking about all of the stress in your life. With yoga, there are two unique benefits. First, you can use some of the more relaxing techniques you learn to de-stress and let go of your negative thoughts. Second, by being required to focus on coordinating your body and your mind in ways that you may not be used to, you are totally in the moment and unable to think of anything else. It's often the only hour in the day in which your mind is quiet and your battery is recharged.

Yoga works by activating the parasympathetic branch of your autonomic nervous system. This branch returns your body to normal after it has been stimulated by the other half of the autonomic nervous system—the sympathetic branch. The sympathetic branch prepares your body for the fight-or-flight response to some sort of threat in the environment. However, what was once a lifesaving reaction to a threat in our prehistorical environment is now stimulated too frequently by our modern world. Defensive driving, a bad fight with your partner, too much stress at work—can all send you into a state of near-constant hypervigilance, in which your sympathetic system is taking over. When active, your sympathetic system causes breathing to quicken, blood to rush away from the skin, and most of your bodily functions, such as digestion, to be put on hold. Needless to say, it is not a good state for your general or sexual well-being. And don't forget about the tend-and-befriend mode women also go into in response to stress. As you learned in Chapter 3, the tend-and-befriend response causes us to reach out for comfort from friends or even chocolate when we feel too stressed. It also activates the body's production of oxytocin, which works against free testosterone levels. Well-being, libido, and sexual response often suffer the consequences.

In contrast, the parasympathetic system calms and soothes the body, allowing it to return to its resting state. Heart rate slows, blood flow returns to the skin and extremities, and your muscles relax. The parasympathetic system creates the ideal environment for deep breathing and clearheadedness. Instead of reacting according to pure, unadulterated instinct, you are able to think and feel things through. You become nonreactive. While the autonomic nervous system is considered involuntary, it can be modified through conscious control. And guess which activity is most conducive for doing so? Yoga! The practice of being in a calm, observant mind-set disposes your body toward a parasympathetic, rather than sympathetic, state of being. When you learn to do it during yoga, you are more likely to do it without thinking in other areas of your life. Or, it's something you can make a conscious decision to do when you are faced with stress or tension. In all of these ways, yoga becomes another tool for staying healthy *and* sexually satisfied. Combined with cardiovascular and weight-bearing activities, it offers the whole-body approach to health, both general and sexual.

Pelvic Push-Ups

So how can you get started without feeling intimidated or operating under the expectation that you will have to twist yourself into a pretzel? Up next, I give you a simple sexual enhancement yoga routine that is specifically targeted to your Kegel and transverse abdominal muscles. Through a combination of controlled deep breathing, mental focus, and a series of physical poses, you gain a new self-awareness. By becoming more in touch with your body and mind, your sex life naturally benefits. The routine can be done in as little as twenty minutes. Done just three times a week, it offers you a whole new world sexually.

Breathing is fundamental to the practice of yoga. Since it is normally a process that most of us do not consciously think about, focusing on the air that comes into and out of your body is the first way that yoga changes your perception. Our breathing is often shallow in day-to-day life. Learning how to breathe deeply brings more oxygen to the body and also removes more toxins from the lungs. You are lengthening the breath—taking in more oxygen and releasing more carbon dioxide. Breathing deeply also relaxes the pelvic floor. It is good to practice during both yoga and sex, since a tense pelvic floor is as bad for sex as a weak pelvic floor. Ideally, your pelvic floor should be strong, yet relaxed when you want it to be. The following exercises teach you to control this response, by learning the difference between relaxation and tension. Contracting and releasing your pelvic floor during sex can heighten your arousal, in addition to the improved muscle tone you are gaining.

Set aside a time and find a place where you are comfortable sitting. Sometimes a carpeted surface provides enough cushion, or you can look into purchasing a yoga mat at a sporting goods store. They usually cost around twenty-five dollars. It's also important to create an atmosphere of relaxation. A quiet room is essential, so you can eliminate the distractions around you and focus on yourself. You can play some soft, soothing music and light a few candles if you find it relaxes you. Sit in a comfortable cross-legged position. Rest your hands on your knees. Breathe in deeply, watching your breath fill your belly. Breathe so you imagine the air is reaching all the way down to your pelvic floor, as if you were trying to breathe the air all the way into your genitals. Your belly should become rounded as you inhale and then collapse back toward your body as you exhale. The space inside your abdomen fills with oxygen as your muscles expand and contract. Visualize relaxing your abdominal muscles, and concentrate on your breath. Breathing in this way opens up the body and allows you to get in touch with your core. In addition to your abdominals, your pelvic floor is an important part of your core.

Breathing deeply and slowly also helps your mind become a nonreactive, yet responsive, observer. You are focusing on what's in front of you, instead of other parts of your life. This is the aspect of yoga that can be most difficult. Trying to tune out the thoughts running through your mind can make you feel like you are paddling upstream. Instead of focusing on controlling your thoughts, take a more passive approach. While your eyes are closed and you are still breathing deeply, observe your mind's thoughts drifting in and out. Instead of paddling upstream, you are observing a river that delivers your thoughts and then carries them away. Focus on your body, scanning it part by part for any signs of tension. Let go of tension in your toes and feet, calves and thighs. Soften your buttocks, pelvis, and hips as you continue breathing and relaxing your entire abdominal area. Let the softness radiate out to your arms and shoulders. Let go of your throat, neck, and head. You should envision your eyeballs gently floating underneath your lids. Your tongue is soft and relaxed in your mouth. All the while, your mind remains light and unattached, observing your thoughts as they come and go.

You can also bring negative internal scripts to the mat so they can be confronted and released. This is not going to happen immediately, but over time and with practice you can modify some of the negative thought patterns you identified in Chapter 4. At this point, pay attention to the emotions that are passing through your mind. Focus on a source of stress that is troubling you—whether something in yourself or an incident or relationship with another. Let the feelings come to the surface. What emotions are you having? Do you feel tension in a certain part of your body when you think about it? Are you nervous? Now think of a time in your life when you felt the utmost love and happiness. It may be when you accomplished something momentous in work or even when in school, or it could be a particular period in your life that you remember fondly. Think about the details of that time. Allow the positive emotions and memories to replace the stress you were previously feeling. Notice the difference in your mind and body as your focus on that time of contentedness. Feel how calm your body becomes, the space inside it. Enjoy the emotions that warm your mind. Then slowly open your eyes.

The benefits of replacing tense, stressful reactions with a loving, peaceful reaction is that you are present in your body's response to stress by learning the difference between the two. As you do it more often while meditating, you become increasingly capable of modifying your response in your everyday life. When you feel your emotional and physical stress reactions triggered by a person or situation, you can make the conscious decision to stop, think, and relax. It won't make the stress disappear, but it will act as a sort of buffer, softening its impact on you.

Once you've spent some time relaxing and breathing, you can move on to the series of poses I developed with the Berman Center's fitness instructor, Becky Jeffers, for enhancing your sexual awareness. There are five in all, each with a corresponding diagram, which can be repeated as many times as you would like. Spend a few minutes on each, with the longest amount of time on the final one.

POSE 1—PELVIC CONNECTING CRUNCH (FIGURE 6)

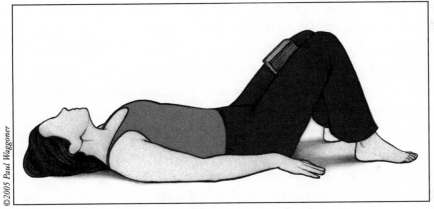

©2005 Paul Waggoner

Fig. 6a. Pose 1: Pelvic Connecting Crunch

This is the exercise that teaches you to access your Kegels and your transverse abdominals. It also engages your inner thighs, or adductors, which are not part of the pelvic floor, but are key to the contraction of it. You will need a block or a book to place between your inner thighs. Holding it between them helps you avoid the most common mistake of using your buttocks instead of your Kegels and transverse abdominals, to strengthen the pelvic floor.

Lie on your back, with your legs bent so your knees are pointed toward the ceiling and your feet are flat on the floor (a typical sit-up position). Place the block or book between your inner thighs, about halfway in. Engage your Kegels as you learned to do earlier. To engage your transverse abdominals, squeeze your Kegels in, up, and back. Visualize the muscles moving toward your head and down toward the floor. It's as if a series of ribbons are being

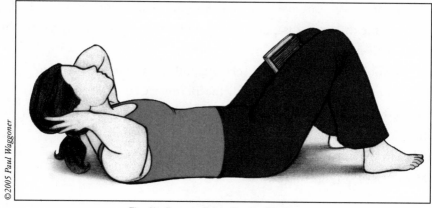

Fig. 6b. Pose 1: Pelvic Connecting Crunch

pulled tighter and tighter around your torso. You are knitting together your muscles, making everything more compact.

Once you've engaged these muscles, lift your head and shoulders slightly off the ground. You can place your hands behind your head to support your neck if you wish. Raising your shoulders will cause your stomach to become even tighter and cave in as you come up. Try to hold it for three complete deep breaths. Your stomach should still expand as you breathe in and contract as you breathe out. You can eventually work toward holding this pose for a full minute. Even if this is the only exercise you do, it will significantly increase your pelvic floor strength by accessing both your Kegels and your transverse abdominals at the same time. Not bad for one minute a day!

POSE 2—SEATED GODDESS (FIGURE 7)

In this pose, you are concentrating on keeping your pelvic floor completely re-laxed, which is also important for enjoyable sex. Especially for women who struggle with pain or vaginismus, learning to relax the pelvic floor can be life-changing. Position yourself so you are sitting on your knees and shins. For women with any history of knee injury, sit on a pillow to reduce pressure on your knees. Bring your torso forward so it is resting on your thighs. Let your head and neck go soft, allowing them to rest on the floor. Extend your arms out in front of you, reaching as far forward as is comfortable. Palms are flat and relaxed on the floor.

Stay in this position for a minute or two. Keep focusing on your deep belly

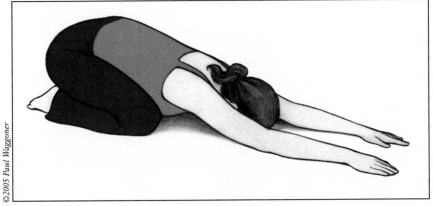

Fig. 7a. Pose 2: Seated Goddess

breathing and on relaxing the pelvic floor. Let thoughts pass in and out of your mind as you focus on the air entering and leaving your body. When you feel

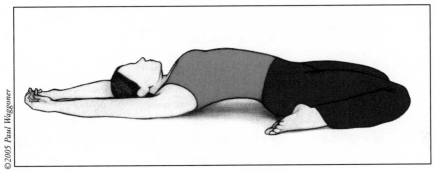

Fig. 7b. Pose 2: Seated Goddess

ready, sit up while remaining on your knees and recline backward, using your arms to support you. Go back as far as is comfortable—for some women this will mean resting on your hands, while others can recline down to their elbows. The ultimate goal is to be lying down, but this is not advised for women with any knee problems. Keep focusing on relaxing your pelvic floor. At the same time, you are lengthening and stretching your hip flexors—another important part of good sex. Flexible hips give you a wider range of motion for trying new sexual positions. Clitoral stimulation in particular depends on flexible hip flexors during intercourse. Stay in the back-reaching position for as long as you are comfortable.

POSE 3—THE WINDMILL (FIGURE 8)

Fig. 8. Pose 3: The Windmill

This exercise combines the pelvic connecting you have been doing with hip flexibility. You will need a strap of some kind to anchor your movement for this pose. If you don't want to buy one, you can use a towel or some type of rope. Move gradually from the Seated Goddess pose to lying on your back on the floor.

Engage your pelvic floor muscles as you did in the Pelvic Connecting Crunch. Knit your Kegels and transverse abdominals together by squeezing in, up, and back. You will use these muscles to anchor your pelvis to the ground. While engaging these muscles, bring one knee to your chest and place the strap (or towel, etc.) around the middle of your foot. Extend the leg out in front of you at an angle that is comfortable. The other leg should be resting flat on the floor.

Holding on to the ends of the strap or towel, move your leg out to the side, hold for a moment and return to center. Then move your leg in the other direction. Hold for a moment and return to center. Your pelvis should be kept firmly grounded the whole time by engaging your pelvic floor. You should also feel your inner and outer thighs engaging, as well as your hamstrings and quads. Repeat as many sets as you can, in which you move in one direction, return to center, and then move in the other direction. Remember to keep breathing throughout. For women with a history of hip injury, hip replacement warning, or sensitive knees, bend the leg and move away from the pain. Women with hip replacement should avoid this exercise.

When you are finished, gently bring your knee to your chest from the central position, release the strap, and return to the floor. Repeat with the other leg.

POSE 4—THE BELLY DANCER (FIGURE 9)

©2005 Paul Waggoner

Fig. 9. Pose 4: The Belly Dancer

Come up onto your knees and place your hands on your hips. For women with a history of sensitive knees or knee injury, place plenty of cushions underneath your knees. Do one set of slow fiber Kegel exercises and one set of fast fiber exercises (the ones discussed earlier in the chapter). As you engage the pelvic floor and then release it, focus on that part of your body as your body's center. Stay mindful about keeping the buttocks soft.

Next, tuck the tailbone and squeeze the buttocks and do Kegels to move your pelvis forward. Then release the muscle tension, allowing the buttocks to move backward as you try to moon the ceiling! Focus on the tension of moving forward and the relaxation of moving backward. Allow yourself to get into a rhythm in which you move your pelvis back and forth, back and forth, twenty times in all.

Next, you are going to move your pelvis from side to side using your Kegels, transverse abdominals, and buttocks. The trick here is that you are practicing using muscles on one side of the body at a time. To move to the right, engage your right buttocks and squeeze your Kegels and transverse abdominals toward the right. Do the same to the left. This may take some practice, but they are two final isolated motions you should be able to do with your pelvic floor. In addition to squeezing in, up, and back, squeezing from side to side gives you a full range of motion.

Moving your pelvis in a circular direction brings it all together. It is the ultimate in pelvic floor coordination, so give yourself some time to master this one. You are combining all of the movements above as fluidly as possible. The circle blends tension and relaxation, forward and back movement, and side to side control. Starting with your left side, you engage the left buttocks, Kegels, and transverse abdominals. Release the tension as you circle toward the right. Engage the right buttocks, Kegels, and transverse abdominals. Relax as you slide your pelvis back. Go round and round in a smooth circle of what will ultimately become intuitive control over your pelvic floor muscles. Do twenty sets of these. You should feel nice and warm and definitely a little sexy! It's also a great technique to practice when you're on top during intercourse. He won't know what hit him, and your arousal will likely be kicked up a few notches, too.

POSE 5—OPEN LOTUS (FIGURE 10)

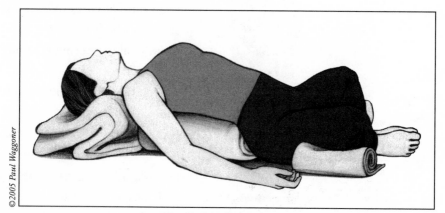

Fig. 10. Pose 5: Open Lotus

This position is the culmination of learning to trust the body to guide you, by having a mind that is present in the feelings and sensations of the moment, which can then be applied during sex. You will need a few extra props for this position; but trust me, it is well worth it! You can once again improvise with household items instead of buying anything new.

You are going to place something under each thigh and also under your torso. Traditionally, wooden yoga blocks would be used for the thighs but you can try books or even rolled up towels for something softer. For under your torso, you will want a pillow, and a couple of more pillows to place under your head. While sitting, place a pillow at the base of your back. A standard bed pillow will work best (even better if it's one of those extra-long king-size pillows), since you want it to provide cushion all the way up to your neck. Behind that, use two more pillows to prop up your neck and head. It may take a little adjustment the first couple of times you do this, but after that it won't seem like so much work.

While you are still sitting up, spread your knees out to the sides so you are in a more open position. Your feet, knees, and pelvis should form a sort of imperfect diamond shape. Once your thighs are bolstered, lie back on the pillows. Your head and neck should feel no tension, and your torso should be propped up slightly. Your rib cage and entire pelvic area should feel as if they are opened wide. Allow your arms to drop comfortably to your sides and rest on the floor. For women with lower back pain or injury, keep legs extended straight instead of spread to the sides. No block will be needed. Now practice the belly breathing discussed earlier on pages 135 and 136.

Once you get the hang of it, this position will make you feel totally open and vulnerable. It puts you in touch with your sensual, primal, and receiving female side. You are at one with your erotic and reproductive potential. Your body has a sense of space that is filled up by the deep belly breathing you are continuing to do. Your eyes are closed and you are feeling the body and mind sensations of being completely open and at rest. Enjoy this moment and make it last as long as you can!

Get Pumped

Each of us requires a different combination of relaxation and activity to keep us looking and feeling our best. We've talked extensively about finding time to relax and slowing down the hectic pace of daily life. We've talked less about getting active. A bubble bath is great, but it's equally important to get your body moving. Getting busy on a treadmill can help you get busy in the bedroom—in more ways than one. It primes both body and mind for sexual arousal and response. Specifically, exercise gets the blood pumping in your body, the endorphins pumping in your brain, and offers the obvious benefit of toning your physical shape. All work as natural aphrodisiacs.

You've learned about the importance of blood flow to your sexual function. It smooths the way for lubrication and swells your genital tissues, helping make sex the delicious sensory experience it should be. When you exercise, your heart pumps blood more forcefully throughout the body. With regular exercise, the walls of the heart grow thicker and stronger, pumping more blood with less effort. The number and size of blood vessels in your body's tissues also increases, enhancing blood flow in all parts of your body—including the genitals. Good blood flow also makes you look better. The rosy glow that a little exercise imparts goes from your face all the way down to your toes. Better blood circulation means that more oxygen and nutrients are being delivered to all parts of your body, and wastes are being removed more quickly. Inside and out, your body is benefiting from the increased blood flow alone.

But it doesn't stop there. Exercise also bathes your brain in feel-good endorphins. These are your pleasure chemicals—the same ones that flood your brain during an orgasm, when you are falling in love, and during almost any of life's most pleasurable experiences. Endorphins work on the brain to create feelings of exhilaration, while also blocking pain. The resulting sense of well-being has countless ripple effects on your sex life. Though you may feel tired when you initially begin an exercise regimen, after one or two weeks you will find that you are more energized. Physical activity boosts energy by improving your body's efficiency and tipping the chemistry of your brain toward more positive thoughts. Taking control of your body gives you a sense of control over your life in general. In fact, regular aerobic exercise can be just as effective as antidepressant medication and therapy in reducing depression. Even if you don't suffer from depression, exercise is a great stress reducer. Every woman could use a little of that, right? The biochemical benefits of exercise translate into real benefits for your sex life, since an energized mind primes you for sexual activity. You reconnect to your physical body, becoming more aware of its sensations and its potential.

Exercise also impacts your hormonal balance—in two ways. It increases the release of growth hormone in the brain, which stimulates the production of testosterone and other sex-friendly hormones. Exercise also reduces body fat, which is a site of additional estrogen production in the body. More body fat equals more estrogen, which through a hormonal chain reaction, reduces levels of free testosterone circulating in your system. Therefore, a woman who exercises regularly and builds lean muscle mass is positively influencing her testosterone levels in two ways. Over a lifetime, this a great way to keep them where they should be for vitality, energy, and libido.

Then there are the tangible benefits for both you *and* your partner. Exercise tones and shapes your body for benefits you can see and touch. Whether it's reducing your weight or sculpting your shape, you can watch as your body responds to the changes you are making. Muscle replaces fat to give you a firmer, more appealing shape. Your body composition becomes more compact and uniform. And your confidence improves as a result. These visible benefits of exercise are just as powerful as what's going on inside your body for your sex life. Maybe you will be inspired to buy that slinky dress you've been eyeing or surprise your partner with a piece of lingerie he's always wanted you to wear. Body image is an essential ingredient of your sexuality. Feeling good about the way you look can open up a whole new chapter sexually. Not to mention the flexibility and stamina that regular exercise gives you. Sex seems like less of an undertaking when you are putting your body to good use on a regular basis. As you train your body and mind during exercise, both are better able to go the distance during sex. You may be inspired to try a new position (and plenty of ideas for that follow in Chapter 8) that would have been uncomfortable—mentally or physically—before. Exercising *with* your partner can also prime you for sex. It gives you good quality time together and gets that blood pumping for later!

Physical activity promotes your vitality in general. Regular exercise activates your immune system, reduces heart disease risk, and helps you achieve or maintain a healthy body weight. It is also an essential part of bone health. Bone loss begins in your thirties and accelerates in the first five years after menopause, increasing your risk of falls and fractures. Regular exercise provides a protective effect against bone loss throughout your life. Younger women can augment their bone density by exercising in their twenties and thirties. Menopausal and postmenopausal women can protect their bone density, minimizing its decline, by participating in regular physical activity. The best news is that the effects of physical activity on bone health are highest in women who are the least active, whatever their age. The loud and clear message is that it is never too late to start exercising!

Sticking to a Routine

How can you determine how much exercise you need? In general, by accumulating thirty to forty-five minutes of physical activity on three to five days of the week you will garner the general health benefits of weight maintenance and reduced disease risk.

The best way to know if you are overweight is by calculating your body mass index (BMI) and taking a waist measurement. Your BMI measures your weight in relation to your height; however, since women with the same weight and height can have different proportions of fat and muscle, your waist measurement is a good backup. This is because fat that is carried around the waist—as opposed to the hips or thighs—increases your risk of developing health problems. Use the following formula to calculate your BMI: your weight (in pounds) × 703/your height squared (in inches). If your BMI falls between 18.5 and 24.9, you are considered healthy. A BMI between 25 and 29.9 is considered overweight and a BMI that is more than 30 is considered obese. Women with a BMI of 25 or greater are generally advised to consider losing weight. To measure your waist circumference, wrap a tape measure around your bare abdomen just above your hip bone. The tape should be snug, but not tight. If the measurement is more than thirty-five inches, you should also consider losing weight.

Getting healthy is different for every woman. Some women require less exercise than others to stay in shape. Other women may prefer a muscular shape that does not come naturally to them. It is each woman's unique combination of genetics, lifestyle, and personal preference that will determine her best fitness routine. Included in lifestyle are eating habits—the other side of the coin in terms of staying in shape—which I discuss in depth in Chapter 9. Without getting into too much detail here, what you eat is as important as how active you are when it comes to keeping your body trim and healthy. Your body uses food as energy to keep itself going. The energy required to maintain your basic functions, such as circulation, breathing, and digestion, is known as your basal metabolic rate. Every woman is different. Any activity above and beyond these basic functions requires extra energy, in the form of calories. This includes turning the pages of this book, getting dressed in the morning, and every other activity you perform throughout the day and night. When there are not enough calories to burn, your body begins burning glycogen (the stored form of carbohydrates) and fat. You begin to lose weight as a result. The goal, then, is to pick an exercise regimen that burns the right amount of calories. Eating 500 fewer calories a day than your body needs to keep functioning can result in one pound of weight loss per week. However, exercise can also be the answer to burning those 500 calories a day. One of the best things about exercise is that it gives you some wiggle room when it comes to what you eat. Keeping active means you don't have to watch your calories quite as closely. If you are just starting out, it is best to work with a personal trainer who can teach you the basics for a few sessions. Many health clubs now offer these assessments as a free bonus for joining. Once you have learned the exercises that are best for you, you can do them on your own.

Regardless of your goals, every woman should choose a fitness regimen that incorporates a balance of cardiovascular exercise, weight training, and stretching. Cardiovascular activity and weight training provide the important benefits to your heart and bones. They are also the keys to weight loss, since they consume calories. Cardiovascular exercise includes many more activities than you might think. Take a look at the calories burned in one hour by these daily activities that get your heart going (figures are for a 140- to 150-pound woman).

Activity	Calories
Aerobic dance	430
Bicycling	530
Gardening	265
Jogging	530
Swimming	395
Tennis	460
Walking	165

The key to finding an exercise routine that you stick with is doing something that you find fun or rewarding. You also want to do an activity that is within your comfort zone. Take a moment to consider whether you prefer being in a group or alone, whether you enjoy or shy away from competition, and whether you like to take risks or are spontaneous. Exercise classes are great if you're highly social but like some structure. Team sports work if you are social but like spontaneity and competition. Walking or running alone is good if you prefer being solo. For risk takers, skiing, rock climbing, and kayaking offer a thrill factor.

And don't forget weights—contrary to popular belief, they are not just for men and won't make you look like one. In fact, weight training adds muscle mass, which increases your metabolism and helps you burn more calories even when you are not working out. Just three sessions a week will help you build muscle, while two will maintain the strength you have. Weights are what give your body tone. With a little work, you can dramatically change the shape of your body. Weight training also improves your strength *and* your bone density. Since muscle mass naturally declines with age, it's all the more important to make weight training a regular part of your fitness routine. Instead of shriveling, you will enhance your muscles' chances of staying strong and durable as you age.

And don't forget to stretch! Often, because of time constraints, women think it is a step they can skip. However stretching is an integral part of your fitness. It lengthens and relaxes your muscles, delivers blood to them, and helps protect against injury, since other muscles will try to compensate for especially sore or tight muscles. Ideally, you should stretch before and after you exercise. If you can't manage it, skip the warm-up stretch and concentrate on stretching after you work out. Even if you are not a routine exerciser, simply stretching a few times a week will benefit your circulation and muscle health.

Start any new exercise regimen slowly and with realistic goals. Try enlisting a friend or your partner if you think it will help you stay on track. And remember that your cardiovascular exercise can be cumulative. Three ten-minute bouts of activity offer the same benefit as one thirty-minute session. For instance, if you are not currently exercising, make it a point to go on a ten-minute walk twice a day for the next week. Then work your way up to two twenty-minute walks. If you feel overwhelmed by the thought of setting aside an hour of time, take a fifteen-minute walk on your lunch break and another one on your way home from work. Take the stairs instead of the elevator when it's feasible. Do some free-weight training while you watch television. Even cleaning the house and bringing in the groceries count!

Be realistic and have patience. The results will not come overnight, but if you stick with it for two weeks, you will begin to see a change in your energy level. After a month, you should start seeing changes to your body, depending on the type of exercise you are engaging in. Change it up and be flexible so you don't get bored or frustrated. If you normally ride your bike, try taking a walk. If you slip up and don't do anything for a few days or even a week, don't condemn yourself. Also, reward yourself along the way as you reach your short-term goals and move onto longer-term goals. Buy yourself a new CD or workout clothes. The idea is to do what you need to do in order to hang in there. Once you get yourself in a regular routine, you will likely find that you are addicted. The benefits to your sex life alone make that almost certain.

EXERCISE TEACHES YOU THAT YOUR body is your haven. Whether lifting weights, taking a walk, or getting mindful with yoga, you find a new appreciation for what your body has to offer. Sex becomes more sensational, your longevity is fortified, and life just feels like it's more yours for the taking. Planting the seeds with good exercise habits yields a harvest of bodily delights.

Good health and good sex are the rewards the body gives us for treating it well. While staying in shape seems to be low on many people's list of *things to do,* it is one of the most vital activities we can undertake. Little changes lead to big changes and exercise is no different. When you think about the payoff for your health and your sexual satisfaction, the road ahead seems clear. It's up to you how you want to navigate it.

PRESCRIPTIONS FOR THE WEEK:
Week 6

✓ Try to incorporate thirty to forty-five minutes of cardiovascular exercise into your schedule at least three days this week and for the next four weeks as well. It can be done throughout the day in small spurts or done all at once, whatever is best for you.

✓ Try to get your partner to exercise with you at least once over the next four weeks, whether it's taking a walk together or going to the gym. If you can convince him to make it a weekly date, all the better, but start off with small steps to get it started.

✓ Try out a yoga class this week. Whether you are a well-established practitioner or a novice, look for a health club or yoga studio in your neighborhood and get yourself to a class this week and for the next four weeks as well.

✓ Make sure you work on those Kegel muscle exercises every day. Once you locate them, you can do them anywhere. You can also make them part of your Pelvic Push-Up sequence. Gradually, you should try to work your way up to a set of ten slow and ten fast Kegel exercises. You can repeat the set up to three times per day.

✓ Do your Pelvic Push-Ups at least three times this week and for the next four weeks. You can do them at the end of another workout or just on their own. It shouldn't take more than twenty minutes and after five weeks you will notice a huge difference.

✓ Don't forget! Masturbate at least twice a week, keep writing about your experiences in your sexual journal, and be sure to take two hours this week, with no work or home demands and no errands. And keep the action with your partner going: at least one sexual experience a week barring illness or extreme relationship conflict!

GUY'S GUIDE:
A Summary of Key Points for the Man in Your Life

1. The pelvic floor muscles are the backbone of a woman's sexual response. They support all of her pelvic organs, including the bladder, rectum, and uterus, as well as the vagina.

2. The Kegel muscles are in the shape of a figure 8, which wraps around the vagina and the anus. In fact, men have them too! They are the same muscles you use to stop the flow of urine midstream. Kegel exercises help strengthen your pelvic floor. Depending on the frequency of Kegel exercises your partner does, results are generally seen within four to six weeks, while significant changes start showing up after about three months. Your partner can also put Kegels to good use during intercourse by tightening and releasing them around your penis. This increases the friction for both of you, enhancing arousal.

3. Regular Kegel exercises are your best bet for mild or moderate incontinence. For a woman, losing control of her bladder when she coughs or laughs is a natural side effect of giving birth or growing older. However, it's a natural side effect she can do something about.

4. Another essential part of the pelvic floor, which gets even less attention than the Kegels, are the transverse abdominals. These are the deepest layer of abdominal muscles in your body that run like a band around your entire torso. They encase the front and back of the pelvis.

5. Sometimes Kegel and transverse abdominal exercises are not enough for repairing a weakened pelvic floor. Every woman experiences a certain degree of pelvic floor weakening as she ages— especially if she has been pregnant or delivered vaginally. Some women never experience any symptoms; however, many others do, including women who have never given birth, since the pelvic floor weakens naturally as a function of age.

6. Yoga can also help with pelvic floor strength, as well as quieting the mind (you already learned about how important that was for your sex life in prior chapters!). Encourage your partner to try yoga. I have given her a series of exercises called Pelvic Push-Ups that will put her pelvic floor muscles in tip-top shape. You can do them with her; it's great for ejaculatory control.

7. Exercise is great to increase your energy, improve your body image, and even make you feel happier via the endorphins that are released when your heart rate has been up for a while. With regular exercise, the walls of the heart grow thicker and stronger, pumping more blood with less effort. The number and size of blood vessels in your body's tissues also increase, enhancing blood flow in all parts of your body—including the genitals. Blood flow, as you already know, is a crucial part of lubrication, engorgement, and sensation for both of you. So encourage your partner to get pumped and join her in her efforts. In general, by accumulating thirty to forty-five minutes of physical activity on three to five days of the week you will garner the general health benefits of weight maintenance and reduced disease risk. Your sex life will reap the benefits.

CHAPTER SEVEN

Making It Pretty Down Under

ANOTHER WAY TO FEEL GREAT about your sexuality is the practice of self-care, and I don't mean getting your nails done. What I'm talking about is care down there—feeling confident about your genitals by tackling any odor and appearance concerns that can cause anxiety. Women who feel sexy in an incredible pair of panties also want to feel sexy when the underwear comes off.

Since women's genitals are often covered by pubic hair and are more internal than men's, we do not get the chance to compare ourselves with one another like they do. As a result, many women do not have a realistic idea of what their genitals should look like. Sometimes this can lead to embarrassment over the shape, size, or color of the sexual anatomy. Many women also worry about their natural smell or taste. The reality is that every woman's genitals are different. Like the face or hands, each and every vulva has its own unique personality. If you have taken my advice and begun exploring your genitals, you are on your way to embracing an important part of your individual sexuality.

Fortunately, there are many techniques for making your genitals everything you want them to be. In addition to learning to accept what's normal, there is an exciting new world of hygiene and grooming choices that will help you feel rapturous about your sexual anatomy. That goes for your partner loving your genitals, too. Also, learn all about an important new concept called genital self-image. It matters for your sex life!

What Is Natural?

Think of the scene: Men stroll around the locker room, maybe on their way to or from the shower. Towels in hand, they show little concern about what may or may not be swinging in the breeze. Same goes for the bathroom, just without the strolling. Now think of a women's locker room. We modestly cover ourselves to hide our bodies. Towels are stretched to their maximum capacity to conceal our "private" parts. For the most part, women just don't let it all hang out like men do. As a result, we lack the day-to-day genital awareness that is a normal part of life for men.

To be fair, a woman's sexual anatomy does not really allow her to strut her stuff in the first place. When's the last time you got a peek at another woman's clitoris? If you're heterosexual, probably never. Since women's genitals are more hidden anatomically, they tend to seem more mysterious. This situation is made worse by messages that discourage us from exploring our bodies. From our childhood homes to clinical visits to the ob-gyn, many women are left in a virtual genital vacuum. The messages to hide, and even ignore, certain parts of our bodies play out in our locker room behavior as grown women. The jump to how such messages affect our bedroom behavior is not hard to make.

Feeling connected to your genitals is essential for lasting sexual satisfaction. And it's difficult to feel good about something when you have little sense of how you stack up. Every woman has wondered about one or more parts of her sexual anatomy, as well as about issues like odor. Unfortunately, many are hesitant to voice their concerns or are not sure where to turn. The first step in becoming aware of your genitals is understanding what's normal when it comes to their look, feel, and function.

Discharge, Lubrication, and Odor

Since a woman's genitals are not roses, they are not going to smell like roses. It's important to remember that the genitals are a body part like any other. You don't expect your mouth to smell like peppermint all the time!

Each woman's genitals has a distinctive smell, which is naturally all their own. From evolution's perspective, it is the genital scent that plays a key role in attracting a mate. Today, a woman's natural odor can be an incredible turn-on to a partner before and during sexual activity. The pubic hair in particular traps a woman's scent, which is why it's always important to keep the hair clean and well-maintained. Genital odor is difficult to evaluate. Women are often very insecure about how they smell, since they're not sure what is normal. A good rule of thumb is this: If you can smell it and it smells bad to you, get it checked by a doctor. Strong genital odor could indicate infection, especially if it is accompanied by a change in discharge. Yeast and bacterial infections are very common culprits, and it's also good to make sure that something more serious—like a sexually transmitted disease—is not the cause. Any change in the color, consistency, or smell of your discharge warrants a visit to the doctor. Itching, rashes, and soreness do as well. Sometimes a strong genital odor is simply your body's natural tendency. Just as certain women sweat more or have stronger body odor, so do some women's genitals smell more strongly than others. If your genitals have been given a clean bill of health by your doctor but you still want to reduce odor, tips on how to do so follow in the next section.

It's important to pay attention to changes in discharge to detect infection and also to learn about what's normal for your body. All women have discharge, which can appear clear or milky white when moist, and pale yellow when dry. A healthy vagina naturally produces secretions to cleanse itself and maintain an appropriately acidic environment. Infections are most common in the days leading up to and during the menstrual cycle, since the vagina is at its least acidic during that time. Discharge is usually heavier around the middle of the menstrual cycle, when ovulation occurs, during pregnancy, and when sexually aroused. Women who use birth control pills also sometimes have more discharge.

Discharge plays a crucial role in making sex comfortable and enjoyable. When aroused, increased blood flow to the genital area causes the vagina to secrete fluids and lubricate itself. Different women produce different amounts, depending on their age, degree of arousal, and use of certain medications. Many women complain about a lack of adequate lubrication during sexual arousal. In Chapter 2, you learned about lubricants and the many options that exist. Give one of them a try if you desire more wetness during sex. Some women complain of too much lubrication during sex, which can lead to feelings of embarrassment or a lack of friction during intercourse. Since it is a natural process, there isn't much you can do to reduce the amount of fluid that's being produced. Lubrication often naturally declines with age. Enjoy it while you have it and wipe away extra fluids with a small towel if they are a nuisance. Tell your partner to take it as a compliment that he arouses you so much!

Appearance

Like so many other parts of our bodies, magazines have created unrealistic expectations for what women's genitals should look like. *Playboy* centerfolds are airbrushed to make the vulva appear uniformly pink, with perfectly proportioned labia. The genitals are almost always portrayed as small and compact. In reality, women's genitals come in all kinds of shapes, sizes, and colors. Their appearance also changes over time. Fluctuating hormones and natural aging change the genitals as much as they do any other part of the body.

Most women's anxiety about their genitals concerns the appearance of the labia, and the inner labia in particular. Natural folds in the skin of the inner labia give every woman a distinctive appearance. Some inner labia have a smooth, sleek shape, while others appear scalloped or with multiple folds. Since the labia expand during sexual arousal, the inner labia's shape often smooths out and becomes more prominent. For some women, the inner labia protrude past the labia majora even when unaroused. All of these variations are entirely normal. Symmetry is also not always the rule. Like the breasts, the labia often don't perfectly match. The labia can also be a range of different colors—pink, brown, black, and everything in between.

Though small, the external appearance of the clitoris can vary, too. Some women's clitorises have a much more obvious glans that sticks out from underneath the clitoral hood. The same size clitoris may appear larger in some women and smaller in others, depending on its proportion to the rest of her genitals. The vagina's structure also changes as a function of age and childbirth. Most of the difference is internal, which women often describe as a loss of tightness. Though the vagina is designed to accommodate a baby during childbirth and then return to its original size afterward, multiple deliveries or difficult labors can damage the vagina's structure. As a woman ages, her pelvic floor muscles further weaken in response to the hormonal changes of menopause. As you learned earlier, the practice of Kegel exercises and general pelvic floor exercises are the best way to prevent and repair structural changes to the vagina. Working those muscles each and every day helps keep your pelvic floor strong (see the previous chapter if you need a brushup on key exercises to strengthen these muscles).

The advent of new procedures like vaginal rejuvenation to increase tightness, and labiaplasty to reduce the size of the labia or make them more symmetrical, is becoming a disturbing trend. Like all types of plastic surgery, the number of women choosing to undergo genital procedures is on the rise. It seems as if the fixation on making our faces and bodies perfect is trickling down to our genitals. Surgery to change the appearance of the genitals should always be the exception, rather than the norm. Though there are those women whose labia interfere with sexual activity or their ability to wear certain clothing, the vast majority of women do not get genital reconstruction out of necessity. Usually, they are trying to attain an ideal of what they think their genitals should look or feel like. Women also need to consider whether they are getting the procedure for their own sexual pleasure or for a partner's. Ironically, genital surgeries often end up making sex *less* enjoyable than before the surgery, since any pelvic surgery poses the risk of destroying nerve endings and blood vessels that are key to sexual function. In my opinion, no woman should undergo a painful and possibly harmful surgery because she thinks it will make her sex life better.

Instead, women need to focus on accepting their genitals like any other part of the body and make the most of what they have. No matter what your genitals look like, they are normal because they're yours! If you're curious about how your genitals compare with other women's, a book by the name of *Femalia* by Joani Blank features a variety of women's genitals in close-up, non-airbrushed photos. There is also a video by Betty Dodson, called *Viva La Vulva,* which features ten women discussing and showing one another their vulvas. The idea is to normalize genital differences so that every woman appreciates her uniqueness.

Genital Self-Image

I call the way a woman thinks and feels about her genitals her genital self-image. Betty Dodson was among the first to suggest that positive thoughts about our genitals are essential to self-acceptance and sexual growth. Now, I can already hear many of you thinking, *What is she talking about? As if I sit around and contemplate my genitals!* However, if you stop and think about it, thoughts about your sexual anatomy are much more common than you might imagine. Everything we've discussed so far—appearance, odor, function—are a part of your genital self-image. Though you may not always express them, thoughts about your genitals are actually quite common.

It is neither strange nor shameful to think about your genitals, any more than it is to wonder if your thighs are getting larger. Most women agree that the way they feel about their bodies affects their sexuality. Why should the genitals be any different? Loving your genitals and feeling confident in them is an integral part of sexual well-being. Unfortunately, too many women are prevented from feeling connected to their genitals. Whether through silence or experiences like having your hand slapped away when you explored your body as a toddler, women receive strong negative messages about their genitals. While men come of age with a sense of pride in their sexual anatomy, women often find that the focus is on inhibition, anxiety, and hygiene. Though it may take a little work, the genitals should be a source of pride for women, too. The tips that follow will help you make the most of your sexual anatomy. It matters for your sex life in more ways than you might think!

Berman Center Genital Self-Image Study

In hopes of shedding some light on genital self-image and its effect on women's sex lives, the Berman Center conducted a nationwide study of a random selection of more than 2,500 women ages eighteen and over. We looked at the impact of genital self-image on sexual response and satisfaction, as well as how body image and genital odor shape a woman's genital self-image. We also investigated the relationship to quality of life. The people at C.B. Fleet, the makers of the Summer's Eve line, provided an unrestricted educational grant to fund the study, gave us access to their scientists, and assisted with the latest technology in odor management.

To measure a woman's genital self-image, we asked her how often she had certain thoughts or feelings about her genitals. For example, whether she felt ashamed of or comfortable with her genitals. We then asked her to rate a series of adjectives in terms of how much they applied to her genitals—whether attractive, embarrassing, healthy, and so on.

We found that how a woman perceives her genitals has a powerful effect on how she functions sexually. Women with more positive genital self-images were found to have more sexual desire and better sexual response. This means they reported more lubrication during sexual activity and better quality orgasms. Women who felt positive about their genitals also experienced an easier time reaching orgasm. Not surprisingly, they reported a higher level of satisfaction with their sex lives overall.

The effects of thinking well about your genitals don't stop in the bedroom either. We found the more positive a woman's genital self-image was, the more satisfaction she reported in her quality of life. Women with a positive view of their genitals indicated they were more satisfied with the meaning and purpose of their lives, as well as with the amount of variety and stress. They also reported higher levels of overall life satisfaction.

What sets apart women with positive genital self-images? In our study, women in steady relationships were more likely to have a positive genital self-image. So were younger women and those with a higher level of education. We found that African American women had a consistently more positive view of their genitals than any other racial group. Most important were the relationships we found between genital self-image, body image, and genital odor perception, since a woman can take a more active role in these areas. Having a more positive body image was found to promote a positive genital self-image. Also, a woman's perception of genital odor, strongly influenced her genital self-image. Feeling a lack of control over odor, worrying or having been told she has excessive genital odor, and concern about that odor affecting her sex life are the three most common ways genital odor negatively impacted a woman's genital self-image.

Finding ways to tackle body image and genital odor concerns are essential to feeling more confident about your genitals, since feeling good about your genitals plays an important role in sex. You've taken steps to begin getting comfortable with your genitals through visual exploration and masturbation. You've also learned that working through body image issues requires the right combination of diet and exercise choices, along with unlearning the negative ways we think about our bodies.

It's also important to understand the way you think about your sexual anatomy. To give you an idea of where you stand, I have developed the Genital Image Scale. This short quiz will give you an assessment of how you think about your genitals. When you have a minute, flip back to the Appendix and take it. Then you can determine what, if any, areas you need to improve on.

As for genital odor concerns, no woman should feel embarrassed about this or any other worries about her sexual anatomy. By bringing the issue of genital odor into the open, women have a better chance of finding concrete solutions. Keep reading to learn about the many ways to keep your genitals feeling, looking, and acting their best. Caring for your genitals is as important as any other part of your body. So go on, it's time to pamper your genitals!

Keeping Your Vulva in Peak Shape

The saying that cleanliness is next to godliness could not be truer than it is for the vulva. Everybody wants a clean lover and, as we've learned, feeling clean may actually make you a better lover—or at least help you enjoy sex more. Keeping your vulva in good condition is easy if you make a few simple choices.

First, you should wash the genital area every time you shower. A mild, fragrance-free cleanser will usually work well. Summer's Eve has a product called Feminine Bath, but many women use their face wash, since it is intended for sensitive skin; however, any cleanser containing glycolic acid or other abrasives should be avoided. You can even gently shampoo and condition your pubic hair to keep it soft and smelling good. Once out of the shower, it's important to thoroughly dry the entire area. Aside from keeping your vulva clean, keeping it dry is most important. A wet or unclean environment promotes the growth of bacteria, which can lead to a yeast or bacterial infection.

What's the best way to keep things dry and clean throughout the day? Three words: comfortable cotton panties. Unless you are a Victoria's Secret model, there is no reason to wear uncomfortable underwear on a daily basis. Nothing compares with cotton for its breathability and stretchability. Both create an ideal environment, in which odor and discharge are kept at their most natural levels. If you think cotton underwear is synonymous with granny panties, check out the choices at Victoria's Secret and GapBody. Both have great-looking lines of cotton panties in a variety of colors and patterns. The string bikinis they make are as cute as your favorite synthetic underwear, without the side effects. Synthetic fabrics promote the growth of bacteria and don't allow air to reach the genitals, both of which increase your chance of infection, as well as excess discharge and odor. I recommend sleeping without underwear to give the genitals a chance to breathe. Anything to keep things airy helps! You can also try going commando during the day—in other words, don't wear any panties. Sometimes not wearing underwear is sexier than any piece of lingerie could be. Surprise your partner by leaving your panties at home the next time you have a date. Don't forget to mention it casually over dinner. As for the lacy, barely-there undies, keep them for special occasions or a short evening out. Great lingerie can make you feel incredible and is always a good way to turn up the heat in the bedroom. They're just not good for you if worn every day.

When it comes to thongs, they are both a blessing and a curse to women. There's no doubt that thongs make your backside look better and have given every woman a whole new perspective on panty lines. What did we do before we had them? Wearing a thong feels pretty sexy, too, until it starts to lodge itself into parts you think it might never return from. Thankfully, there are some choices you can make to ensure thongs are a healthy part of your lingerie selection, instead of a painful one. A bad thong usually consists of inflexible fabric and a skimpy, string-like design. Aside from often being uncomfortable, bad thongs are also hazardous to your sexual health. They can transfer bacteria from the anus to the genitals and cause infection. Even without any bacterial exchange, if the fabric is chafing, it can cause irritation and tiny tears in the genital tissues.

Good thongs make your body feel good, in addition to making it look good. How can you tell the difference? Most important is a wider panel of fabric in the crotch area that goes from the front all the way to the back. Next in importance is a flexible, breathable material. Keeping things airy is still essential. Fortunately, you have many excellent options for comfortable, but cute, thongs. Obstetrician Lisa Masterson has developed a great line of underwear with the right fit. The Butterfly line is a sort of hybrid thong, which has more fabric across the back, but leaves enough exposed to keep it sexy *and* avoid panty lines. There are lots of colors available, all in a great mesh material with a cotton crotch. For you low-rise women, the Hanky Panky line of stretch lace thongs will make your day (or your night). The material allows the thong to stay comfortably in place underneath the hips for as long as you want it to.

Aside from wearing the right underwear, you should never try to mask your genital odor with deodorant soaps, sprays, or douches. They often irritate the vagina and lead to even more problems by destroying healthy bacteria. The issue of genital odor is one I've struggled with as a clinician. On the one hand, I want to tell women, *Love your genitals exactly as they are!* And an important part of loving your genitals is embracing your natural scent. Many of us in the field of women's sexual health are taught that it is antiwoman to even have a conversation about genital odor. The rule of thumb is that odor is natural and good and not something to be masked. But I've worked with too many women who are debilitated by their concerns about odor, many of whom do have quite a strong scent that is inhibiting to them and their partners. The bottom line is that a woman's scent is natural; however, you shouldn't be embarrassed about seeking help if it is negatively affecting your sexuality. I think it's important for every woman to have the tools she needs to feel her best sexually. There are several options for improving your genital odor that do not place your reproductive anatomy at risk.

Douching with a simple water and vinegar solution, it turns out, may not be such a bad thing. For years women and health-care professionals alike, myself included, have been warned about the dangers of douching; however, recent research has found that it may not always be such a bad thing. A study conducted by researchers at Mount Sinai Medical Center in New York City discovered that women who douche once a week or less with water and vinegar have no more risk of vaginal infection than women who didn't. The study still found women who used fragranced douches, or douched with anything more than once a week, had double the risk of vaginal infection.

While perfumed products are never good, odor-neutralizing and unscented alternatives are usually fine. These can be especially useful for women who struggle with a strong natural odor. What's the difference between unscented and odor-neutralizing products? Unscented products for the genitals do not contain any ingredients added for the sole purpose of fragrance. The product may still have a scent, since the ingredients can contribute a natural smell. Odor-neutralizing products contain ingredients that actively reduce odor. This can include antibacterial or antiperspirant agents, which work to reduce genital odor. Different women will respond to these products in different ways. Always check the ingredients before using a product, so you can determine what has been added. If you want to give an unscented or odor-neutralizing product a shot, I tell patients to try feminine cleansing cloths. They are great for staying fresh during the day and freshening up on the go. Summer's Eve makes these, as well as other companies. When all else fails, you can even use unscented baby wipes. The cloths remove odor-causing bacteria from the genitals. They may be just what you're looking for to reduce natural genital odor. However, if any irritation develops or your symptoms do not improve, you are better off without them.

Too often, women believe that their genitals are dirty and need to be cleaned. The reality is that a healthy vagina regulates itself, with little need for extra cleaning. In fact, if you clean it too much, you can offset the natural balance of bacteria that always exists in a healthy vagina. The best way to keep your genitals feeling their best is by taking the simple steps listed above. Eating well and drinking water help, too, since they keep the entire body in good health. And safe sex is a must! Always use a condom with a new sexual partner until you are sure you are both disease-free. Even if a new partner is clean and uses a condom, women often develop urinary tract or yeast infections as their body adjusts. It can also happen to women who've been with the same partner for years after a particularly overzealous session of lovemaking! For women who haven't had sex in a while, such infections are even more common. Urinating immediately afterward can help reduce your risk. If you have any itching, burning, or changes in discharge or odor, it could be a sign of infection. While many over-the-counter remedies exist, it's always important to have the symptoms checked out by a doctor to confirm nothing more serious is causing them.

Grooming and Beyond

Women spend endless hours at the salon, in bathrooms, and in front of mirrors messing with their hair. I say it's time to give the hair downstairs a little love and attention. In addition to daily washing, there is an endless array of choices for grooming and even decorating your genitals.

To trim or not to trim? For many women, the thought of trimming their pubic hair, aside from the bikini line, has never crossed their minds. Like all areas of personal style and hygiene, every woman is different when it comes to her genitals. Grooming is simply another way to feel great about your sexual anatomy, and you need to do what's most comfortable for you. Even if you do not want to do anything radical, reducing the volume of pubic hair with a little trim can help. It not only tidies things up, but also makes the scenery better for your partner. Though some men enjoy a bohemian bush, many appreciate it when you show a little effort. And don't hesitate to tell *him* if he's in order for some trimming, too.

I would venture to say that every woman has shaved her bikini line at some point in her life. For some women, the grooming stops there. For others, it is merely the tip of the iceberg. Whatever your preference, getting a clean shave is easy if you follow a few simple steps. Always wait to shave until the end of your bath or shower. This allows the hair to soften and the pores to open, which makes removal easier. The next most important tip is to use a sharp clean razor. Using the old razor that's been in the shower for months is just going to irritate your skin. Same goes for using your partner's razor! If you really want to get fancy, apply some shaving cream with a badger brush (these are the little brushes they use when shaving men at old-fashioned barbershops). The brush helps exfoliate the skin and raises the hairs for a cleaner shave. Finally, make sure you are pulling the skin taut when you shave. Extending your leg to the side usually does the trick. If you decide to skip a few of these steps and end up with razor burn, a little Visine will take the redness right out of those little bumps until they heal. It's a good last-minute remedy. But remember that when you shave, the hair often grows in thicker, at least initially.

Some women and men go crazy over a completely bare vulva. Women often say it heightens their sensitivity and makes them feel sexy in a totally new way. Many men say it looks and feels great during sex. Going completely bare, however, is no small task. While you can get waxed, which I discuss next, many women choose to shave. Some even let their partner get in on the activity, which can be incredibly erotic. Whether you do it or your partner does it, this is a delicate undertaking and several precautions need to be followed.

It once again helps to let the hair and skin soften during a warm shower or bath. If you are removing hair for the first time, you will need scissors as well as a good razor. A small pair of scissors usually works best. Once you've let the hair soften, use the scissors to trim the hair so it is close to the skin. Since it's going to take you longer to shave the entire vulva, turn off the shower or drain the water from the tub. Next, apply shaving cream with either your fingers or a badger brush. Using a brush now will really make a difference if you are shaving virgin hair. When you're ready, start shaving from the outside part of your vulva in. It will probably work best to stand up for the top portion of the hair, and to sit down for the lower part. A hand mirror also comes in handy for this area, unless you are incredibly flexible or letting your partner shave you. You will need to rinse your razor repeatedly to keep removing hair. Pay attention so the razor does not come into contact with any hairless parts of your vulva. Usually women are so sensitive during shaving that this is not a problem. After you've finished, gently rub the area with a washcloth to remove any final hairs or potential pore-cloggers. Apply a mild moisturizer and if your skin feels irritated, you can also apply some hydrocortisone cream.

The smooth finish should last for a day or so, since shaving is only tempo-rary. Be prepared for the hair to itch as it grows back in! This is true for any form of hair removal, especially when it's a dense area that's never been groomed before. Gently exfoliate every other day to prevent ingrown hairs. Also, continue to moisturize the area lightly so it does not become inflamed.

If that seems like a lot of work for one night, but you like the hair-free feel-ing, or if you have coarser hair and are worried about the increased stubble, waxing is likely your next best option. Waxing hurts. There is no getting around it. But no form of hair removal compares with it for the long-lasting results at an affordable price. Many women find that waxing becomes less painful over time as the hair thins. It also might be that they just adjust to the pain! Some women wax themselves at home, but it's usually best to have a few experiences at the salon before you try that.

If you decide to wax an area that you normally shave, you'll need to let the hair grow in for at least a month. Hair also needs to grow back in between ap-pointments, which can be a potential downside. Women usually get waxed every four to six weeks. Depending on your hair, regrowth begins two to four weeks after a wax. The same rules apply for maintenance as they do for shaving—gently exfoliate to prevent ingrown hairs and lightly moisturize or use hydrocortisone cream. After a wax especially, the skin is likely to be slightly red and inflamed. This usually subsides after a day or two.

There are four main hairstyles when it comes to waxing: the bikini, the Brazilian, the playboy, and the sphinx. The bikini removes hair from the bikini line only. This is good for beginners or for the weak of heart. The Brazilian is where the real pain begins—this and anything beyond it are only for the brave. Though painful, many women swear by them. The Brazilian and playboy are very similar. Both remove virtually all of the hair, except for a narrow landing strip. The technical difference is that the playboy removes all hair from the labia, so a patch of hair remains only just above the labia. The Brazilian leaves a strip of hair that extends down the entire length of the labia. Both get into the nether regions and remove hair from the peri-anal area. Get one and you will understand once and for all why Brazilian women can wear the bikinis they do. Finally, the sphinx is a completely bare wax. Every last hair is whisked away by the expert hands of your aesthetician. Speaking of which, it is always important to make sure you visit a licensed salon with licensed aestheticians. You wouldn't want to put hot wax and your genitals into untrained hands. Also, a good waxing professional will take the time to pluck out ingrown hairs and give you tips for taking care of your newly waxed skin at home. Fragranced products are always a no-no for the first forty-eight hours after a wax.

Once your skin has recovered, decorating with stick-on jewels or temporary tattoos can be really fun for a special occasion. Many salons offer the service, or you can buy your own and get creative. Tattoo a private message for your partner or use the stick-on jewels to make a design. There are also salons that will dye or shape your pubic hair into endless creations. A little red heart works for Valentine's Day or a peach shows him how sweet you are. If you want to try changing the color of your southern locks at home, opt for a colored mousse or gel. You should never use permanent hair dye when not under the supervision of an experienced aesthetician. You run a serious risk of irritation, infection, and worse if it gets inside your genitals. For 170 pages of everything you've ever wanted to know about genital grooming, take a look at *Hot Pink: The Girls' Guide to Primping, Passion, and Pubic Fashion,* by Deborah Driggs and Karen Risch.

Beware of depilatory creams. They can be incredibly harsh on the skin and most women's pubic hair is too coarse to be removed by them anyway. If you're interested in permanent hair removal, laser and electrolysis are both options. They are quite expensive and will usually run you upward of $1,000 by the time you are done. However, if you add up the cost of bimonthly waxes over the course of several years, the cost seems less outrageous. Electrolysis is more tedious than laser, since the hairs are destroyed one at a time by sending a slight electric current into the root. It can also be more painful, since hair is removed continuously throughout a thirty- to sixty-minute session. Laser hair removal is more like waxing—there are brief periods of pain as the laser targets the hair, but they end quickly. Women with lighter skin and darker hair are the best candidates for laser. New technology is constantly evolving, but women with light hair or dark skin may not respond well to laser hair removal. With both laser and electrolysis, it's important to remember that whatever hair you take off is not likely to come back. Choosing conservatively is always best.

Beyond taking care of your hair, it is also important to attend to your skin. Nothing feels better than soft, smooth skin, and it's not difficult to get. Exfoliate once or twice a week from head to toe. Always moisturize after you shower. A moisturizer with alpha-hydroxy or glycolic acid is best, since it will help your skin stay smooth, but keep the acids away from the genitals. Oil is another great moisturizer, especially if you put it on before you go to bed. Try some on your newly groomed hair, too, to help keep it soft. It's all about feeling good about your body.

Living with a Chronic STD

A chronic sexually transmitted disease (STD) can challenge a woman's sense of confidence in her body and her sexuality. Women often beat themselves up over past choices that compromised their sexual health. Some feel betrayed by partners who were not upfront with them about their sexual history. Others are shocked to learn they contracted an STD even after practicing safe sex with a condom, since genital warts and herpes can be transmitted even if you use one. However, it's important to remember that every woman has some aspect of her sexuality with which she struggles. Even if you have a chronic STD—such as herpes, genital warts, Hepatitis B, or HIV—a full and satisfying sex life is still within reach. And you are not alone; one in three Americans develops an STD before age twenty-four.

Chronic STDs are the result of a virus that can never be eliminated from the body; however, many options exist for managing them. All are contracted through unprotected sex. Some can be contracted through oral sex or genital-to-genital contact, in addition to vaginal or anal sex. The physical symptoms of a chronic STD may take years to emerge, or never become evident at all. Because of this, safer sex is always a must. Regular testing for common STDs is also a good idea, even if you are in a monogamous relationship.

Women must learn to forgive themselves for the decisions that led to their diagnosis. Every relationship involves a leap of faith and this is especially true for intimate relationships. There is nothing wrong with having mistakenly put your trust in someone who, ultimately, turned out to be a different person from what you thought. Learning that you have a chronic STD intensifies the normal emotions of anger, regret, and loss that accompany the end of a relationship. Once you have let yourself feel what's only natural, the goal is to work on redefining your sexuality, which is both an emotional and physical undertaking. In addition to approaching sex with a different mind-set, a chronic STD also requires certain physical modifications.

After a chronic STD diagnosis, safer sex becomes an absolute if it hadn't been in the past. All chronic STDs can be passed on to a partner, whether or not any physical signs are present. Many times, the symptoms are so mild that they are absent or unnoticeable. For herpes and genital warts, sexual activity should be avoided entirely when there are visible symptoms. This means oral sex, too, since herpes and genital warts can both be passed on from mouth-to-genital contact.

A young college student I recently treated came to my center seeking help for a string of events set in motion two years earlier by a herpes diagnosis. I'll call her Sarah. Cute, athletic, and energetic, Sarah had contracted herpes from oral sex with a former boyfriend, who had falsely assured her he was disease-free. This is not surprising—it is estimated that one in five Americans has herpes, and 90 percent do not know they have it. Sarah was currently in another relationship and managing the outbreaks. She had not told her new boyfriend about her herpes diagnosis until the relationship was well established. Though he was supportive when she confided in him, he admitted that he probably would not have continued the relationship had she told him at the beginning.

In addition to struggling with the physical symptoms of herpes, Sarah was experiencing a sense of emotional conflict about her relationship. She was relieved that her new boyfriend accepted her, but also felt as if he were taking pity on her. The sense of gratitude she felt toward him created an imbalance in their relationship. I understood that since Sarah felt lucky to have a boyfriend, she was hesitant to stick up for her own needs a lot of the time. We discussed her feelings of guilt and anxiety over waiting to tell him about her herpes. Sarah, like many women and men with a chronic STD, felt torn about discussing it. She explained that if she told her boyfriend about her situation at the beginning of the relationship, she would not have been given a chance. By telling him later, however, it felt like betrayal.

Sarah and I worked on counteracting her feelings of shame and anxiety. Like many others, Sarah was not given much advice from her doctor about how to manage the disease beyond medication. Since she did not know where to turn for help, she experienced a strong sense of isolation and anxiety. Sarah even believed she would not be able to have children, since no one told her that the risk of passing herpes on to a baby is incredibly low if the virus was not contracted during the pregnancy. Sarah began accessing support resources to learn about how to lessen her chances of an outbreak. As with any chronic health condition, stress reduction is very important. Getting enough sleep, learning to relax, and reaching out for support are all helpful. Eating right and exercising also reduce the frequency and severity of outbreaks. Sarah continued taking a prescription medication to treat, as well as prevent, future outbreaks.

Slowly, Sarah began to feel that she did deserve a satisfying sex life, even if some of the conditions had changed. She realized the importance of being honest about her diagnosis from the start with any future partners. Her relationship with her boyfriend ended as they were unable to move beyond his resentment over her lack of honesty at the beginning. I suggested that Sarah check out one of the online dating sites for people with chronic STDs. Though she would not have to limit herself to that forever, it was a good place for her to begin reestablishing herself in the dating world. Sarah also took advantage of support systems for people with herpes, like the H.O.P.E. patient support network run by the drug company Novartis. Meeting other people who were dealing with a chronic STD created a feeling of connectedness and hope. It offered Sarah further insight into how other people move on with their lives, sexually and otherwise, after learning they have a chronic STD. For a list of resources for coping with herpes and other chronic STDs, visit the Resource Guide at the end of this book.

The bottom line is that every woman must learn to embrace her own sexual reality, no matter what the particulars. A chronic STD does not have to mean the end of a satisfying sex life. Like Sarah, it's essential to take a diagnosis one step at a time by reaching out for help. Arming yourself with information is the best way to prevent a chronic STD from taking your sex life hostage.

It's important to know what the signs of a chronic STD are, so you can detect it as soon as possible. A healthy awareness of your sexual anatomy helps send up a red flag when something may be wrong. Though not all STDs cause noticeable symptoms—making regular testing essential—you can never be too aware of your own body. Genital warts appear as tiny, flesh-colored or cauliflower-like bumps on the vulva and perineal area. Warts can also appear internally in the vagina and on the cervix, which is why it's important to get an annual gynecological exam. Genital warts are caused by a strain of the human papillomavirus (HPV), which is also associated with an increased risk of cervical cancer if left undetected.

There are two types of herpes: type 1, which most often causes oral herpes; and type 2, which normally causes genital herpes. Oral herpes appear as cold sores on the face and mouth. Genital herpes appear as a rash or bumps on or around the genitals or anus, accompanied by itching or burning. They can develop into blisters or sores in more severe outbreaks. Sometimes flu-like symptoms are also present. As mentioned earlier, herpes outbreaks are not always accompanied by physical symptoms. The number of outbreaks, if any, varies widely from person to person depending on the strength of the virus and lifestyle choices. Some people experience one outbreak and never again have another, while others have several outbreaks a year. A typical outbreak lasts from two to twelve days.

Hepatitis B is transmitted through unprotected vaginal, anal, or oral sex, but does not have any sexual side effects. It can also be passed on through intravenous drug use. Hepatitis B is the most easily prevented STD, since a vaccine exists to prevent infection. The most common symptoms of Hepatitis B are jaundice, fatigue, abdominal pain, nausea, and loss of appetite. The Hepatitis B virus can become chronic and attack the liver in certain cases. Thirty percent of people with Hepatitis B experience no symptoms.

HIV is transmitted through unprotected vaginal, anal, or oral sex and, often, through contact with an infected person's blood. The early symptoms of HIV are difficult to detect and may be dormant for several years. For that reason, the only way to know if you have HIV is to get tested. Warning signs of HIV may include weight loss, fatigue, swollen lymph glands in the armpits, groin, or neck, diarrhea that lasts for more than a week, or unusual spots under the skin or inside the mouth, nose, or eyelids. HIV infection often progresses to AIDS, which is the permanent weakening of the immune system.

TAKING CHARGE WITH GROOMING, SELF-CARE, and an acceptance of your individuality is an important part of feeling confident about your sexual anatomy. Whether you're challenging how you think about your genitals to get over feelings of shame or embarrassment, or tackling a physical concern, you are on your way to reconnecting with an essential element of your sexuality.

Every woman deserves to feel attractive. In addition to exercise and diet, keeping it pretty down under gives you another advantage in getting the sex life you want. It's fun to put some effort into a part of our bodies that is often overlooked. Your sexual anatomy is not simply functional, but also a source of connection to who you are as a woman. Show it some love like you do any other part of your body. Your sex life will thank you for it.

PRESCRIPTIONS FOR THE WEEK:
Week 7

✓ Your hormone tests should be back by now. Make sure you check in with your doctor to get your results and see if your levels are low.

✓ Take the Genital Image Scale (Appendix page 262) to get a sense of the problem areas in your genital self-esteem. If you know where you are struggling, you will have a better sense of what to do about it. If it's odor, make sure you see your doctor. If it's the shape or size of your genitals, make sure you read the chapter to get some ideas, but don't worry—if you keep doing those Pelvic Push-Ups three times a week it will make all the difference for your concerns about tightness.

✓ Go through your panty drawer and take inventory! Throw out the bad panties that may compromise your physical and sexual health and make a list of the new brands listed in this chapter that you'd like to try. Hit the lingerie shops and stock up!

✓ Try a new hairdo down under . . . whether it's a wax, shave, or dye job, try a new coif and see how your genital confidence soars!

✓ Schedule your annual Pap smear to be tested for STDs, HIV, and any other possible infections that may be present.

✓ By now you should have talked to your doctor about any hormonal irregularities and may be on the way to treating them. If you have a sexual function complaint, you've either contacted your doctor or a therapist, depending on what you discovered when you took the Berman Sexual Assessment mentioned in Chapter 3.

✓ Don't forget! Masturbate at least twice a week, keep writing about your experiences in your sexual journal, and be sure to take two hours this week, whether it's with friends or by yourself, but with no work or home demands and no errands. And keep the action with your partner going: at least one sexual experience a week barring illness or extreme relationship conflict! Also remember to do your Kegel exercises on a regular basis, incorporated into or separate from your Pelvic Push-Ups three times a week, and thirty to forty-five minutes of cardiovascular exercise three times a week as well.

GUY'S GUIDE:
A Summary of Key Points for the Man in Your Life

1. Every woman's genitals are different. Like the face or hands, each and every vulva has its own unique personality. *Playboy* centerfolds are airbrushed to make the vulva appear uniformly pink, with perfectly proportioned labia (the majority just don't look that way—I promise!). In reality, women's genitals come in all kinds of shapes, sizes, and colors. Their appearance also changes over time. Check out the book *Femalia* if you want to see some realistic pictures of women's genitals.

2. Each woman's genitals have a distinctive smell, which is naturally all her own. From evolution's perspective, it is the genital scent that plays a key role in attracting a mate. Today, a woman's natural odor can be an incredible turn-on to a partner before and during sexual activity.

3. When aroused, different women produce different amounts of lubrication, depending on their age, degree of arousal, and use of certain medications. Many women complain about a lack of adequate lubrication during sexual arousal. Give one of the lubricants listed on pages 28 and 29 a try if you desire more wetness during sex. Some women complain of too much lubrication during sex, which can lead to feelings of embarrassment or a lack of friction during intercourse. Reassure her that it's OK, and wipe away extra fluids with a small towel if they are a nuisance. You should take it as a compliment that you arouse her so much!

4. I have found that how a woman perceives her genitals has a powerful effect on how she functions sexually. Women with more positive genital self-images have more sexual desire and better sexual response—meaning they report more lubrication during sexual activity and better quality orgasms. They also have an easier time reaching orgasm. Guess what I've found to impact a woman's genital self-image most negatively? A partner telling her something negative about her genitals. So help her learn to love and celebrate her sexual anatomy, and your sex life will thank you!

CHAPTER EIGHT

Show Him

■◣◣◣◣■

YOU'VE WORKED HARD TO GET yourself where you want to be. Now it's time to bring it all together. It's opening night for your new and improved sex life and getting your partner on board in bed is your final act. Good technique is what will make it worthy of a standing ovation.

Many men do not understand the different physical and emotional needs that women have when it comes to enjoyable sex. Many women are left understandably dissatisfied by partners who don't take the time they need to warm up and reach orgasm. When women and men enter the bedroom, all too often she's hoping for a marathon and he's getting ready to do the fifty-yard dash!

The average man takes between five and ten minutes to reach orgasm, while the average woman takes a half hour. Though a woman's sexual pleasure is on a different schedule from a man's, it's nothing that a little gentle instruction can't clear up. The days of women putting their sexual satisfaction on the back burner are coming to an end.

Lucky for your partner, you should now be a seasoned expert in all of your pleasure hot spots. Time to show him, ladies!

What You Want and Need

Women's feelings of arousal come from their brains as much as from the physical sensations they feel in their genitals and elsewhere. This is not to say that physical pleasure does not matter—it does! But when sex is good, it's usually because the woman feels she has achieved a deepened sense of intimacy with her partner, which is what she originally sought. As I revealed in my last book, *Secrets of the Sexually Satisfied Woman,* our national survey of more than 1,500 women found that sexually satisfied women had one primary characteristic in common: a sense of intimacy and connection to their partners. This helps explain why good sex is less about what happens physically than it is about the sense of connection women feel during it. It is a completely subjective experience, with no definite pattern. Depending on the kind of sexual activity engaged in and a woman's individual preferences, orgasm is not always the final outcome of good sex. A woman's sexual response neither starts nor ends in the same place every time. One woman who does not orgasm may consider herself as sexually satisfied as another woman who orgasms multiple times. Unlike men, for women there is no absolute physical definition of sexual satisfaction.

Our sexual needs also change from day to day, and even from hour to hour. You may find yourself overwhelmed with sexual desire for your partner at 4:00 in the afternoon while sitting at your desk or while you are making dinner, but at 9:00 P.M. when you finally have a moment, you are too exhausted and the mood passes. Then there are those days when you find it amazingly easy to respond sexually and reach orgasm and others when you just know it isn't going to happen, but still enjoy the closeness and intimacy with your partner.

Women definitely can have that physical, primal urge for sex. When enthralled by a new sexual partner, or the early days of being sexually active, the body's craving for sex is definitely strong. The same can be true for women who have been in a relationship for years, depending on the situation. The point is that your mind-set about your relationship has the strongest influence on your desire to be sexual, while for men it is a more purely physical drive.

Since the process of getting in the mood begins in two separate places, how then do men and women come together? Good sex always depends on finding the middle ground. Up next, you will map out your own personal road to sexual pleasure. Teaching your partner to pay attention to these key areas is your surest route to satisfaction in bed. Coupled with an understanding of your body, you become your own guide in discovering good sex.

Knowing Yourself

Setting up realistic expectations before sex begins is essential. Maintaining those expectations throughout is equally important. To define your expectations when it comes to sex, you need to understand what's realistic—both as an individual and in general.

We'll start with the individual. Most women have an ideal of mind-blowing sex stuck somewhere in their mind. It could be a one-night episode, or maybe it was in a former relationship. Either way, it is the sex that to one degree or another still lingers in the back of your mind—the sex that was *so* good, even if the person you had it with was so wrong. I think it is precisely this sex that can be most instructive when you are trying to figure out exactly what you want in bed. Individually, this will be different for each woman. Try thinking about the best sex you ever had. Close your eyes and allow the feelings and sensations of the moment to wash over you. Next rank the characteristics in order of importance. Below is a list to get you started, but you should add your own.

Best Sex Ever: Your Great Sex Template

I felt a sense of trust toward the person.

I felt a sense of danger with the person.

I had one or more orgasms.

I was really lubricated.

I liked the way he kissed me.

I liked the way he touched me.

We had sex in an adventurous location.

We had sex in a familiar location.

We tried unusual positions.

He told me how attractive I was.

He performed oral sex on me.

I performed oral sex on him.

He took charge.

I took charge.

He knew what to do without being told.

I told him what to do.

He paid attention to other parts of my body (list parts).

We had a deep connection to each other before sex.

We did not know each other very well before we had sex.

He pursued me.

I pursued him.

The sex was unplanned.

The sex was planned.

Once you have a list of characteristics together, it should help you to understand what made the sex so memorable. While some of the characteristics may be unrealistic—like not knowing each other well—most will be qualities that you can work to incorporate into your current sex life. Enjoy a sense of being in control? Surprise your partner by initiating sex after he is dressed and ready to go to work in the morning. He probably won't mind being a little late. Like having other parts of your body admired? Let him know in a subtle way that you enjoy hearing what he thinks about your nonsexual parts. Or, compliment him on a part of his body you've never paid attention to before. He'll likely return the favor. There are ideas throughout this book for adding novelty to your sex life. The most important part of bringing it all together is having a clear picture of what good sex looks like for *you*.

Besides understanding your individual expectations for good sex, it is important to know what's realistic generally. Though it's helpful to use your best sex ever as an ideal to work toward, it should not be your benchmark on an everyday basis. You would be setting yourself up for a lot of disappointment! Like the opening of this chapter explained, sex is different for every woman, as well as on each and every occasion. Even if you are with the same partner, in the same bed, doing the same stuff—the sex is going to feel different. So it's best to approach sex with a law of averages in mind. Sometimes it's great, sometimes it's good, and other times it's bad. What you hope for is that over the long run it evens out to good enough. By managing your own expectations, you can also manage your partner's. And he might just be relieved to find out that mind-blowing sex is not required of *him* every time either.

In addition to knowing what you want, it's important to understand what you can expect from your body. You've already read about what happens to your body during sexual arousal. In large part, good sex comes from knowing how your sexual organs and functions work. Use your results from the Berman Sexual Assessment you completed in Chapter 3 to help you identify any problems you might be having with your sexual function. Or, take it again by flipping to page 252 in the Appendix if you think you've begun to see some changes as a result of everything you've been doing!

Time to Warm Up

Once you've gotten your expectations nailed down, most women still need time to transition from mom, professional, or housekeeper to sexy vixen in the bedroom. Men, on the other hand, often need little more than a good kiss to get their attention. In fact, the ease with which many men get erections often leaves them astonished that women are not the same.

In part, this can be explained by our evolutionary background. We evolved as a hunter-gatherer society—men were the hunters and women the gatherers. As hunters, men who survived were those who could focus and be completely goal-oriented. In prehistoric times, they would gather together with the other hunters, draw out a plan for how they were going to drive their prey into the ravine, and then carry out that plan in an organized fashion—totally focused on the task at hand. Echoes of the hunter remain in the modern man who can focus on his work or other tasks to the exclusion of everything else. This can be frustrating for their partners—who want to be able to carry on a conversation with them while they are driving or working on another project. However, it works great in the office and it also works to their advantage sexually. When it's time to get busy, men can tune out everything else and focus on the sexual moment.

Women had to be multitaskers to survive. They needed to do many things simultaneously: scan the area for nuts and berries, make the social connections that were a key to their survival, carry and care for their small infants, and be on alert for predators or danger. This is why women today can make dinner, help their child with homework, and talk on the phone, all at the same time. We are able to manage many different tasks at once, much to our male partners' amazement, but it can be a curse sexually. It's often very difficult for us to turn off the noise and tune into a sexy mind-set. Women find their minds racing, worrying about how they're going to get the kids to soccer practice, the arguments they got into with their bosses that morning, or whether the windows are closed. Another common problem is that if you're not feeling great about yourself or the person you're with, it's really hard to turn those thoughts off and focus on the sexual act in progress.

The best way to work around this is by giving yourself some time to relax before sex. This means carving out some time to quiet the mind. For some women this means reading something pleasurable, like a novel or a trashy magazine. For others it's just a matter of spending time cuddling on the couch with your partner before bed. Ask your partner to rub your back or your feet to help you get out of your head and in touch with your body. The idea is to give yourself an opportunity to cleanse your mind of the day's stresses. Like I said before, it is also helpful for creating an emotional connection to your partner. Nonsexual together time—especially right before sex—is often the best foreplay.

And remember, you deserve it! Too many women assume there is something wrong with them because they are not instantly game for sex. The difference is that women need time to warm up; men don't. Don't feel bad about asking for some time to get in the mood. Your sexual satisfaction is important, and you should do what's necessary to set the stage for it. If you have some nonsexual time to quiet the mind, your sexual response is likely to move along much more quickly. It is the first stop on the road to good sex.

The Big "O"

To orgasm, or not to orgasm? That is the question. Women and men alike fret over the female orgasm—that elusive benchmark we tend to measure ourselves against when it comes to good sex. The problem with women and orgasm is the more you think about it the less likely you are to have one. And the more your partner focuses on it, the less likely you are to have one. Many women feel incredible pressure to have an orgasm every time they have sex.

Quite a tall order, when you consider that only about one-third of women consistently climax from penetration alone. Surprising, isn't it? Look around you, or think about your friends—only one out of every three women regularly orgasms from intercourse. Yet somehow, women continue to operate under the idea that penetration is their surest route to sexual satisfaction. In reality, clitoral stimulation is almost always necessary and even then not all women orgasm. Manual or oral stimulation of the clitoris, or use of a vibrator, are your best bets when in search of orgasm.

So why do we make such a big deal about orgasms? Probably because a good orgasm can be staggering—a peak physical experience that actually takes you right out of your body for a few precious seconds. Strong orgasms feel electric since they race from your genitals to your mind and all places in between. Orgasms can also be soft or barely noticeable. Your body may tense and convulse, or relax and open up. You may moan or scream when it happens, and your skin is often hot and flushed. Like sex, orgasms fluctuate depending on a number of factors. For this very reason, an orgasm should not be chased but allowed to happen naturally. The key is to let your body flow with the sexual experience.

Women have three kinds of orgasm—vaginal, clitoral, and combined. The trick is finding your way to at least one of them, which is a matter of both body *and* mind. Instead of focusing on what kind of orgasm you are having or want to have, it is better simply to focus on the sensations of the moment. There is enough of a focus on orgasm already! We don't need to be analyzing it even further, especially when many of the same structures are probably involved in all kinds of orgasm. Unfortunately for women, Freud had everyone under the mistaken impression that vaginal orgasms were the only real orgasms, until about thirty years ago. Freud considered clitoral orgasms to be immature since they were not the result of penetration. We now know that clitoral orgasms are actually more common for many women than vaginal orgasms. Even women who have so-called vaginal orgasms are probably receiving some kind of clitoral stimulation.

The bottom line: Orgasms are great, no doubt. But men and women make a woman's orgasm the end-all-and-be-all of sex. In reality, we now know that orgasm is not an accurate measure of women's sexual satisfaction. Instead, it is the emotional and physical intimacy women feel during the act of sex that matters most.

Whoa, now! I can see some of you twisting in your seats saying, *Well, yes, actually orgasm* does *matter to me.* Of course it does. All I am saying is that orgasm is not the only part of sex that matters, and women and men stand to gain a lot by understanding this. Sex is about pleasure, not some goal at the end of the line. By focusing on the sensations and enjoyment of the moment, sex is good no matter what. And orgasm, ironically, is much more likely to happen. If your goal for good sex is to have an orgasm, there are many suggestions in the pages that follow to make it more likely. But remember, mind control is just as important as body control. Focus on the sexual experience instead of on your orgasm. If you build it (and just try to enjoy it), you will come.

Good Technique

Good technique matters! It is the bridge across the gap that separates men and women sexually, which is a matter of both time and anatomy. Time because men often finish before women, and anatomy because women's sexual organs are often less understood than men's. Good technique solves both dilemmas. Properly arousing a woman takes time. As a result, pleasure increases for you, and he is able to garner more endurance.

Sexual pleasure is about communication with your body and your mind. Good sex should be a delicious sensory experience that engages you and your partner on every level. Technique is an important part of making this happen. By learning to enjoy yourself, sex is instantly better. And there isn't much that a man likes more than the sight of a woman experiencing sexual pleasure at his hands. The task is to make those hands (and other parts) do what you need them to do!

Foreplay before the foreplay is always a must. You've heard the saying that if a man is like a microwave oven, then a woman is like a standard oven—we need more time to warm up. And it all begins with a kiss. The best way to kick off sexual activity is with a little lip service. I think most women would agree that they love to be kissed—on the mouth, the neck, just about anywhere. In fact, kissing can be downright erotic if it's something you haven't done in a while. Try spending a little time just kissing your partner before things go any further. Tell him how good it feels. Whether tender or passionate, a nice kiss can often do wonders for the sex that follows.

Though your man may feel ready to go sexually, he needs to remember that you probably do not. It's good for him to test the waters a bit. Here's a hint to making it go well: The most sensitive part of a woman's anatomy is her clitoris. If you teach him to pay attention to your clitoris, the doorway to sexual satisfaction will be thrown wide open. Now, this does *not* mean he should tear off your clothes and go right for the gold! What women want and need is foreplay. Going back to the oven analogy, women ease their way into sexual arousal. Along with kissing, massaging the breasts, buttocks, and other parts of the body is a good prelude to genital stimulation.

Once you're ready for genital stimulation, guide him to focus first on your entire genital area. There are many incredibly sensitive parts besides the clitoris and vagina. Have him stroke your pubic hair. Rubbing the outside of the vulva is a great way to warm up. It also feels good to gently grind against each other's pelvic bones while your hands are focused elsewhere. Once you're ready, let his fingers move down to your labia. They contain all sorts of nerve endings that are satisfying to touch. He should gently part your outer labia and stroke the inside. If you spent some time warming up beforehand, you may already be lubricated. If you're not, have him add a little saliva or lubricant to his fingers and gently rub your labia, both inside and out. Ask him to use a sweeping motion that extends from your clitoris all the way down to your vaginal opening, so you can discover what feels good.

There are endless possibilities for stimulating the clitoris, both manually and orally. Some women enjoy direct contact, while for others indirect touching is better. This also varies as you become more aroused. Sometimes working just one spot can lead to overstimulation, while other times, finding that magic spot is all you need. Speak up! It's the only way he's going to know what is working for you and what's not. The best technique for doing this is to show him he's bringing you pleasure with either words or moans. If you don't like what he's doing, gently move his attention elsewhere, or focus on him for a while.

The last thing foreplay should be is a mechanical process, and this is especially true for clitoral stimulation. The pleasure is in the details. And if you don't try, you might never know what feels the best. Manual stimulation can be just as much of an art form as oral stimulation. For women who prefer less direct contact, moving his fingers in a figure-8 often works, since it engages many delightful nerve endings. The figure-8 can be small, where it moves mostly around the clitoris, or large to work the entire length of your vulva. He can also hold open your labia while he uses his middle finger to stroke you up and down. For women who like direct pressure on the clitoris, one or two fingers can be used to tap or rub it constantly. Many women enjoy having their vaginal opening massaged, which is full of sensation-friendly nerve endings. The perineum is another area many women find arousing.

Only after some attention has been paid to your external genitalia should he try inserting a finger or two to stimulate you internally. He should start by entering you shallowly. By moving his fingers around in a circular motion, he stimulates the most sensitive part of your vagina—the opening. Only the first third or so of the vagina is very sensitive to touch; the rest responds more to pressure after you are really aroused. Tell him this when he wants to go deep before you are turned on!

The same guidelines apply for oral stimulation. Though it can be intimidating, most women love it when a man performs orally. It is often the best way for a woman to reach orgasm. Have him start by kissing your abdomen and inner thighs. Tell him to tease you a bit. Alternating between genital stimulation and focusing on other parts of your body is great way to leave you craving more. His tongue is a wonderful tool for stimulating your clitoris, since it is soft and wet. While he is working your clitoris with his mouth, have him insert one or two of his fingers into your vagina with a gentle thrusting motion. If he tilts them upward slightly, he can try to hit your G-spot. The G-spot can be found about one or two inches in from the top of your vagina. It feels like a spongy bump. Most important, keep letting him know what's working and what isn't so he feels confident. If you think he is feeling reluctant or needs some pointers, there is a great book called *She Comes First* by Ian Kerner that gives men a step-by-step guide to oral sex. It explains the importance of oral stimulation for women and tells him just how to do it if he is feeling a little uncertain.

Done right, clitoral stimulation is the best way to bring you to the edge of orgasm and also to take you right over that edge. It all depends on what works for you as a couple. Some women will take their orgasms where they can get them and if that's the case, you should keep going until you get there. Other women prefer to orgasm during intercourse. If that's your preference, manual or oral stimulation should be used to achieve maximum arousal before penetration. This gets you both ready to go at the same time and makes orgasm more likely.

If orgasm is a priority, you should ideally go first. It helps if your partner stays mindful of the desire to climax and stops or switches positions if you're not there yet. There should be no sense of rushing, as this is the surest way to prevent you from having an orgasm. One significant way that women and men differ sexually is in what happens to them after they climax. For men, the game is over. His refractory period can last for several hours and his energy is usually tapped, too. Women, however, have great potential for arousal after they have orgasmed. This explains why some women have multiple orgasms. By putting in the effort so that you orgasm first, there is more of a guarantee that both of you end up satisfied. Even if your partner does orgasm before you, he should continue to stimulate you either manually or orally until you are satisfied.

There are several positions that make orgasm more likely for you during intercourse. It all depends on your preferences both individually and as a couple. Some women enjoy thrusting and a faster rhythm, especially as arousal intensifies. Other women like a more gentle rocking motion that maintains maximum contact between her and her partner's bodies. Often, having him move his pelvis in a circular motion feels good since it stimulates more of your sexual anatomy. Different degrees and angles of penetration also play a part. Some women like deep penetration that hits the back of their vaginal walls and maybe even their cervix. Other women may want an angle that hits their G-spot or allows for clitoral stimulation. The following positions all offer different benefits. Reason enough to change it up in the bedroom and try a new position (or two, or three).

The standard missionary position is the one that many women feel most comfortable in (see Figure 11). It offers a feeling of connectedness, since your body and face are lined up with your partner's. Many women also enjoy feeling that their partner is in control. Like any position, however, missionary gets very

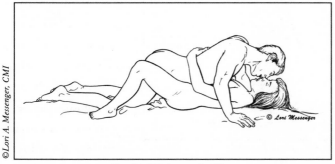

©Lori A. Messenger, CMI

Fig. 11. Missionary Position

boring over time. Fortunately, there are several variations that can take missionary in a fresh and exciting direction. Placing a pillow under your pelvis gives the position a whole new angle, which may lead to different sensations. For the flexible, putting your legs around your partner's shoulders will increase the degree of penetration.

As shown in Figure 12, a position called CAT, or the Coital Alignment Technique, is good for maintaining full-body contact while stimulating both the clitoris and the G-spot. During CAT, the man lifts up and over the woman

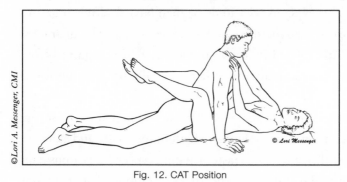

©Lori A. Messenger, CMI

Fig. 12. CAT Position

so that the base of his penis and his pelvic bone stimulate her clitoris, all while deeply penetrating. The trick is to maintain constant contact with a gentle rocking motion, instead of thrusting. At the same time, the woman squeezes her pelvic floor muscles in and up to increase friction on the G-spot, which also increases friction on the penis. In fact, squeezing your pelvic floor muscles is great in any position, since it heightens arousal for both of you.

Woman-on-top is another good position because it allows you to control the degree of penetration and also to receive clitoral stimulation (see Figure 13). You can either lean over your partner so your clitoris rubs against his pubic bone, or one of you can stimulate it manually or with a vibrator. Many

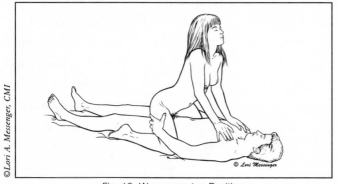

©Lori A. Messenger, CMI

Fig. 13. Woman-on-top Position

women like this position because it gives them a sense of power. Men like it since it allows them to see more of a woman's body during intercourse.

Most rear-entry positions also allow one of you to stimulate your clitoris. Getting on all fours, as shown in Figure 14, can be a highly erotic position. It allows the man to see himself entering you and also to stimulate your clitoris. Angling yourself down so you are on your elbows increases G-spot stimulation. You can also try lying on

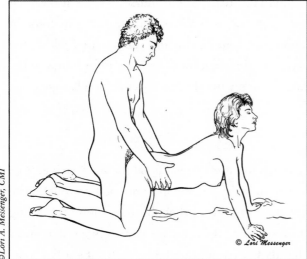

Fig. 14. Rear Entry Position

your stomach while he penetrates you from behind.

Two side-by-side positions are the spoon and the scissors. In the spoon you lie on your sides, with him behind you (see Figure 15). In the scissors you lie facing one another (see Figure 16). These positions are good if you like less penetration and a slower rhythm of movement. They are also great if you are feeling tired, since they don't require much movement! Both positions allow either of you to stimulate your clitoris, which again can be done manually or with a vibrator.

You can also take another look at the Passion Prescription Pad recommendations in the Appendix. There are lots of ideas to help with orgasm, adding

Fig. 15. Spoon Position

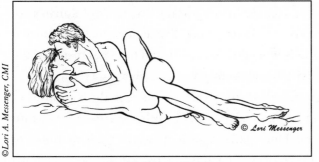

Fig. 16. Scissors Position

©Lori A. Messenger, CMI

novelty and virtually any other sexual want or concern. One final and important element of good technique is that sex should not be defined by its outcome. As you have learned (and may already know yourself), sex is also valued for the pleasure and intimacy it provides. For women, pleasure can come in waves. It is not a steady climb to orgasm. By you and your partner taking the time to understand how sex may be different for you than it is for him, you become even more in sync. And finding your rhythm together is what good sex is all about.

Return the Favor

In fact, sex would not be much fun if it weren't good for your partner, too. Understanding the male sexual anatomy helps you know how to touch him. You feel more confident as a lover. Plus, when he likes how he's being touched, he is more likely to want to do the same for you. While it may seem like his sexual pleasure is slightly less complicated than yours, it's still important to make sure you understand his body. A quick anatomy lesson followed by a few hints about what men really want should do the trick! Check out Figure 17, too.

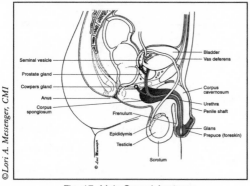

Fig. 17. Male Sexual Anatomy

©Lori A. Messenger, CMI

The penis is made up of a spongy, erectile tissue, which is what gives it the ability to expand in size when engorged with blood. There are three cylinders of this tissue—two run across the top of the penis and are called the corpus cavernosa and one runs along the bottom, known as the corpus spongeosum. You can see the important structures of a man's reproductive organs in Figure 17. During the Excitement phase of sexual arousal, a man's penis expands in length and width and becomes firmer as the spongy erectile tissue fills with blood—otherwise known as an erection. Muscle tension builds in the groin and erectile tissue elsewhere in the body also becomes engorged, including his nipples and lips. He feels a sensation of warmth in his genitals and in general. During the Plateau phase, the penis continues to increase in diameter and the color may change to a reddish-purple. The testicles also increase in size and are drawn tightly toward the body. The longer a man remains in the Plateau phase, the more obvious the change in his testicle size will be. Sometimes, they can double in size.

In the Orgasm phase, two separate processes begin taking place. Sperm begins traveling from the epididymis through the vas deferens. As it passes the seminal vesicle and prostate gland, it picks up seminal fluid that encases the sperm. The fluid energizes the sperm and increases their chances of survival once inside the vagina. The prostate signals the spinal cord that ejaculation is on its way. The Cowper's glands secrete a small amount of pre-ejaculate, also known as pre-come, to neutralize the acidity of the urethra, which the sperm will pass through (pre-come can contain sperm, which is why it's possible to get pregnant or infected with an STD even if he pulls out before ejaculating). The prostate also clamps down on the bladder to prevent urine from mixing with the semen. The pubococcygeal muscles, vas deferens, and prostate then contract to produce the spasms of orgasm. Ejaculation and orgasm usually involve three or four involuntary, rhythmic contractions. The anus often also contracts at this time. Orgasm is swiftly followed by the Resolution phase. The penis and testicles return to their unaroused state and size. If your partner gets up or uses the bathroom, the change is rapid. If he stays in bed with you, the return to normal is more gradual and it can take longer for him to become completely flaccid. The Resolution phase also marks the beginning of a man's refractory period. During this time, he cannot reach full sexual arousal or orgasm. For some men, it is a matter of minutes while for others it is a matter of hours, even days.

So now that you've had a brushup on what happens to your man's body during sex, here are some tips on how you can make it go better for him. In general, the most sensitive part of the penis is the head, or glans. Like the glans of the clitoris, the penis glans is a concentration of many nerve endings. Can you say sensation? In uncircumcised men, the glans is covered by foreskin, which retracts during sexual arousal. Focusing on or teasing the head of the penis is likely to send him into the stratosphere. You can do this with either your hands or your mouth. Another highly sensitive spot that's close by is the frenulum. It's located on the underside of the penis where the head connects to the shaft and looks like an upside-down V. Spend some time on these parts—you'll notice his response. To work the glans and frenulum, you can gently rub the palm of your hand over the top of his penis. When you close around it, lightly twist your hand to stimulate the head only. Alternate by using your thumb to massage the frenulum. You can also make special use of the glans and frenulum during oral sex. Licking everything *but* the head and frenulum can get him super aroused. I would not be the first to tell you that men love oral sex. Maybe it's the thought of you pleasuring only him, maybe it's that he gets to watch you do it, or maybe it's the different stimulation that only a tongue can give, but make no doubt—he *loves* it. Many women give up on oral sex because they find it unpleasant or figure they can just have intercourse instead. However, most men rate oral sex as right up there with intercourse and sometimes even better. If you've had problems with oral sex in the past, give it another try. It can be a great way to show your partner you care about pleasing him. And the good news is that almost anything will feel good if it's something you haven't done in a while! Focus on breathing through your nose and using your hand to supplement your mouth. That way you are able to control how much goes in your mouth and are less likely to gag. If you do not want to swallow, let it go on his stomach or switch to intercourse before he has finished.

Another very sensitive area—and I mean that in both senses of the word—are the testicles. You will have to let your guy be the judge on this one. Gently rub his testicles with the pads of your fingers. If he likes it, keep going. If it hurts, he may not be a testicle-stimulation kind of guy. You can also try licking them or cupping them in your mouth. Just be mindful of your teeth. While you're in that area, and, again, depending on your and your partner's tastes, you can try stimulating his prostate. The prostate feels like a walnut-sized bulge. It's located about two inches inside his anus, toward the bellybutton. Sounds like the female G-spot! In fact, the prostate has been called the male G-spot, since it's capable of the same miracles and letdowns as the female one is. Some men are brought to the brink of orgasm, while others just find it uncomfortable. What men do have in common is that they like to have their genitals touched. If you want him to take the time to warm you up properly, give him what he wants by going for his genitals faster. That's right—the next time you're starting to get it on, unzip his pants and give him a nice touch. He'll feel like you read his mind.

Beyond Penetration

Sometimes it helps to go back to the sexual basics when you need to break out of a routine or have a fresh start. It can also increase your chances of orgasm if you are not having success. Starting from scratch means removing the penetration focus from sexual activity altogether in order to find new ways to please yourself and your partner. It's a program I developed in the late 1980s to help teenagers practice safe sex, but I realized it was also helpful to couples who were in a sexual rut. All too often, couples fall into a pattern over time in which sex consists of the same moves and ends quickly—even if it is satisfying. The program helped couples who wanted to break out of their sexual routine, as well as women who were left unsatisfied by intercourse and couples dealing with impotence.

The program is called VENIS, short for Very Erotic Non-Insertive Sex. In VENIS, sexual contact occurs without penetration. The focus is on eroticism, and the verbal and physical communication between you and your partner. Women in particular love it. They often find that they are doing new things in bed and having a lot more fun than when sex was all about intercourse. Many times, they also find that they are having more orgasms, too.

VENIS expands your sexual horizons by pushing you to get creative sexually. When intercourse is not an option, new activities are discovered. So are fresh sensations and sources of pleasure. VENIS works for women especially because it refocuses sex on the parts of their anatomies often left behind by intercourse. It also removes the pressure of goal-oriented sex. Instead of experiencing sex as a baseball game, in which you go up to bat in hopes of a home run, it is all about enjoying the moment.

When things are shaken up, sex becomes less predictable. Women find themselves more at ease, which leads to more pleasure. Orgasm often happens effortlessly. If you present the idea to your partner this way, he is more likely to get on board. Tell him it is a new adventure in your sex life that will help rekindle the passion. I often tell couples to set aside a VENIS-only night. Also, it's important he knows that orgasm is still part of the picture for him during VENIS. The difference is that instead of intercourse, foreplay now becomes the home run.

VERY EROTIC NON-INSERTIVE SEX (VENIS) ACTIVITIES AND PROPS

VENIS techniques and activities are not just fun, but creative, too. Allow yourself to let go of the conventional ideas of how sexuality is expressed. The key is to let your mind and body move toward pleasure that is not goal-oriented. Following is just a beginning set of activities and props to spark the imagination. Let yourself experiment, even if something initially makes you uncomfortable. Discuss your options with your partner and decide together what you would like to try. Most of all, have fun! Props are a great place to start, since they often get the creative juices flowing all on their own. Here are some ideas I often recommend to my patients.

Bathing together as a couple brings a whole new dimension to exploring each other sexually. Light some candles to create a soft relaxing mood. Pour some scented oil or bubble bath into the tub before you fill it. Make sure you have some fun sponges or loofahs handy, as well as shampoo. VENIS activities can be as active or relaxed as you want them to be. A bath is a great place just to be together as a couple. Try rubbing each other with your hands, sponge, or loofah. Or, you can try washing one another and enjoy the different sensations of letting someone else take care of you. Wash each other's hair. There are also some vibrating bath toys like *I Rub My Ducky,* which is a vibrating rubber ducky, as well as some vibrating sponges that you can use to wash each other's most sensitive parts.

If getting in the bath is not appealing, or seems like too much work, try the bedroom. Take turns massaging each other with oil or lotion. Let a body massage progress to an intensely pleasurable genital massage. Eating off of each other can also be very sensual. Try foods like honey, whipped cream, ice cream, peanut butter, and hot fudge. They not only taste good to eat, but also feel sensational for the person being eaten off of. There are also edible body paints, edible tattoos, and edible panties that can be incorporated.

Sharing fantasies opens the door to many VENIS activities. Communicate your desires. Don't be afraid to tell each other what turns you on—sometimes it's good just to share your fantasies. If you want to act out some of your erotic wishes, costumes can help you become someone else for a little while. Other props like furry handcuffs and blindfolds also help with role-playing.

In addition to paying attention to your imagination, think about other ways to give physical pleasure that do not involve penetration. Try kissing all over your partner's body and have him do the same. Kiss each other's feet and toes, neck, back, nipples, and fingers. Blindfold each other and take turns running feathers up and down each other's bodies. Once arousal gets too hot, you can move onto using your hands and vibrators for stimulation. Blindfolding yourselves at the same time while touching and fondling each other takes your senses into a whole new dimension.

Erotic wrestling can be great for body-to-body contact. You can do it on the bed or put a towel or mat down on the floor. *Slippery Sex Sheets* by *Hustler* are a great option as well. The kit includes not only an easy-to-clean plastic bed sheet, but also scented, squirtable body paint that glows in the dark! Just lather each other up with oil and go where your body leads you. You'll find that limbs rub against limbs against genitals against genitals and that the sensation is extremely erotic. Although you can't do anything involving penetration, rubbing and touching are often enough to bring you to orgasm. Mutual masturbation also works. One of you can watch the other masturbate, or you can masturbate together at the same time.

VENIS can also include plain and simple making out in a bed. Maybe it will take you back to the passionate days before you became sexually active. When intercourse is not an option, it's amazing how hot it can get. When was the last time you and your partner just made out? Remember the whole range of activities we engaged in before we started having intercourse—heavy petting, dry humping, and lots of kissing and rolling around? VENIS can help take you back and reawaken the sexual spirit you once had.

The VENIS Kit helps you and your partner get creative beyond penetration. To get your creative juices flowing, try all or some of the following:

❑ Massage oil

❑ Plastic sheet or *Slippery Sex Sheets*

❑ Blindfold

❑ Feather

❑ Furry handcuffs

❑ Waterproof vibrator

THE SAME OLD BEDROOM ROUTINE officially has been replaced! Gone are the days when you view sex as just another chore to cross off your list. Armed with an understanding of what you need physically *and* emotionally, your sex life won't know what hit it. By bringing back the pleasure, your motivation to be sexual is reinvigorated.

And it's worth it. Good sex gives you the gift of enjoyment—of the moment, of yourself, and of your partner. Making time for you to get in the mood, learning about pleasure-friendly techniques, and getting a little creative are the final steps to a satisfying sex life. They are also the long-term practices that will ensure your intimate relationship goes the distance in the bedroom, as well as outside of it.

PRESCRIPTIONS FOR THE WEEK:
Week 8

✓ Fill out your Great Sex Template, discussed on page 177.

✓ Try to take orgasm out of the equation with your partner this
week if you haven't already. Remember, orgasm is much more
likely if it's not the primary goal! Just focus on sensation,
sensuality, and pleasure, and see what happens. If he's read the
Guy's Guide, he knows not to expect orgasms from you every
time.

✓ Give your partner a tour of your genitals this week. If you haven't
already done so, make sure you explore the different kinds of
clitoral stimulation described in this chapter to see which type
works best for you.

✓ Try at least one of the sexual positions described in this chapter
this week and for the next three weeks. See which one provides
you with the most pleasure and the best clitoral stimulation.

✓ Take a shot at one or two techniques discussed in this chapter for
stimulating your partner during your next sexual encounter and
see how that works.

✓ Have a VENIS night this week! Perhaps during your one
sexual encounter this week (or a second or third). Read up on
the activities and props you'll need and make it a night of non-
insertive pleasure. Don't worry, he's read all about it in the
Guy's Guide.

✓ Don't forget! Masturbate at least twice a week, keep writing
about your experiences in your sexual journal, and be sure to take

two hours this week, whether it's with friends or by yourself, but with no work or home demands and no errands. And keep the action with your partner going: at least one sexual experience a week barring illness or extreme relationship conflict! Also remember to do your Kegel exercises on a regular basis, incorporated into or separate from your Pelvic Push-Ups three times a week, and thirty to forty-five minutes of cardiovascular exercise three times a week as well.

GUY'S GUIDE:
A Summary of Key Points for the Man in Your Life

1. Sexually satisfied women have one primary characteristic in common: a sense of intimacy and connection to their partners. This helps explain why good sex for women is less about what happens physically, as it is about the sense of connection they feel during it. It is a completely subjective experience, with no definite pattern. This is not to say that physical pleasure does not matter—it does! But when sex is good, it's usually because the woman feels she has achieved a deepened sense of intimacy with her partner.

2. Most women need time to transition from mom, professional, or housekeeper to sexy vixen in the bedroom. Men, however, often need little more than a good kiss to get their attention. In fact, the ease with which many men get erections often leaves them astonished that women are not the same.

3. When it's time to think about sex, men can tune out everything else and focus on the sexual moment. Women, however, are often worrying about a million little details instead of focusing on what's happening during sex. This is because we evolved as hunters and gatherers, in which men survived by being focused and women survived by multitasking. Help your woman tune into sex by giving her time to quiet her mind. Take care of the kids or chores and send her off to take a bath or read a trashy magazine. You'll likely find a vixen waiting for you afterward!

4. Foreplay before the foreplay is always a must. You've heard the saying that if a man is like a microwave oven, then a woman is like a standard oven—she needs more time to warm up. And it all begins with a kiss. The best way to kick off sexual activity is with a little lip service. I think most women would agree that they love to be kissed—on the mouth, the neck, and just about anywhere.

5. Good technique matters! It is the bridge across the gap that separates men and women sexually, which is a matter of both time and anatomy. The average man takes between five and ten minutes to reach orgasm, while the average woman takes a half hour. Though a woman's sexual pleasure is on a different schedule from a man's, it's nothing that a little more foreplay and good communication can't clear up. Sometimes working just one spot can lead to overstimulation, while other times, finding that magic spot is all you need. Ask her! It may be the only way you're going to know what is working for her and what's not.

6. Depending on the kind of sexual activity engaged in and a woman's individual preferences, orgasm is not always the final outcome of good sex. Most women do not reach orgasm every time, so don't feel bad if your partner is one of them.

7. However, many women feel incredible pressure to have an orgasm every time they have sex. Take the pressure off her by letting her know it's OK if she doesn't. In fact, not focusing on orgasm is the surest way to help her have one.

8. Only after some attention has been paid to your partner's external genitalia—hint, the clitoris—should you try inserting a finger or two to stimulate her internally. You should start by entering her shallowly. By moving your fingers around in a circular motion, you stimulate the most sensitive part of her vagina—the opening. Only the first third or so of the vagina is very sensitive to touch; the rest responds more to pressure after she is really aroused. Don't go deep before she is turned on!

9. Though it can be intimidating, a woman loves it when a man pleases her orally. It is often the best way for a woman to reach orgasm. Start by kissing her abdomen and inner thighs. Tease her a bit before going for the genitals. You can insert one or two of your fingers into her vagina with a gentle thrusting motion. If you tilt them upward slightly, you can try to hit her G-spot. Remember, the G-spot can be found about one or two inches in from the top of her vagina.

10. During intercourse, stay mindful of your desire to climax and stop or switch positions if your partner is not there yet. By putting in the effort to help your partner orgasm first, there is more of a guarantee that both of you end up satisfied. Even if you orgasm before she does, you should continue to stimulate her either manually or orally until she is satisfied.

11. A program I developed called VENIS, short for Very Erotic Non-Insertive Sex, helps you get back to the sexual basics when you need to break out of a routine or have a fresh start. It can also increase her chances at orgasm if you are not having success as yet. Sexual activity occurs without penetration. The focus is on eroticism and on the verbal and physical communication between you and your partner. Women in particular love it. They often find that they are doing new things in bed and having a lot more fun than when sex was all about intercourse. Try it once or twice and see what happens.

CHAPTER NINE

Nutrition

FOOD HAS MANY SIMILARITIES TO sex. It's a craving that can bring much pleasure and also much peril. Most of us have found ourselves standing in the dark, devouring a box of chocolate—sensually stimulated and yet with a feeling of guilt or even shame. Sound like something else we've been talking about? Food has become as much a source of shame and anxiety as sex in our culture. Women are pressured at every turn to deny ourselves for the sake of our bodies, our health, and our longevity. And you know what they say—it's the forbidden fruit that always tastes the sweetest. The minute chocolate chip cookies are off-limits, you find yourself thinking about them obsessively! Has food replaced sex as women's dirty little secret?

Making the right food choices is absolutely essential for a healthy sex life and for your health in general. It's just that food is not the enemy. Rather, eating should be about staying healthy and also relishing in the sensual pleasure that food is meant to provide. In fact, one of the primary ways you can wrestle yourself away from the food demons is to get back to focusing on food as a sensual pleasure. From preparation to enjoyment, getting back in touch with *all* of your senses will allow food to satisfy you, not taunt you.

Why Eating Right Matters for Sex

The benefits of eating right are obvious in many ways. Together with regular exercise, a healthy, well-balanced diet can help boost your body image. Getting rid of excess weight makes you feel more comfortable in your own skin. It also perks up your stamina—during sex and otherwise—since you have less weight to carry around and feel better about yourself in general. However, the benefits of a good diet go much further than skin-deep. Eating healthy foods fortifies the libido, stimulating body and mind from the inside out.

How, you ask? Food is fuel for our bodies. When we eat, our stomachs sort the contents into proteins, carbohydrates, and fat, which the body uses for different purposes. Both enzymes and hormones help the food break down, and this is where the problems begin. If the body is off balance hormonally, its ability to proceed with digestion is interrupted. The result is a sort of domino effect on the rest of the body. Organs like the pancreas and gallbladder can be forced to work harder than they normally would—which ultimately translates to more wear and tear on the body. The chemical messages the body is sending to your brain can begin to get confusing, too. If digestion is not taking place as it should be, feelings of fullness do not register in the brain. This is when you start eating more than you should, which continues throwing the body further and further out of balance.

Declining levels of estrogen is a common culprit. In particular, when the estradiol level drops during perimenopause, menopause, or for any other reason I've covered in previous chapters, so does a hormone called cholecystokinin produced during digestion. This hormone signals the gallbladder that it's time to empty. In our body's language, this tells our mind we are full and to stop eating. If you aren't a calorie-counter, it is reasonable to assume that you will eat until you feel full. However, through the chemical chain reaction just described, the body begins tricking the mind into thinking it needs to eat more. Most women would never suspect that it is their hormones driving their hunger instead of their stomachs. Out-of-balance estrogen also causes insulin levels to go up—for yet more unneeded wear and tear on the body at the cellular level—and thyroid levels to go down. Diminished thyroid levels not only lower your energy levels and your libido, but also slow down the body's metabolism, for the ultimate double whammy. You are eating more and burning less as effective fuel for your body.

As this continues, the weight begins to accumulate. It can be absolutely maddening for women who eat only when they are hungry to watch themselves gain weight. And if you weren't already upset, lowered estrogen levels also affect your brain's serotonin levels, which can leave you more prone to depression. When we're depressed, food often takes on a new meaning as we tend to "stuff our feelings" with those fattening comfort foods. Not to mention that when our hormone levels start to shift, our ability to manage stress changes as well. And higher levels of stress are associated with increased body fat, especially in the abdominal area. When we are stressed, cortisol levels rise, which can also make you want to eat more *and* disrupt your ability to sleep— yet another important regulator of appetite and metabolism. So hormones affect your digestion, mood, and stress levels, and then depression and stress levels have chemical effects on your body and its storage of fat. But don't worry; it does not have to be a vicious cycle! Your way out is not only by incorporating healthy variety into your diet but also by reaching the right ratio of the nutritional triumvirate—carbohydrates, protein, and fat.

And remember, severely reducing your caloric intake will only slow down your metabolism. Gradual is best, especially to prevent yourself from getting on a cycle of yo-yo dieting, in which you repeatedly lose and gain weight. This can permanently affect your ability to stay trim. Chronically deficient caloric intake causes your body to begin breaking down muscle for energy. Aside from losing muscle mass, which helps fuel your metabolism, too few calories leads to fatigue, nutritional deficiencies, and irritability—bad for your health, bad for your sex life.

Balance for Bodily Bliss

Carbohydrates are the main source of energy for the body. There are two kinds of carbohydrates—simple and complex—and the difference for your health couldn't be greater. Simple carbohydrates include white sugar, honey, corn syrup, and fructose. They are found most often in breads, candies, desserts, and crackers. Simple carbohydrates are quickly broken down into glucose and absorbed into the bloodstream for an initial burst of energy that is often followed by a crash. Simple carbohydrates require more insulin—the hormone responsible for regulating your blood sugar levels—which is produced by the pancreas. Too many simple carbohydrates can stress the pancreas over time, compromising insulin's ability to deliver glucose to your cells. Type 2 diabetes is the most common result. More insulin also causes the body to hold onto fat, rather than use it for fuel, since there is the glucose from the simple carbohydrates available for that immediate purpose.

Alternatively, complex carbohydrates are the body's slow energy suppliers. They are found in whole grains and vegetables. Complex carbohydrates take longer to break down and so are absorbed more slowly into the bloodstream. Less glucose flooding the bloodstream means far less stress for the pancreas *and* less insulin—the body's fat-storing hormone. It also means the body must take from its reserves to keep itself going. Your fat, instead of that cake, begins to get burned for fuel. This is the underlying mechanism of the Atkins, or low-carb, diet craze. Moderation is the key to maintaining any eating lifestyle, and many people have a hard time maintaining a low-carb diet due to all the things they can't eat. However, I've seen the benefits of cutting carbohydrates, even in moderation, in many of the patients we treat. Since the body is forced to burn fat in the absence of carbohydrates, it can be a great way to lose weight and reinvigorate your sex life. At the end of this chapter, you'll find some recipe ideas that prove eating right can still mean eating delicious food. Just remember that complex carbohydrates are still a beneficial part of any diet. It's those simple carbohydrates you want to minimize or even avoid.

Eating protein also promotes the breakdown of fat stored in your body. Protein is used by the body for the building and repairing of all its tissues. There are twenty-two amino acids in all—the building blocks of protein—nine of which must be absorbed from food since the body cannot produce them. Eating protein stimulates the production of glucagon, which tempers the effects of insulin. Basically, it forces the body to make use of its own fuel reserves, instead of relying solely on what's being eaten.

And finally there is fat. If there ever was a part of the food chain that gets an unfair rap, it's fat. Women especially make the mistake of thinking that buying something that is low-fat is the best decision for their health. Low-fat cookies, low-fat ice cream, low-fat everything! While some alternatives are beneficial, such as reduced-fat meat and dairy products, others are just as bad as eating the real thing. In fact, they may be even worse. Low-fat products often contain astronomical sugar levels to help make up for the lack of taste in low-fat foods. Look out in particular for high fructose corn syrup—a particularly nasty and ubiquitous sugar ingredient that depletes the body of vitamins and minerals. In the end, sugar equals simple carbohydrates equals more fat on your body. Instead of trying to have your cake and eat it too, why not nibble on the real version. It is far more satisfying to eat a few delicious bites of real chocolate cake than to overcompensate with an enormous slice of reduced-fat cake that tastes like cardboard! We need fat—for proper vitamin absorption and to keep our bodies and minds functioning smoothly. While saturated fats need to be kept in check, monounsaturated sources are actually *good* for you.

Saturated fats include butter, most meats, and full-fat dairy products. You have to keep all of these to a minimum, especially butter. However, instead of turning to margarine and other similar butter substitutes that are often full of chemicals, try making olive oil your new fat. It is chock-full of good fats and antioxidants. It can replace almost anything you use butter for, and if the taste is too strong for a certain dish, try canola oil—another excellent, good-fat alternative. And before you go for only nonfat yogurt, milk, and cheeses, research has shown that fat in dairy products is a good thing. Try 2 percent or 1 percent milk instead of skim, and reduced-fat yogurt and cheeses instead of nonfat. The calcium in these dairy products binds to the fat and prevents your body from absorbing it (the fat, that is). Research has repeatedly found that women who include several daily servings of dairy in their diet lose more weight than those who don't. Plus, it gives you much-needed calcium.

Moderation and balance are the keys. Eat what you crave in tiny amounts instead of denying yourself, since that's when the rebound happens. Getting back to whole grains, fruits, and vegetables as your carbohydrate sources can begin to turn things around. Focusing on lean protein sources, such as nuts, beans, and healthy meats ensures you are eating calories that are beneficial, instead of empty or harmful. All of these foods contain fiber—another essential to feeling full after you eat and staying healthy through regular bowel movements.

By the way, it's really common for people to fall off a dietary regime because they cheated, splurged, or had a bad-eating day. So remember that if you cheat, or you have a bad-eating day, don't throw in the towel. Just get back on the diet. It's too easy to say, "I messed up so just forget it. I can't do it." All that matters after you have a slip is how vigorously you can recommit to what you began. The past cannot be changed, but the future is still in your hands. That's why the moderation we talked about is so important and indulging your cravings in small amounts is not a bad idea.

The Right Ratio

Eating complex carbohydrates, protein, and fat in the right proportion is the key to weight loss and to keeping the weight off in the long term. It also helps to eat five or more mini-meals throughout the day, if you are able. This keeps your metabolism and blood sugar levels more constant and your digestive process running more smoothly. Instead of a deluge of food, you are spreading it out more gradually for your body to process. This is especially important for sex, since too much food at one sitting can make you feel tired as your body focuses on digesting. Stretching out your meals is also helpful in menopause in terms of regulating insulin and cortisol levels.

Try for a balance of 40 percent protein, 35 percent carbohydrates, and 25 percent fat (only 10 percent of the total calories should be saturated fat). If you are eating 1500 calories a day, this roughly translates to 150 grams of protein, 130 grams of carbohydrates, and 40 grams of fat (15 saturated). At first, you may have to become a fastidious label reader, but over time you will grow accustomed to knowing what you can and can't eat to stay within this range. The fifteen grams of saturated fat should give you some flexibility when it comes to indulging in something sweet or a little butter for your vegetables. Speaking of which, you should get creative to get your five to ten servings of fruits and vegetables a day. There's no doubt that eating antioxidant, nutrient-rich fresh fruits and vegetables will make a noticeable difference in your short- and long-term health. Make a point to eat at least five servings a day this week.

Also, remember that you can eat nuts and other nonanimal sources of protein to meet your daily requirements. Keep a bag of nuts in your purse or at work for when hunger strikes. Just a small handful will make you feel full, while giving you the added benefits of those good fats. Starting each day off with protein jump-starts your metabolism for the rest of the day. Yogurt, eggs, and cheese, which often have a higher caloric content, are best eaten in the morning so the body can burn them off over the course of the day. Many women also need the boost that protein provides first thing in the morning. Combined with some whole grain toast or granola and a piece of fruit, it lives up to its reputation as the most important meal of the day.

Romancing the Kitchen

You've learned how food fortifies us for better sexual function by providing fuel for the body and helping to maintain a healthy weight when the right choices are made. Food also feels and tastes good to eat. Like sex, food can stimulate all of the senses if done properly. The smell of food in particular speaks directly to one of the most primal parts of our brain—the limbic system—which in turn communicates with our hormones. The aroma of different foods can evoke all sorts of memories and emotions, including sexual excitement. The other senses can be put to good use, too. The sight of appetizing or even phallic-looking food can be highly erotic. Taste, touch, and sound all take off from there. Learning to make food an enticing, sensual form of foreplay or part of sex itself brings you full circle in appreciating food's effect on your sex life.

If you don't already know, find out what your partner's favorite foods or aromas are. Tell him you want to have a date night this week, in which you cook together and make eating and drinking the centerpiece of the evening. If you have kids, send them to their grandparents' or a friend's for a sleepover. You want this to be a totally sensual evening with no sense of time limits.

Depending on what your partner asks for, you can also make use of some tried-and-true sensual edibles. Any food that resembles the sex organs is a good choice. Red juicy tomatoes or strawberries work. Asparagus, cucumbers, and carrots are suggestive vegetables. An avocado is said to be the ultimate sexy food since its texture and appearance are creamily evocative. Cut the tomatoes and avocado into pieces that allow you to feed each other. Strawberries are perfect for licking, dipping in sugar, chocolate, or whipped cream and slowly nibbling. The vegetables work best with a creamy dip that you can have some fun with. The idea is to include a range of textures and tastes. Crunchy carrots contrast with soft tomatoes to keep the sensory experience unpredictable.

Some other edible props that might help include olives, whose salty taste contrasts nicely with the fruit's sweet taste, and hot peppers, if you can handle it. Jalapeños or other peppers make your heart beat faster, make your face flush, and your body come alive. Chocolate and coffee also work wonders in mimicking the signs of arousal. Both stimulate, while chocolate provides the added boost of feel-good endorphins washing over your brain, much like when you fall in love or have an orgasm.

And now, the best news of all about nutrition: Chocolate can improve overall sexual function and increase sexual desire! A recent study completed by an Italian researcher, Dr. Andrea Salonia, demonstrated a link between satisfying sex and chocolate. Now, don't go eat tons of it—that would be counterproductive by making you gain weight—but feel free to make a reasonable amount your daily treat. And guess what? Yet another study found dark chocolate improves heart health with its naturally-occurring polyphenols—the same substances that make red wine good for you. Hooray for chocolate!

Red wine can be an aphrodisiac and it's also good for you, in small amounts. Or, try some white wine or champagne kept on ice next to the blanket. The ice cubes will come in handy for running up and down each other's bodies, or to give each other a cold kiss on the lips or elsewhere. Hot drinks, either virgin or alcoholic, can be relaxing after you finish eating. And don't forget dessert—whipped cream, honey, and hot fudge all beg to be eaten off your favorite parts of each other's bodies. Focus on all of the sounds, sights, and tastes of your sensual dinner together.

And remember, keep it light. You want your energy to go into foreplay and sex, not digesting. Take your time cooking and preparing the food together—all the while paying attention to your senses. It might be fun to set up an indoor picnic somewhere comfortable. Put a blanket on the floor and set it with plates, but no silverware so you have to use your hands to eat. Surround yourself with candles to make the mood right. If you're really daring, you could even cook and eat while you are naked!

Even when you don't make a night of sensual eating, learning to savor your food has real benefits. It is yet another way to stir up the senses and get closer to the physical pleasures of the body. Eating in a way that is mindful also leaves you feeling more satisfied and less likely to overeat. Following next are low-carb and low-fat recipe guides to give you some more ideas for eating well and eating sensually. All of the recipes are good for you and all of them taste wonderful! I am speaking from experience—I have had the good fortune of enjoying chef Jeremy Charles's cooking. He specializes in gourmet diet cuisine, which is a key to staying on any diet. All of the recipes were developed by Chef Charles to combine good health with good eating. Remember to use food for your sensual enjoyment as well as its nutritional benefits. These recipes can be great for a romantic meal, or for everyday healthy weight management. Enjoy!

Low-Fat Recipe Guide

Cauliflower Couscous

1 head of cauliflower
2 tablespoons of butter
2 tablespoons of chopped fresh chives or parsley
Salt and ground black pepper

1. *In a medium saucepan, over high heat, bring salted water to a boil.*

2. *Core and separate cauliflower into florets.*

3. *Quickly blanch florets, 5 to 6 seconds, and place directly into a bowl filled with ice water to stop the cooking.*

4. *Drain and grate florets on a box grater.*

5. *In a medium-size pan, sauté butter, cauliflower, and herbs for 2 to 3 minutes.*

6. *Season to taste.*

Broccoli Cheese Soup

2 bunches of broccoli
2 cups of chicken stock
3 cups of sharp cheddar cheese
½ onion
2 balls of fresh buffalo mozzarella
2 tablespoons of olive oil
1 fresh bay leaf
Salt and ground black pepper

1. *In a medium saucepan, sweat diced onion and bay leaf in 2 tablespoons of olive oil for 3 to 4 minutes.*

2. *Add chopped broccoli and cover with chicken stock.*

3. *Bring to a boil, cover, and simmer 10 to 12 minutes.*

4. *Add cheddar cheese, remove bay leaf, and puree with a hand blender or food processor. Salt and pepper to taste.*

5. *Before serving, garnish with chopped buffalo mozzarella.*

Guacamole

3 Hass avocados
2½ tablespoons of white wine vinegar
2 tablespoons of olive oil
1 teaspoon of kosher salt
Freshly ground black pepper

1. *Carefully cut the avocado in half, remove the pit, and scoop out the flesh.*

2. *In a mixing bowl, combine the finely diced avocado with white wine vinegar and salt.*

3. *Add olive oil and freshly ground pepper.*

Duck Confit

Start this recipe a day in advance. The duck needs 24 hours to cure before cooking. See steps 1, 2, and 3.

6 duck legs with thighs
6 cups of duck fat
2 bunches of fresh thyme
1 fresh bay leaf
1½ cups of kosher salt
Freshly ground black pepper

1. *Place a cooling rack on a cooking sheet of equal size. Place duck legs, skin side down, on the cooling rack.*

2. *In a food processor, puree kosher salt, ground pepper, bay leaf, and bunches of fresh thyme to form an herb salt.*

3. *Generously rub the duck legs with the salt mixture. Cover with plastic wrap and refrigerate for 24 hours.*

4. *The following day, preheat oven to 300°.*

5. *Brush salt mixture off duck legs.*

6. *In a preheated sauté pan, over medium-high heat, brown duck legs on skin side for 5 to 6 minutes.*

7. *In a medium saucepan that is oven-safe, melt duck fat over low heat. Add browned duck legs to fat and bring to a light simmer.*

8. *Cover and transfer to oven and confit (in other words, allow to cook slowly and soften) for 2 hours.*

9. *Remove from oven the crisp duck legs in preheated sauté pan and serve. Duck legs keep in the refrigerator, in the duck fat, for up to one month.*

Mushroom Sauce

1 pint of button mushrooms, chopped
4 tablespoons of butter
2½ cups of chicken stock
½ cup of white wine
1 fresh bay leaf
1 cup of 35% cream
Salt and ground black pepper

1. *In a medium sauté pan, heat butter and chopped mushrooms, and caramelize 7 to 8 minutes.*

2. *Deglaze with white wine, add bay leaf, and reduce over medium heat for 3 to 4 minutes.*

3. *Add chicken stock and reduce over medium-high heat for 7 to 8 minutes.*

4. *Finish with cream and reduce to desired consistency. Season with salt and pepper to taste. Serve with chicken, fish, pasta, or vegetables.*

Creamed Spinach

2 bags of baby spinach
2 tablespoons of unsalted butter
1/4 teaspoon of freshly grated nutmeg
3/4 cup of freshly grated Parmesan cheese
1/2 cup of 35% cream
Salt and ground black pepper

1. *In a large saucepan, over medium-low heat, wilt spinach in butter for 2 to 3 minutes.*

2. *Add grated nutmeg and cream, reduce over medium-low heat for 5 to 6 minutes.*

3. *Season with salt and pepper to taste and carefully add spinach mixture and Parmesan cheese to food processor. Pulse for 2 to 3 seconds to maintain texture.*

4. *Serve immediately.*

Curry Chicken Salad

2 boneless organic chicken breasts
1/2 cup of curry powder
2 celery stalks
2 Belgian endives
1/2 cup toasted walnuts
1 cup of mayonnaise
2 hearts of romaine lettuce
Juice of 1 lemon
Salt and ground black pepper
Vegetable oil

1. *Preheat oven to 425°.*

2. *Season chicken breasts with salt, pepper, and a light dusting of curry powder.*

3. *Put vegetable oil in a medium preheated sauté pan and sear chicken breasts over medium-high heat for 6 to 7 minutes.*

4. *Finish in the oven for 8 to 10 minutes.*

5. *Combine mayonnaise and curry powder, and season to taste with salt, pepper, and lemon juice.*

6. *Chop celery, endive, and romaine lettuce.*

7. *Slice chicken breast.*

8. *In a large salad bowl, toss all ingredients with walnuts and combine with curry mayonnaise.*

Salmon with Black Olive Tapenade

2 six-ounce portions of Atlantic salmon
1½ cups of pitted olives
1 tablespoon of capers
¼ cup of olive oil
3 tablespoons of vegetable oil
Salt and ground black pepper

1. *Place the olives, capers, and olive oil in a food processor and puree.*

2. *In a medium preheated sauté pan, over medium heat, heat vegetable oil and sear the salmon, seasoned with salt and pepper, on one side for 5 to 6 minutes.*

3. *Carefully flip to the other side and cook for an additional 2 to 3 minutes.*

4. *Serve salmon with a tablespoon of the olive tapenade and any vegetable of your choice.*

Grilled Buffalo Rib Eyes with Blue Cheese Butter

2 twelve- to fourteen-ounce buffalo rib eyes
2 sticks of unsalted butter (brought to room temperature)
6-ounce portion of blue cheese
Kosher salt
Freshly ground black pepper

1. *Preheat your grill.*

2. *Place butter and blue cheese in mixing bowl.*

3. *Whisk together to form a compound butter.*

4. *Place the blue cheese butter in plastic wrap and roll to form a log. Place the log in the refrigerator to chill before slicing. If you are running short on time, place it in the freezer for 10 to 15 minutes, but don't forget about it!*

5. *Season rib eye steaks generously with kosher salt and ground black pepper.*

6. *Place steaks on grill and cook 10 to 12 minutes, until medium rare.*

7. *Slice butter log into rounds and serve on top of steaks. Enjoy with some grilled asparagus and a simple chopped salad.*

Crustless Cheesecake

2 pounds of cream cheese (brought to room temperature)
1¼ cups of sugar
4 eggs
2 teaspoons of vanilla
¼ cup of 35% cream
¼ cup of sour cream
Zest of 1 lemon

1. *Preheat oven to 325°.*

2. *Using an electric mixer, combine cream cheese and eggs, one at a time, until well-blended.*

3. *Add lemon zest, vanilla, sugar, sour cream, and cream. Mix well.*

4. *Pour mixture into a springform pan that has been covered with aluminum foil around the bottom and up the sides.*

5. *This will be cooked in a water bath to keep it moist. To make one, place springform pan in a roasting dish. Pour in enough boiling water so that it goes about one-quarter up the springform pan.*

6. *Bake for one hour. Turn off oven and leave cake inside for an additional 45 minutes.*

7. *Remove from water bath and chill 4 to 5 hours. Unmold cake from springform pan and serve with fresh strawberries.*

Low-Fat Recipe Guide

Kale Slaw

1 bunch of dinosaur kale
½ head of cabbage
1 head of radicchio
3 tablespoons of white wine vinegar
1 tablespoon of sugar
½ cup of low-fat mayonnaise
Salt and ground black pepper

1. *Carefully remove the rib of the kale and rinse under cool running water.*

2. *Roughly chop cabbage, radicchio, and kale. Combine in a large bowl.*

3. *Add the vinegar, sugar, and mayonnaise; toss well and season to taste with salt and pepper. Serve immediately or refrigerate until ready to use.*

Spinach Salad with Citrus Vinaigrette

1 bag of baby spinach
1 Belgian endive
2 cups of freshly squeezed orange juice
1 orange (or grapefruit) cut into segments
1 teaspoon of Dijon mustard
3 tablespoons of white wine vinegar
1 tablespoon of vegetable oil
Salt and ground black pepper

1. *In a medium saucepan, bring orange juice to a boil and reduce by half.*

2. *Add mustard, oil, and vinegar to the reduced juice.*

3. *In a tightly sealed container, season with salt and pepper and shake well to form an emulsion.*

4. *Slice endive and combine with spinach and orange segments.*

5. *In a large bowl, toss with vinaigrette and season to taste.*

Artichoke and Spinach Dip

1 can of artichoke hearts
1 bag of baby spinach
1 can of garbanzo beans
2 cloves of garlic
1 tablespoon of olive oil
½ jalapeño pepper
Juice of 1 lemon
Salt and ground black pepper

1. *Under cold running water, quickly rinse the artichoke hearts and garbanzo beans.*

2. *Finely chop the garlic and jalapeño pepper.*

3. *Combine all of the ingredients in a food processor and puree for 20 to 30 seconds. If mixture is too thick, add water or vegetable stock to thin the puree to the desired consistency. Season to taste with salt and pepper.*

4. *Enjoy with crackers or toasted pita.*

Sweet Miso Soup

1 container of sweet white miso paste
2 postcard-size pieces of kombu (seaweed)*
1 package of bonito flakes*
1 package of firm tofu
1 bunch of scallions
10 cups of cold water

1. *Rinse kombu under cold running water.*

2. *In a medium-size pot, add water, kombu, and bonito flakes. Bring to a light simmer, but not to a boil. Remove from heat and steep for 10 to 15 minutes.*

3. *With a fine mesh sieve, strain the broth.*

4. *Place the broth back into the pot over medium-high heat and bring to a simmer. With the use of a sieve, whisk in the miso paste to prevent lumps and remove impurities.*

5. *Finely dice tofu and slice scallions. Add to broth.*

Kombu and bonito flakes are available at Asian markets and specialty food stores.

Pork Tenderloin with
Caramelized Peaches and Arugula

    1 pork tenderloin
    1 fifteen-ounce can of peaches
    1 bag of arugula
    1 tablespoon of butter
    Vegetable oil
    Salt and ground black pepper

1. *Preheat oven to 425°.*

2. *Lightly rub pork with vegetable oil and season with salt and pepper.*

3. *Place pork in a preheated sauté pan and brown on all sides.*

4. *Finish in the oven for 12 to 14 minutes.*

5. *While pork is resting, strain peaches.*

6. *Place the peaches in a preheated sauté pan and caramelize well over medium heat. Finish the peaches by adding ½ tablespoon of butter.*

7. *Sauté arugula in the remaining ½ tablespoon of butter. Season well and serve with the sliced pork and caramelized peaches.*

Rigatoni with Mushrooms, Asparagus,
and Sun-dried Tomatoes

    1 box of rigatoni pasta
    10 to 12 sun-dried tomatoes (not packed in oil)
    1 bunch of asparagus
    1 pint of button mushrooms
    4 cups of vegetable stock
    1 tablespoon of butter
    2 tablespoons of low-fat Parmesan cheese
    ½ cup each of freshly chopped basil, parsley, and chives
    Salt and ground black pepper

1. *Rehydrate sun-dried tomatoes in 2 cups of warmed vegetable stock for 15 to 20 minutes. Reserve liquid.*

2. *Trim, peel, and blanch asparagus in boiling salted water for 35 to 40 seconds. Quickly place in a bowl filled with ice water to stop the cooking and release chlorophyll.*

3. *In a preheated sauté pan, brown mushrooms in butter and deglaze the pan with 2 cups of vegetable stock. Bring to a boil and reduce by a third.*

4. *Chop the asparagus and slice the tomatoes.*

5. *Bring a large pot of salted water to a boil over high heat. Add the pasta and cook for 3 to 4 minutes, or until al dente, then strain.*

6. *In a large pot, over medium-low heat, combine all ingredients and toss with fresh herbs and Parmesan cheese. If necessary, add reserved vegetable stock to loosen pasta. Season to taste with salt and pepper.*

Ratatouille

2 plum tomatoes
1 zucchini
1 onion
1 small eggplant
1 red pepper
1 clove of garlic
2 tablespoons of olive oil
Chopped fresh basil and parsley
Salt and ground black pepper

1. *Finely dice all vegetables, keeping size consistent.*

2. *In a medium sauté pan, sweat the chopped garlic and onions in 1 tablespoon of olive oil for 3 to 4 minutes.*

3. *Add zucchini to onion and garlic. Continue cooking 2 to 3 minutes, then remove from heat.*

4. *With the remaining tablespoon of olive oil, sauté the eggplant 5 to 6 minutes. In the final 2 minutes of cooking, add the red pepper and continue to sauté.*

5. *Over medium heat, combine all the ingredients and sauté for 1 to 2 minutes.*

6. *Finish with fresh herbs, season to taste with salt and pepper, and serve.*

Orange Roughy with French Lentils and Sherry Vinegar

2 six- to eight-ounce orange roughy fillets
1½ cups of French lentils (Du puy)
1 plum tomato
1 carrot
1 celery stalk
1 onion
1 clove of garlic
1 fresh bay leaf
1 leek
3 tablespoons of sherry vinegar
1 bunch of chives
1 tablespoon of olive oil
3 cups of vegetable stock
Zest of 1 lemon
Vegetable oil
Salt and ground black pepper

1. *In a fine-mesh sieve, rinse lentils thoroughly, discarding any stones you may find.*

2. *Roughly chop celery, carrot, onion, and leek.*

3. *In a medium saucepan, combine lentils, garlic, and bay leaf with chopped vegetables.*

4. *Cover the lentil mixture with vegetable stock and over a medium-low heat, bring to a gentle simmer for approximately 30 to 35 minutes.*

5. *Dice tomato and slice chives.*

6. *When the lentils are cooked, discard the aromatic vegetables and combine with sherry vinegar, olive oil, lemon zest, chives, and tomato. Season to taste with salt and pepper.*

7. *Lightly rub the fish with vegetable oil and season generously with salt and pepper.*

8. *In a preheated sauté pan, place the fish in the pan and sear on one side for 5 to 6 minutes. Carefully flip the fish over and finish on the other side for 1 to 2 minutes.*

9. *Quickly warm lentil mixture and serve with fish.*

Poached/Baked Asian-Glazed Chicken Breast with Steamed Bok Choy and Grilled Shiitakes

1 boneless, skinless organic chicken breast
1 knob of sliced ginger
4 cups of vegetable stock
1 clove of garlic
½ pint of shiitake mushrooms
2 to 3 baby bok choy
½ cup of mirin (sweet Asian cooking liquid)*
1 tablespoon of sesame seeds
2 tablespoons of freshly chopped chives
Salt and ground black pepper

1. *Preheat grill.*

2. *In a medium saucepan, bring vegetable stock to a boil with the sliced ginger and garlic.*

3. *Add chicken breast, turn off heat, and cover for 15 to 20 minutes.*

4. *Steam bok choy for 2 to 3 minutes.*

5. *Lightly spray mushrooms with vegetable oil and season with salt and pepper.*

6. *Grill mushrooms for 4 to 5 minutes, slice, and toss with chives.*

7. *Remove chicken from poaching liquid and blot on paper towel. Lightly rub with vegetable oil and season.*

8. *In a preheated sauté pan, over medium-high heat, brown the chicken breast 2 to 3 minutes. Remove chicken breast and deglaze with mirin. Reduce liquid by one third, and place chicken back in pan to glaze.*

9. *Slice and serve mushrooms and bok choy. Sprinkle with sesame seeds.*

*Mirin is available at Asian markets and specialty food stores.

Peaches and Pine Nuts Dessert

3 fresh white peaches
½ cup of white wine
½ tablespoon of honey
¼ cup of toasted pine nuts

1. *Remove pits from peaches by slicing in half.*

2. *Cut each half into quarters, leaving skin on.*

3. *Whisk honey and white wine together, then add peach quarters.*

4. *Marinate for 12 to 15 minutes.*

5. *Sprinkle peaches with pine nuts and serve immediately.*

IF YOU'RE NOT READY TO get gourmet, some general eating guidelines apply to make the most of your sexual health. You should do everything in your power to incorporate more fresh fruits and vegetables into your diet. They add fiber, which promotes regular bowel movements and helps get rid of excess estrogen in your system. Too much estrogen is what causes those nasty PMS-like symptoms and throws your body out of whack hormonally. Fiber also leaves you feeling more satisfied for a longer period of time after you eat. In fact, fruits and vegetables are an excellent source of bulk with minimal calories and no fat. They also provide many essential vitamins and antioxidants to keep your body in peak condition inside and out. Eat as if you are envisioning the colors of the rainbow. Leafy green vegetables, tomatoes and strawberries, oranges and carrots, yellow peppers and squash, blueberries and grapes—incorporate as many as possible into your daily (and seasonal) diet. Try keeping a bag of dried fruit in your purse or some baby carrots at work to meet your minimum five-a-day requirement. Add spinach or another favorite vegetable to your typical pizza or omelet.

Fresh, wholesome food choices don't stop in the fruit and vegetable aisle, either. Limiting your intake of processed, sugary, and salty foods is another staple of good eating. We've talked about the effect too much sugar has on the body. Too much salt is just as bad. It often makes you bloated and can raise your blood pressure. Processed foods tend to contain more salt and are never good choices for other reasons. They are full of refined flours and sugars, which are literally empty calories stripped of their nutritional value. These are the simple-carbohydrate ingredients that spike your blood sugar, cause your mood to temporarily soar and then crash, and turn your body into a fat-storing machine instead of a fat-burning one. Unfortunately, many options at the supermarket and everywhere else these days are processed. Cutting down on crackers, pretzels, cookies, breads, and prepackaged meals is the best way to begin changing your diet. Fruits and vegetables help fill in the void. Whenever possible, try making choices that are whole, natural foods. For instance, it is always better to eat a chicken breast than high-salt, processed lunch meat. Stick to lean sources of protein in general, such as chicken and fish, with red meat less often. If you need a snack, celery stalks spread with a little peanut butter are healthier and more filling than pretzels. Your guiding principle about food should be: If you don't need to prepare it, you probably shouldn't eat it. While it may take a little adjusting to at first, in the long run you will hardly notice the time it takes to prepare and eat the right kinds of foods. Caring about what you put in your body is an investment in your quality of life and your health with major payoffs.

How about when dining out? Most restaurants have become more health-friendly and the choices are there if you want them. Think about what you would be eating at home. I know, that's why you're going out to eat—to eat what you would *not* be eating at home—but it's a good exercise to keep you balanced. If a monster plate of fettuccini alfredo would feel funny at home, why not try the linguini with spicy tomato sauce? Or split the fettuccini with your dinner date and skip dessert. While you're at it, you can add some spinach or mushrooms for fiber. If you eat out on a more regular basis because of work or lifestyle, choose healthy, filling meals. It may be a good idea to say no thank you to the bread basket to avoid the temptation of filling up on empty carbohydrates. If you do opt for it, choose the dark, whole-grain breads, which have the lowest conversion rate to sugar (unlike white breads). For your entrée, salads with good sources of protein, like chicken, nuts, or fish, are satisfying. Soups fill you up and often provide many healthy vegetables; just beware of cream soups. Even a hamburger can be indulged in safely if you take away half of the bun and skip the cheese. Instead of the standard french fries or hash browns that accompany many meals, you can often ask for other options at no extra charge. Tomato slices, fresh fruit, cottage cheese, and a side salad are just some of the typical choices. And while we're at it, fried food itself should be avoided. Period! You can indulge here and there, but as a rule, fried food is the ultimate poor choice. It is full of saturated fat—and trans-fat at that, which has been shown to increase cancer and other health-disease risk. It contains virtually no nutritional value and often makes you feel sluggish after eating it. Fortunately, most people do not eat fried food unless they are out at a restaurant. Eating at home can help for this reason alone, but it is no reason to avoid restaurants. Whether at home or out, nutritious, healthy food choices are the goal. I believe that we know when we're not making the right food decisions, but choose to ignore or justify it.

Another way to kick up your metabolism and take some stress off your body is to drink water. Eight glasses, or sixty-four ounces a day, is the minimum recommendation. Unlike soda, juice, and other beverages, water cleans the body and keeps toxins at a minimum by eliminating them via your urine. It has no adverse side effects, as other drinks do, and the difference really adds up over time when you grab water instead of something else. Juice contains sugars and debate remains what, if any, vitamins are absorbed once the juice has been pasteurized or regularly exposed to light. Better to eat fruits and vegetables than to rely on juices for those nutrients. The only exception would be freshly squeezed fruit and vegetable juices or smoothies. And though they don't contain sugar, diet sodas are no better and possibly worse than regular soda. Artificial sweeteners are, in the end, artificial and not good for our bodies. Carbonation of any kind increases bloating and puffiness, and some sodas may leach calcium from the body's bones over time. Drinking a soda when you're thirsty does nothing to give your cells the water they are signaling they need. It just tricks your brain into thinking you are no longer thirsty, which can lead to chronic dehydration. Limiting your intake of alcoholic beverages and caffeine is another given—for good hydration and good health.

The changes in this chapter may be easier to make for some than for others. Eating is an emotional act. We choose the foods we do because they are comforting and sensual, and old habits die hard. However, our bodies pay the price. As you've learned throughout this book, a healthy, active sex life is fueled by a body that's in similar condition. While you can eat that cookie when no one's looking, there is always a day of reckoning!

I think it is far more satisfying to get our pleasure from sex and intimacy rather than from food. While the two may be similar, only one allows us to connect to another person. Making the decision to make the right food choices is a way of showing that you care about your sex life. Plus, it makes the food that much more delicious when you do decide to indulge on special occasions!

PRESCRIPTIONS FOR THE WEEK:
Week 9

✓ If you feel you want to lose some weight, you are hopefully following some of the steps outlined in Chapter 6. Now it's time to make sure your diet is working as well. Choose a balanced low-carb or low-fat routine and make the decision today to move toward a healthier lifestyle.

✓ If you don't already know, find out what your partner's favorite foods or aromas are. Tell him you want to have a date night this week, in which you cook together and make eating and drinking the centerpiece of the evening. Make foods that will appeal to his senses and make sure you use all of your senses while you are eating (and make sure the kids are out of the house as well).

✓ Prepare one of Chef Charles's gourmet diet recipes.

✓ Eat a piece of chocolate this week and savor every bite!

✓ Don't forget! Masturbate at least twice a week, keep writing about your experiences in your sexual journal, and be sure to take two hours this week, whether it's with friends or by yourself, but with no work or home demands and no errands. And keep the action with your partner going: at least one sexual experience a week barring illness or extreme relationship conflict! Also remember to do your Kegel exercises on a regular basis, incorporated into or separate from your Pelvic Push-Ups three times a week, and thirty to forty-five minutes of cardiovascular exercise three times a week as well.

GUY'S GUIDE:
A Summary of Key Points for the
Man in Your Life

1. Food has many similarities to sex. It's a craving that can bring much pleasure and also much peril. Making the right food choices is absolutely essential for a healthy sex life and for your health in general.

2. Most women would never suspect that their hormones may be driving their overeating instead of their stomachs. Declining levels of estrogen can affect a hormone called cholecystokinin produced during digestion. The result is that feelings of fullness do not register in the brain and women begin overeating.

3. Out-of-balance estrogen also causes insulin levels to go up and thyroid levels to go down. This slows down her body's metabolism for the ultimate double whammy, and also affects her energy level and libido. When weight begins to accumulate, it can be absolutely maddening for women who are eating only when they are hungry.

4. Too little estrogen also affects her brain's serotonin levels, which can leave her more prone to depression. When depressed, food often takes on a new meaning as we tend to "stuff our feelings" with those fattening comfort foods.

5. Higher levels of stress are associated with increased body fat, especially in the abdominal area. When we are stressed, cortisol levels rise, which can make you want to eat more and disrupt your ability to sleep—yet another important regulator of appetite and metabolism.

6. So hormones affect a woman's digestion, mood, and stress levels, and then the depression and stress levels have chemical effects on her

body's storage of fat. The way out is by incorporating a healthy variety into your diet and eating the right ratio of the nutritional triumvirate—carbohydrates, protein, and fat.

7. Complex carbohydrates are the body's slow energy suppliers. They are found in whole grains and vegetables. Complex carbohydrates take longer to break down and so are absorbed more slowly into the bloodstream. The body must take from its reserves to keep itself going. Your fat, instead of that cake, begins to get burned for fuel. This is the underlying mechanism of the Atkins, or low-carb, diet craze. Since the body is forced to burn fat in the absence of carbohydrates, it can be a great way to lose weight and reinvigorate your sex life.

8. Low-fat products often contain astronomical sugar levels to help make up for the lack of taste in low-fat foods. Look out in particular for high fructose corn syrup—a particularly nasty and ubiquitous sugar ingredient that depletes the body of vitamins and minerals. In the end, sugar equals simple carbohydrates equals more fat on your body.

9. Saturated fats include butter, most meats, and full-fat dairy products. You have to keep all of these to a minimum, especially butter. However, instead of turning to margarine and other similar butter substitutes that are often full of chemicals and just as bad for the body, try making olive oil your new fat. It is chock-full of good fats and antioxidants. It can replace almost anything you use butter for, and if the taste is too strong for a certain dish, try canola oil—another excellent, good-fat alternative.

10. Eating complex carbohydrates, protein and fat in the right proportion is the key to weight loss and to keeping the weight off in the long term. Try for a balance of 40 percent protein, 35 percent carbohydrates and 25 percent fat (only 10 percent of your total calories should be saturated fat).

11. It also helps to eat five or more mini-meals throughout the day, if you are able. This keeps your metabolism and blood sugar levels more constant and your digestive process running more smoothly. This is especially important for sex, since too much food at one sitting can make you feel tired as your body focuses on digesting.

12. One of the best ways to support your partner on a diet is by dieting with her! This may just mean cutting back on the junk food a little more, but if you exercise with her and also don't flaunt bad food choices in front of her, she's not only going to love you for your support, but it will also give you some nonsexual bonding time—a powerful aphrodisiac for women!

CHAPTER TEN

Eastern Alternatives

THE ANCIENT CAN INFORM THE modern, especially when it comes to our sex lives. Eastern alternatives consider the whole person to be a reservoir of energy. This energy drives everything we do, from having sex to cleaning the floors. Learning how to cultivate and nourish your energy is the goal. Sex provides the perfect opportunity to do so, and sex flourishes when the energy is flowing. From erotic massage to getting Tantric, the alternatives are fun at the very least and therapeutic at the very best. Putting them to use during sex adds a new dimension to intimacy. Think of yourself as experimenting with the ancient approaches of our Eastern neighbors to unite body, mind, and spirit.

Alternatives such as acupuncture and reflexology additionally benefit your well-being. While it's always important to keep the dialogue open with your primary physician, complementary medicine can provide other options for treating a range of health conditions. Keep your mind open, too, since there are many benefits these less invasive alternatives may offer for your general and sexual well-being.

Sexual Healing

Energy, referred to as Chi by Eastern medicine, circulates through our bodies along a series of pathways known as meridians. You can think of these pathways as invisible veins. Each meridian is related to a specific organ or bodily function. When energy flows freely through the meridians, the body is balanced and healthy. When energy is blocked, it results in physical or emotional ailments. According to Eastern philosophy, an energy imbalance is the root of everything from a bad temper to headaches to chronic disease. Energy can be thrown out of whack by virtually any internal or external event, such as emotional turmoil, physical illness, or even the weather. The goal of Eastern healing is to realign your body's energy flow and fortify your well-being. It is predicated upon the body's natural ability to heal itself when properly stimulated.

One of the primary ways to restore the body's energy is through sex. Unlike the Western view of sex as a pleasurable or shameful activity (or both), Eastern philosophy considers sex to be a spiritual energy exchange. Pleasure and intimacy, *and* spiritual growth and awareness, give sex its special power. Having sex unites polar energy opposites—woman and man, yin and yang, which depend on each other for completion and growth. Together, these two energies represent a complete whole—a creative energy force that permeates every aspect of the universe.

Getting in touch with this energy allows you to drive your sexual experience. Sex becomes about the dynamic flow of energy between you and your partner. It is this tenet of Eastern philosophy that I find most appealing for couples—the idea of sex as a harmonizing activity for couples. According to the Eastern view, men and women may be at odds with each other in many ways, but together we are a powerful source of connection and energy. Sex offers us the opportunity to appreciate each other and come together despite our differences.

This matters not just for couples, but for singles, too. Your sexual energy can be transmitted to every part of your life. Whether to your health, vitality, career, or vibrant personality—putting your energy to good use helps make your life more positive in all ways. So are you ready to get in touch?

Your Microcosmic Orbit

I know, it sounds funky. But getting in touch with your microcosmic orbit is the key to all of the hands-on Eastern-inspired activities for your sex life that come next. It is also how singles can best get in touch with their energy. In layman's terms, your microcosmic orbit describes the circulation of energy through all of the body's meridians. Finding it opens up your energy center to let the healing come inside. As you learned in Chapter 6, breathing is a fundamental part of the sexual experience.

Working with your internal energy is something you can do on your own if you are not interested in seeking the services of a professional acupuncturist or reflexologist (more on that follows in the next section). According to Eastern philosophy, the microcosmic orbit is your access to your body's vital energy current. Making a simple meditation a regular part of your daily activity allows you to modify your energy. The microcosmic orbit nourishes all of your body's meridians and, thus, all of your body's organs and systems. Circulating energy through it helps eliminate blockages and allow your Chi to revitalize your body.

The microcosmic orbit consists of two channels—one that goes up the back of the body and one that goes down the front of the body. The first channel, the Governor meridian, begins at the perineum (see Figure 3 on page 12) and goes up the back of the body. As you breathe deeply, you envision energy traveling from your perineum to the tailbone, up through the spine, and into the brain. The second channel, the Conception meridian, goes down the front of your body. Energy moves from the throat, down through the stomach to the genitals and the perineum. Your tongue acts as a switch to connect these two currents. When touched to the roof of your mouth, it allows the two channels to become a circuit in which the energy loops around. This continual circle of energy gives all of your cells what they need to function and heal.

It is best to practice the microcosmic orbit when you are alone, like when you do your Pelvic Push-Ups. The focus is on your breath and internal energy. Start with the energy in your eyes and allow it to go down the front of your body and into the perineum. Then allow the energy to loop past the perineum to begin traveling back up the spine. When you imagine the energy moving into your brain, touch your tongue to the roof of your mouth to begin its descent down your throat and back to the perineum. Like yoga, this is about visualization. Think about the energy as it moves through all of your body parts, instead of any one specific image. Synchronize your breath along with your energy to help you feel connected. Sometimes it helps to imagine the breath as a white light that travels through your body and as you close your eyes you can imagine its circular travel.

The microcosmic orbit is just an extension of the breathing exercises you learned in Chapter 6, which puts you further in touch with your internal energy. Now it's time to put this energy to work for your sex life.

Eastern Massage

The use of touch is an excellent mechanism for balancing your energy and connecting with the energy of another. Through massage and stimulation of different pressure points on the body, your energy becomes something you can consciously modify. The benefits are both direct and indirect for your sex life—some work for a specific aspect of your sexual function, while others improve your general health (intimately tied to your sexual health). Most of the massage techniques can be practiced by yourself or with another. Of course, it always feels best when someone else is doing the massaging!

First, there are a few pressure-point massages that can alleviate some common general health deterrents to your sex life. These were introduced to me by Dr. Ka-Kit Hui of the Center for East-West Medicine at UCLA. In each case, the pressure point should be located and gently massaged for several minutes. Depending on your symptoms, you can make one or all of the exercises a regular part of your wellness routine.

Pressure Point	How to Locate	Benefits
Hand	Place your thumb inside the fleshy area between the other hand's thumb and forefinger—known as the web. Massage with a gentle and consistent kneading motion.	Headaches, stress, anxiety, depression, and menstrual problems.
Wrist	Located three finger widths in from the wrist, between the two forearm tendons.	Anxiety, insomnia, and depression, as well as nausea and vomiting.

Pressure Point	How to Locate	Benefits
Wrist (*continued*)	Gently massage the area in between the two tendons.	
Lower Leg	On the backside of the leg, you can find it four finger widths below the kneecap, toward the outer edge.	A similar set of symptoms as the wrist pressure point, as well as immune dysfunction, digestive problems, and fatigue.
Ankle	It's located four finger widths above the ankle bone (on the inside of the leg).	Extremely useful for both men's and women's sexual health. Helps with pelvic pain, infertility, menopause, impotence, and difficult childbirth. Put it to use for you, your partner, or a friend.
Foot	Located between the first and second toes (the toes that come after your big toe). Two finger widths in from where the toes meet is the spot you should massage.	Head, neck, chest, and back pain, hypertension, and general health and well-being.

Each of these exercises stimulates a particular organ by massaging a pressure point located along its meridian. Eastern medicine considers the body to have five vital organs: the kidneys, heart, lungs, liver, and spleen. These organs are powerfully connected to your general health and to your sexuality as well. Each organ is associated with a particular earth element, which has unique significance for your sex life. Like balancing yin and yang, balance among the five vital organs is another goal of Eastern healing. When sexual energy is out of balance, it is reflected in the health of one or more of your internal organs. Likewise, an out-of-balance organ will in turn weaken your sexual energy. Targeted massages stimulate each organ's energy flow, which then boosts your sexual energy. What follows is a description of each organ, its corresponding element, and the aspect of your sexuality it governs. Massage techniques are given to help repair a sexual complaint and can either be done on yourself or another. Remember, a little oil or rich lotion makes every massage go more smoothly! It is also helpful to be somewhere warm and relaxing, so both body and mind are at ease.

THE KIDNEYS The kidneys are considered your main source of sexual energy. They are associated with the water element of the body. For women in particular, sexual energy is like water. Arousal and sexual satisfaction are similar to boiling water, in that they occur more gradually than in men and take longer to cool down afterward. Water is associated with gentleness. Kidneys that are in good health will imbue the person with a high-spirited, healthy sexual vigor. Try the following exercises for diminished interest in sex or general feelings of fear, which are associated with imbalance in the kidneys' energy.

There are two massages designed to stimulate and energize the kidneys. The first targets the kidneys themselves. Begin by locating the kidneys on the lower back, just above the last rib. Massage the area briskly with the palms, using a circular kneading motion. Keep massaging until you begin to feel heat in the area, which will penetrate the kidneys. Visualize it warming them. Then start rubbing a larger area, extending from the kidneys all the way down to the lower back, still with a circular motion. Feel the entire area warm up and open up. Afterward, cover the kidneys with your palms for a minute or two to keep the newly generated energy inside them. A second exercise stimulates the ears, which are an extension of the kidneys' energy. The ears also happen to be hubs of some major nerve endings, which activate your sexual energy (this one you may have already figured out on your own). Grasp the ear between your thumb and forefinger. Massage the entire ear gently, but with some pressure to stimulate the body's energy. Run your finger through the grooves. Knead the fleshy lobe between your forefinger and thumb. If you are doing this to somebody else, give a little kiss or nibble with your lips or tongue. Who knew this was good for your kidneys?

THE HEART Next is the heart, the body's second-most important organ according to Eastern tradition. The heart is associated with the fire element, the energy center of passion and attraction. Like fire, the heart warms the rest of the body by delivering blood and energy to it. A balanced heart allows joy and positive emotion to flow through it. It is the center of loving energy, which allows you to connect deeply with a partner during sex. When the heart's energy is blocked, it can play out as trouble connecting with your partner. In other words, congestion in the heart runs parallel to congestion in the relationship.

To open the heart, you can use one of two different techniques. While lying down, begin massaging the lower part of the sternum with your fingers (the sternum bone can be found just between the breasts). Use your fingers to keep massaging all the way up the chest. Press into the body gently but firmly with your fingertips. You can also use your knuckles as you knead the entire chest area. While massaging, visualize a bright red glow in the heart. Focus on the heart glow connecting to the genitals, letting the warmth join them together. A second exercise uses the tongue, which is an extension of the heart's energy. Using the tongue while kissing naturally makes use of its sexual energy. You can also actively cultivate this energy on your own. To do so, bring the tip of the tongue over the upper teeth, so it is touching the inside of the lip. Circle the tongue down so it slides across the lower inner lip. Continue circling in one direction and then switch directions, repeating multiple times.

THE LUNGS The lungs are associated with the metal element. Like metal, the lungs are conductors that move energy through the body. Through breath, the lungs keep us connected to the universe and to ourselves. Deep breathing is essential to sexual arousal. Healthy lungs help the body fill with breath and respond. Imbalanced or weak energy in the lungs can interfere with sexual arousal.

To stimulate the lungs, use your fist to gently knock below each side of the collarbone. Continue to knock outward and inward, across the chest, for a few minutes. Focus on the new sensations and tingling in the chest area once you stop. Then take five deep breaths, inhaling and exhaling all the way down to your perineum. Feel the energy of your lungs open up to stimulate the rest of your body.

THE LIVER The liver is connected to the wood element, and with kindness and forgiveness. It regulates the flow of energy throughout the body by acting as a sort of root. Imbalance in the liver's energy is associated with anger and sexual frustration. A harmonized liver provides the vital energy for sexual response. Since this response grows out of feeling relaxed, stimulating the liver is said to help with erectile dysfunction and difficulty with orgasm in women.

The liver meridian travels down the legs and ends at the feet. Therefore, a foot massage is the best way to activate it. A foot massage is both relaxing and stimulating at the same time. Sexual energy is released. Spend at least five minutes massaging each foot. Use your palms and fingers to rub the arch, kneading the top and bottom of the foot simultaneously. Massage each toe, as well as in between them, paying special attention to the big toe. A nibble on the big toe can provide an energy surge that goes up the leg to the genitals.

THE SPLEEN The final vital organ is the spleen, associated with the earth element. A healthy spleen fuels balance and vigor. Too much worry or anxiety is at odds with the spleen's energy. When out of balance, it can translate to trouble with sensation during sex. This makes sense if you think of too much activity in your mind as preventing you from getting in touch with your body—which is a common sexual problem for women. Restoring the energy flow allows you to rediscover sensation and trust the body to guide you.

To stimulate the flow of energy, massage the abdomen in a clockwise direction if you are doing it to yourself and a counterclockwise direction if doing it to your partner. The abdomen is the seat of much of the body's energy. Massaging it helps release the energy to nourish the rest of the body. Breathe deeply as you continue massaging in a circular manner. Focus on locating and releasing any areas of tightness.

Positions for Healing

Now it's time to move on to the positions that can be used during intercourse to make the most of your synergistic energy as a couple. Doing the massages *beforehand* gets you nice and warmed up, but it's not a must. In fact, some of the most powerful healing points on the body are located on the genitals.

The idea is that by making use of different positions to target specific spots, you make a pleasurable act also a healing act. Like the massage techniques, these are a sampling of positions that offer unique benefits to your sex life. The healing positions for women are ones in which you take a more active role to receive your partner's energy. The healing positions for men call on them to be more active. However, both partners benefit from any of them, since connected sex is always about the exchange of energy.

There are three positions you can try out for you and three you can try out for your partner. You're up first. The degree of penetration is the key to these positions, since the penis is used to stimulate different energy points inside the vagina. In all positions, the man is supposed to remain still while the woman moves her pelvis to stimulate the vagina (and other parts of the vulva in the process). It is the man's responsibility to let his partner know if he is getting too aroused, so she can slow down or stop temporarily. The idea is that since you are in an unusual position that takes more focus, he will be distracted from climaxing as quickly as he might normally. In addition to healing, it adds a little novelty, too! In fact, any of these positions can be good for discovering new hot spots for you or your partner.

The first position is intended to heal fatigue in women, which can impact libido. In it, the woman lies flat on her back, with the man on top of her but between her legs. He penetrates with his penis as deeply as he can, while you move your pelvis in circular motions beneath him. The circles can be in either direction. Orgasm is not the ultimate goal for you, but if it happens that's fine, too. The focus is on remaining in the position for a short while to stimulate the right spots—in other words, for as long as it feels good.

The second position is supposed to restore energy flow that protects against headaches and poor blood circulation. In this one, the man is on his back, while the woman straddles over him resting on her knees. Your body is leaning forward, slightly off to one side, supported by your elbow. Holding the base of his penis, you allow him to penetrate you shallowly. Move your pelvis to stimulate the internal part of your vagina. Since the first third has the most nerve endings, this position has a lot of potential for satisfying stimulation. However, you are still focusing on propping yourself up with your elbow, which may not be easy. After a while, you may want to switch sides and rest on the other elbow.

The third position for you can also help with blood flow. The woman is lying on her back, knees pulled up to her chest, while the man rests on his knees in front of her and penetrates. Your pelvis can be raised slightly on a pillow if you wish, and your feet should be dangling in the air. This helps open up the vagina for deeper penetration. Once again, you rotate your pelvis in whatever way feels best to stimulate the area. The penetration should never be painful, so your partner may need to refrain from penetrating totally. Holding the base of his penis can help (and it will also help him maintain his erection since it is similar to the squeeze technique you learned about in Chapter 5).

Now, for the men's positions. Like the vagina, the penis gets stimulated in specific spots to offer special kinds of healing. The first position is a revision on missionary. It is supposed to help with erectile dysfunction and premature ejaculation. The woman lies on her side slightly with her pelvis rotated forward. The man is above her, between her legs, supporting himself with his arms and chest. He should focus on penetrating and doing what feels best, while you lie still. Since he has to concentrate on a somewhat awkward position, there is less chance of quick orgasm. It may take some practice to get comfortable.

The second position aims to restore overall energy levels. The woman is on her back, her torso and head propped up by one or two pillows. The key to this position is bending your head and neck forward, which is thought to curve the vagina and offer the penis the right stimulation. Try the position for a few days to see if it boosts his energy level. It is a great position in general for intercourse, since both of you are comfortable and at a good angle for mutual stimulation.

The final position is thought to help with his blood flow. It is a variation of the woman-on-top position. As the man lies on his back relaxed, the woman kneels over him slightly up on her knees. There should be some space between your and your partner's pelvises. While you remain still, he thrusts his penis in and out of you. He keeps moving in whichever way feels best, while you remain elevated and still.

Getting Tantric

Like the positions you just learned about, which are focused on using your sexual energy as a healing force, Tantric sex also focuses on your energy potential during sex—but it is less about healing than it is about communication between you and your partner. And the good news is that it can be done in any position. Getting Tantric is all about the right mind-set, rather than any physical gymnastics. Tantrism puts the union of opposing energies—yin and yang—to work for your sexual satisfaction. It can be a great way to prolong intercourse, which is good for any woman's satisfaction. As you learned in Chapter 8, time is a huge part of men and women getting on the same page sexually, since we are often on different schedules when it comes to our arousal.

Tantric sex is firmly rooted in the Eastern view of sex as a powerful furnace of energy. The longer sex goes on, the more potential for stoking the flames (energetically and otherwise). Strict Tantrism teaches that orgasms are meant to be lived instead of released, since ejaculation is a drain on all of that wonderful energy created by sex. However, you have to be realistic. The average guy is probably not going to be interested in giving up ejaculation. If you are interested in pursuing that goal with your partner, there are a few good books on the subject listed in the Resource Guide. Otherwise, you can practice the spirit of Tantrism by working to delay orgasm as long as possible. This keeps the energy flowing between you and your partner and offers the added bonus of a more intense erotic experience.

One terrific Tantric warm-up that I like to recommend to patients is called soul gazing. You can be nude if it's a prelude to sex, or you can be clothed if you just want to use it for reconnecting and getting on the same page after a hectic and disconnected day (or period of days). You sit comfortably and cross-legged facing each other. Stare softly into each other's eyes for several minutes. You should be focusing your gaze on your partner's left eye, above his or her heart. Keep holding the gaze as you tune into your partner's heartbeat. Remain silent and try to open yourself up to your partner's energy. If you want to take it to the next level, you can put your hands over each other's hearts and try to synchronize your breathing. You can even use elements of the microcosmic orbit as you imagine not only the breath flowing like energy through your body in a circular motion, but also flowing through your arms to the other's body. It may feel like an eternity at first, especially if this is new to you, but you will find that it is not only relaxing, but also a fabulous way to quiet your mind and connect with your partner on a deep spiritual and physical level.

To practice Tantric sex, your partner should focus on a slower rhythm of movement, sometimes with periods of no movement at all. When he gets close to the desire to climax, he should pull back and return to a more medium level of arousal. Then you get to work your way back up. He learns to control his level of arousal with different movements and pacesetting. Both of you are focused on what it feels like to slow things down. All the while, you should be looking at each other in the eye, getting inside the feelings and sensations of the moment. Your mind is supposed to be immersed in the moment completely—its energy and physical pleasure. If and when orgasm finally does happen, it is likely to be explosive! You especially have a better chance at multiple orgasms the longer your partner is able to last. Be patient and keep trying if it doesn't work the first couple of times. Getting Tantric means getting past the old way of doing things in bed. It may take a little time, but the benefits are well worth it. Tantric is meant to increase your feelings of connectedness— with each other, yourself, and, ultimately, the universe. It can help to teach you to strip away the fears and boundaries that hold you back from a satisfying erotic connection.

The Energy Alternative

Acupuncture and reflexology are two professional practices that aim to grease the wheels of your energy flow. Acupuncture is one of the oldest forms of surviving medical treatment in the world. It is known to have been practiced more than 2,000 years ago in China and may have been around well before then. Acupuncture heals body and mind by unblocking energy along a series of 2,000 points located on the body. The points are dotted along the body's meridians and, therefore, correspond with various organs and functions. Using needles, the body's energy flow is stimulated at precise points in order to treat and prevent illness. It may not always be at the site of the symptoms.

I know what you're thinking: needles, ouch! But the needles used in acupuncture are hair-thin. They are regulated by the FDA, which requires that the sterile needles be used only one time. Most people feel little or no pain during treatment. Depending on what's being treated, some people feel energized while others feel relaxed. While acupuncture is touted for every condition imaginable, the World Health Organization (WHO) has recommended it for more than forty conditions based on clinical data reviews. These include headache, painful menstruation, depression and a host of chronic and acute pain conditions. It has also been found effective for women undergoing in vitro fertilization, increasing chances of pregnancy. There are many other conditions that the WHO considers likely to benefit from acupuncture, but they are awaiting more clinical data. Ultimately, it is up to you (and your physician) to decide whether it's worth a shot. If it is not a life-threatening problem, acupuncture may be a good first option to try since there are no known side effects when done properly. As you learned in previous chapters, medication and surgery are often taxing to both body and mind. For more serious conditions, acupuncture can be a good adjunct to medical treatment.

However, acupuncture is a good practice even without a specific complaint. Prevention is as much—or more—the aim of Eastern medicine as treatment. Keeping your energy moving is the key to longevity and well-being. Stress, in particular, affects our sexual function and many experts believe that acupuncture is an effective stress-relieving treatment. By unblocking the body's energy pathways, well-being is enhanced, even when nothing seems out of sorts. Though outside the bounds of Western medicine, there is a medical theory as to why acupuncture might work. It's been proposed that acupuncture stimulates the nervous system to promote the release of endorphins, our body's natural pain reducers. Acupuncture may also alter brain chemistry, affecting the release of neurotransmitters and neurohormones, which are connected to immune response and blood flow. Whether the mechanism is spiritual or physical—I say if it works, go with it!

Technique matters, which is why it's important to choose a qualified practitioner. There are some resources listed at the end of the book for finding an acupuncturist in your area; however, keep in mind that training and licensure requirements differ from one state to the next. Ask how long the acupuncturist has been in practice and what type of training was received. Treatment may take as little as one session or occur on a regular basis for several weeks or months. It is best to get the treatment when you have not just eaten or had sex, and to practice good personal hygiene both before and after (in other words, don't go three days without showering!). A session typically runs between fifty and one hundred dollars per session. Many health insurance companies cover acupuncture as part of their complementary and alternative medical therapy coverage.

Reflexology is similar to acupuncture in that it involves manipulating certain parts of the body to energize or heal others. In this case, all of the points are located on the feet; massage, rather than needles, is used. Sometimes the hands and ears are also manipulated. Many of the pressure-point exercises described earlier are based on reflexology. Like acupuncture, reflexology encourages the body to restore itself. It is yet another ancient healing technique that was practiced by cultures in Egypt, India, and China. The underlying principle of reflexology is that tension in some part of the foot (or hand or ear) indicates tension in that part of the body. Each foot is divided into five sections, each of which corresponds to a specific part of the body. Reflexologists usually do an initial foot massage and examination of your bare feet. Based on your therapeutic goals, he or she then applies different degrees of pressure to various spots. Lotion or aromatic oils are used for lubrication. Special massagers, wooden sticks and other instruments are also often used. A typical appointment lasts between thirty and sixty minutes.

Reflexology is theorized to work by a mechanism similar to that of acupuncture. Stimulation of the feet may unblock the vital energy flow to certain parts of the body. It also may stimulate the release of endorphins via the nervous system. However, reflexology is not currently regulated or clinically researched to the degree that acupuncture is. It is said to induce a state of relaxation, but anyone who has had a good foot massage could tell you that. There is some preliminary evidence that reflexology can help with stress, headache, and premenstrual syndrome, but it's nothing definitive. Either way, it offers one more option for taking charge of your well-being, sexually and otherwise.

Herbs: Friends or Foes?

Do plants have the power to heal, excite, and soothe? Or are they merely an ineffective, possibly even dangerous, palliative? Plants have been used since the earliest of times for their medicinal properties. Herbal remedies—as they are called—can be made from any part of a plant. The flowers, leaves, stem, roots, bark, seeds, and fruit can be processed in a variety of different ways to unlock their secret potential. Herbal remedies are not regulated by the FDA, so the lack of regulation makes it difficult to standardize the quality of herbal remedies. You could be getting less concentration of the herb than the packaging advertises, with other substances used as filler. Or companies can make claims on their product that do not have to be clinically proven. Finding a brand you can trust puts the focus back on the herb, instead of the skepticism. It is helpful to look at the packaging to determine if any placebo-controlled clinical trials have been carried out on the herbs you are considering trying.

While this is not a requirement, many companies that are of high quality and standards will carry out clinical trials to support their claims. You can either check out a local health food store for their suggestions, or consult a local acupuncturist or reflexologist for their suggestions. Many Eastern medicine practitioners hand-mix their own herbs for their clients.

Considering that every culture has used herbal remedies to treat body and mind, there is likely some benefit to be had by the contemporary use of them. Like other forms of Eastern medicine, herbs are intended to support the body's systems so it can naturally heal itself. Most are adaptogenic, which means they work to make a system more resilient by toning it, instead of treating a specific problem or symptom. Herbs may work by supporting the endocrine, nervous, and neurological systems. When these systems are working properly, the body is regulated both chemically and hormonally. Many herbs provide vital amino acids, vitamins, and enzymes to the body in addition to other unique healing properties.

In other words, herbs can be good for you—especially for your sex life! You just have to exercise some common sense in using them. Just because it's herbal doesn't mean it's safe. Always inform your physician of the herbs you plan on trying out and also tell your Eastern practitioner (if you have one) about any medications you are currently taking. If you have a chronic health condition, you should also discuss taking any herbs with your physician first. You should always follow the dosage instructions on the bottle. Stop taking herbs at least two weeks before any kind of surgery and of course stop if you notice any side effects. Pregnant and breast-feeding women should avoid herbal remedies.

So which herbs are rumored to be aphrodisiacs? The list is long, so to make it easy I am giving you a smattering of options you and your partner can put to the test. They can be taken daily over a period of three or four months, with a break in between and then resumed use, or in preparation just before an amorous encounter. Experiment and see what works for you. Most herbs are available in capsule form, liquid form that are taken as drops, and as dried forms of the herb itself, usually requiring that it be boiled or soaked in water and prepared as a tea to unleash its medicinal properties. Again, pay attention to the specific dosage that's called for or ask a practitioner for assistance. (Note: Herbal remedies with stars next to them have been tested in clinical trials that support their claims or are currently being tested.)

Herb	Benefits
For You	
Black Cohosh*	May reduce hot flashes, vaginal dryness, and general menopausal symptoms. Since it may work on the body's estrogenic receptors, controversy remains about use in women with a history of breast cancer.
Damiana Leaf	May increase circulation and sensation in the genitals, while acting as a relaxant. Rumored to induce erotic dreams when consumed before bedtime.
Licorice Root	May strengthen adrenal glands and enhance energy levels. Contains substances similar to those in estrogen. Also may increase testosterone levels, improving libido.
For You and Him	
l-Arginine	May increase blood flow to the genital region to help with lubrication, engorgement, and clitoral sensation in women and erectile ability in men. Should not be taken if you have herpes, as it may increase or worsen outbreaks.
Epimedium	Nicknamed horny goat weed, may boost libido in both sexes and help with erectile dysfunction in men. Also thought to regulate cortisol levels to restore energy and metabolism.
Ginkgo*	May help with arousal in both men and women by enhancing blood flow, and with erectile dysfunction in men specifically.
Ginseng*	An overall stimulant and libido booster that may enhance well-being and stamina, sexually and otherwise.
Maca	This ancient Peruvian root is said to enhance libido, arousal, and well-being in both sexes. It may help with menopausal symptoms in women and erectile dysfunction in men.
Muirapuama and Catuaba	Together they have been popular in Brazilian culture for fueling libido and increasing sexual potency. According to folklore, men become like boys again and women get a boost, too!
Rhodiola Rosea	May boost sexual desire and energy levels in general, increasing stamina. Positive effect on well-being has been indicated

for the treatment of depression. Improves body's natural
defenses to stress.

Yohimbine   May increase blood flow to the genital region to help with
lubrication, engorgement, and clitoral sensation in women and
erectile function in men.

Energy is everywhere. You can feel it when someone walks in a room, when you intuitively know the mood of a loved one without saying a word, and, now, as you get more in touch with your own. Our energy flow matters for our bodies and our minds. The electricity that runs through all of us has many tangible effects—for good health and good sex.

The energy mind-set also offers up a natural way to spice things up and get back in touch erotically. By encouraging the joining together of body and mind, man and woman, the quality of sex is redefined. As a couple, you come together as two halves of a whole. You realize that each one needs the other and that love blossoms from among your differences. Ultimately, the East may give us our most important message yet: In a relationship there are two that join to make one. They don't cancel out each other, but create something new together.

PRESCRIPTIONS FOR THE WEEK:
Week 10

✓ Get in touch with your microcosmic orbit. Find a time to practice this simple meditation, perhaps after an exercise session or while doing your Pelvic Push-Ups.

✓ Once you've tried the microcosmic orbit alone, try it during sex with your partner and see if increasing the flow of energy through your body increases your sexual response as well.

✓ Try a new Eastern technique learned in this chapter. Whether it's an organ massage, acupuncture, or reflexology, give one of them a try. You can go to a specialist with a specific complaint if you have one, or just for a Chi checkup and some stress reduction. (See the Resource Guide for acupuncturist and reflexologist referrals.)

✓ Add one of the positions for healing to your repertoire of new positions and try it out with your partner.

✓ Do a Tantric breathing exercise with your partner. Don't worry; he's read about it in the Guy's Guide. You can try it during a nonsexual time, or just before sex and see if it creates a greater sense of connection between you.

✓ Don't forget! Masturbate at least twice a week, keep writing about your experiences in your sexual journal, and be sure to take two hours this week with no work or home demands and no errands. And keep the action with your partner going: at least one sexual experience a week barring illness or extreme relationship conflict! Do your Kegel exercises on a regular basis, incorporated into or separate from your Pelvic Push-Ups, and thirty to forty-five minutes of cardiovascular exercise, three times a week. And if you are trying to lose weight, you should have started a balanced low-carb or low-fat diet. Don't give up. If you cheated you can always start again tomorrow!

GUY'S GUIDE:
A Summary of Key Points for the Man in Your Life

1. The ancient can inform the modern, especially when it comes to our sex lives. Eastern alternatives consider the whole person to be a reservoir of energy. Learning how to cultivate and nourish your energy is the goal. From erotic massage to getting Tantric, the alternatives are fun at the very least and therapeutic at the very best. Putting them to use during sex adds a new dimension to intimacy.

2. One of the primary ways to restore the body's energy is through sex. Unlike the Western view of sex as a pleasurable or shameful activity (or both), Eastern philosophy considers sex to be a spiritual energy exchange. Pleasure and intimacy, *and* spiritual growth and awareness, are what give sex its special power. Having sex unites polar energy opposites—woman and man, yin and yang, which depend on each other for completion and growth.

3. The use of touch is an excellent way to balance your energy and to connect with the energy of another. Through massage and stimulation of different pressure points on the body, your energy becomes something you can consciously modify. Most of the massage techniques can be practiced by yourself or with another. Of course, it always feels best when someone else is doing the massaging! If you are interested, read some of this chapter to get some techniques to try.

4. There are also three intercourse positions you can try out for you and three you can try out for your partner. Like the massage techniques, they are intended to heal. Some of the most powerful healing points on the body are located on the genitals. The degree of penetration is the key to these positions, since the penis is used to stimulate different energy points inside the vagina, and vice versa. In addition to healing, it adds a little novelty, too! In fact, any of these positions can be good for discovering new hot spots for you or your partner.

5. Tantric sex is firmly rooted in the Eastern view of sex as a powerful furnace of energy. The longer sex goes on, the more potential for stoking the flames (energetically and otherwise!). You can practice the spirit of Tantrism by working to delay orgasm as long as possible. This keeps the energy flowing between you and your partner and offers the added bonus of a more intense erotic experience.

6. One terrific Tantric warm-up that she'll love is called soul gazing. You can be nude if it's a prelude to sex or you can be clothed if you just want to use it for reconnecting. You sit comfortably and cross-legged facing each other. Stare softly into each other's eyes for several minutes. Remain silent and try to open yourself up to your partner's energy. If you want to take it to the next level, you can put your hands over each other's hearts and try to synchronize your breathing. You can even use elements of the microcosmic orbit (don't worry; you can learn more about it in this chapter) as you imagine not only the breath flowing like energy through your body in a circular motion, but also flowing through your arms. It may feel like an eternity at first, especially if this is new to you or you feel awkward, but you will find that it is a great way to connect with your partner on a deep spiritual and physical level.

7. Acupuncture and reflexology are two professional practices that aim to grease the wheels of your energy flow. Stress, in particular, affects our sexual function and many experts believe that acupuncture can be an effective stress-relieving treatment. Reflexology is similar to acupuncture in that it involves manipulating certain parts of the body to energize or heal others.

8. Which herbs are rumored to be aphrodisiacs? The list is long, so to make it easy I have listed a smattering of options for you and your partner to try on pages 243 and 244. They can be taken daily over a period of three or four months, with a break in between and then resumed use, or just before an amorous encounter. Experiment and see what works for you. Be sure to pay attention to the specific dosage that's called for or ask a practitioner for assistance.

9. Ultimately, the energy mind-set offers up a natural way to spice things up and get back in touch erotically. By encouraging the joining together of body and mind, man and woman, the quality of sex is redefined. As a couple, you come together as two halves of a whole. You realize that each one needs the other and that love blossoms from among your differences. Ultimately, the East may give us our most important message yet: In a relationship there are two that join to make one. They don't cancel out each other, but rather, create something new together.

Final Thoughts

You did it! Hopefully you've moved through the different steps, ten weeks have passed, and you find yourself in a very different place from when you began this journey. I congratulate you on your commitment and openness to the process, and thank you for letting me into your life (not to mention your bedroom). I really hope it helped.

Every woman's path will be unique in making her sex life what it can and *should* be. Some women will need to continue to rebuild certain parts of their sex lives; others will feel they completed the work they needed to, at least for now. You have been given the tools—now it is for you to decide where you go from here. Feeling passionate inspires every aspect of who we are, as women, mothers, wives, and girlfriends, and well beyond. I find that women are incredibly invested in their personal lives and that success in this area spills over into the many other roles we play. A passionate, healthy sex life is at the heart of feeling successful in your personal life.

I hope that you have been able to rediscover your passion. My intention in writing this book was to empower every woman to feel in charge of her sexuality. The information and activities presented are designed to help you look inside and make your sexual dreams a reality. And more than any one activity, it is the willingness to open yourself up and try new things that is the ultimate gift for your sex life. You act as a model for your partner and a trailblazer for your own pleasure. You discover that two people come together, but only you can make it happen. It is a good lesson for life in general.

I also think it's important to become more comfortable with our sexuality so we can act as good role models for others, especially our children. Viewing sex as a natural, healthy expression of who we are helps work against negative messages that harm all of us. Each and every woman makes a difference in making this happen. So embrace who you are, ask for what you want, and give of yourself in the best way you know how. Make sex a microcosm of how you want to be in every part of your life. That's the passion prescription.

Appendix

—◼\\\\\\\\\\\\◼—

THIS APPENDIX CONTAINS THE THREE self-assessment tools included as part of your homework. Each has been developed to give you a better understanding of your sexuality. They include:

Berman Sexual Assessment (Chapter 3 and, if you wish to retake it to check your progress, Chapter 8)

The Passion Prescription Pad (Chapters 2 and 8)

Genital Image Scale (Chapter 7)

Each quiz is designed for you to take and score yourself with the paper version that follows. You also can access the quizzes online at www.drlauraberman.com to receive your score automatically, as well as tailored recommendations and discussion. Click on the appropriate icon, located on the Web site's home page.

Berman Sexual Assessment

1. **During sexual stimulation, foreplay, and/or intercourse, I experience the following sexual complaint(s) (check all that apply):**

   ❑ A. vaginal dryness
   ❑ B. lack of genital sensation, tingling, and/or warmth with sexual arousal
   ❑ C. difficulty achieving orgasm
   ❑ D. loss of intensity of orgasm (orgasms feel muffled)
   ❑ E. genital pain either with or without sexual contact
   ❑ F. lack of sexual interest
   ❑ G. none of the above

2. **I feel that my sexual complaint(s) have affected my desire for sex. (In other words, if sex weren't painful, frustrating, or no fun, I would be more interested.)**

   ❑ I have no sexual complaints, just lack of desire.
   ❑ I agree.
   ❑ I disagree.
   ❑ I'm not sure.

3. **I notice that I have the same sexual difficulties with my partner as I have alone during self-stimulation or I am equally unmotivated or uninterested in self-stimulating as being sexual with my partner.**

   ❑ Yes
   ❑ No
   ❑ Don't know
   ❑ Don't self-stimulate

4. **There was a time when I was satisfied with my sexual response and/or interest.**

   ❑ Yes
   ❑ No
   ❑ Don't know

5. I am presently being treated with medication and/or psychotherapy for:

- ❑ depression
- ❑ anxiety disorder
- ❑ any psychiatric illness
- ❑ none of the above

6. I feel that:

- ❑ My partner knows what to do to satisfy me sexually.
- ❑ I am comfortable giving my partner direction about how to stimulate me sexually.
- ❑ I am connected to and emotionally intimate with my partner.
- ❑ My general/sexual communication with my partner is adequate.
- ❑ not applicable; I don't have a partner at this time.

7. I have a history of sexual abuse or trauma.

- ❑ Yes
- ❑ No
- ❑ Don't know

If yes,

- ❑ I never told anyone.
- ❑ I never pressed charges.
- ❑ I did not receive counseling.
- ❑ I feel this history affects my present sexual life.
- ❑ none of the above

8. The following conditions apply to me:

- ❑ I have had a hysterectomy or other pelvic surgery.
- ❑ I am postmenopausal.
- ❑ I have diabetes.
- ❑ I have cardiovascular disease.
- ❑ I smoke.
- ❑ I am taking SSRI's (e.g., Zoloft or Prozac).
- ❑ I am taking birth control pills.

❑ I have had one or more prolonged labor and deliveries (e.g., needed ventouse/suction).

❑ I have a history of straddle injury (fell on a bicycle, balance beam, etc.).

❑ I have had a back injury and/or back surgery.

❑ I have had a spinal cord injury.

❑ I have had genital circumcision.

❑ I have multiple sclerosis or another neurological disorder.

❑ I have had two or more children.

❑ none of the above

Berman Sexual Assessment Scoring

1. **If you answered yes to:**

   1A or 1B–You have symptoms of difficulty with arousal.
   1C or 1D–You have symptoms of orgasm difficulty.
   1E–You have symptoms of sexual pain.
   1F–You have symptoms of low libido.

Now let's see if there are clues about what kind of intervention might help.

2. **If you answered yes, your low libido may be the result of problems with arousal and your sexual response. In other words, if sex is frustrating, painful, or no fun because of how your body responds, you may have lost your motivation to have it. Treatment should be focused on these specific complaints as much as, or more than, your diminished desire.**

3. **If you answered yes, this is an indication your sexual complaints may be medically based. If you answered no, you are certainly not alone! Many women find it difficult to reach orgasm with their partner, but have no problem achieving orgasm by themselves. You may want to look into the possibility that there are other problems playing a role in your sexual response, such as stress in your relationship.**

4. **If you answered yes, this is an indication that your sexual complaints may be medically based. If you answered no, meaning your complaint has always existed, you have what is called a primary complaint. There may be a medical basis and you should seek a physician's help. At present, however, most med-**

ications and interventions are focused on women who were satisfied with their sexual response at one point, but now no longer respond as they did. You may want to talk to your physician about neurologic testing, as well as the possibility of seeking support from a general therapist or sex therapist.

5. If you answered yes, although there may be medical issues to consider, you may also want to look into the possibility that your sexual complaints are related to your anxiety, depression, or other mental health concerns.

6. If you answered yes to all sub-questions, this is an indication that your complaints may be more medically based. If you answered no to one or more sub-questions, there may be issues or conflicts in your relationship that are contributing to your sexual complaints.

7. If you answered yes and also answered yes to any of the sub-questions, you may want to explore the possibility that your sexual complaints could be related to this traumatic history.

8. If you answered yes to any of the sub-questions, this is an indication that your sexual complaints could be medically based.

Now, what do you do with these clues about your sexual function? Obviously you cannot be evaluated or diagnosed solely on the basis of this questionnaire. However, it can help you discover areas that may need to be investigated further.

For medically based problems, consult a physician to help you target the source and investigate appropriate treatment alternatives, in addition to reading up on how to help yourself in Chapter 3. If you believe there is a relationship or emotionally based problem contributing to your sexual complaint, seek out the help of an individual, couples, or sex therapist. A more thorough discussion and suggestions for this can be found in Chapters 4 and 5. And remember, it is the rare case that is purely physiological or purely emotional. Usually sexual difficulty is a combination of both and each piece of the puzzle needs to be addressed to provide lasting relief. Hopefully by the end of this book, you will be closer to finding your unique answers.

If you want more information, completing the online questionnaire will provide you with a personalized report about the state of your sexual health. It may be another useful tool in understanding your needs and seeking the appropriate treatment.

The Passion Prescription Pad

(Note: Kit recommendations are described following the quiz starting on page 252.)

1. How does your relationship feel?

    A. I am a swinging single at the moment.

    B. Like the honeymoon has never ended.

    C. We're comfortably settled, but still discover new things about each other.

    D. Sometimes I can't remember what attracted me to my partner in the first place.

2. How satisfied are you with your sex life?

    A. Sex? Sorry, I forgot what that was for a moment.

    B. When we hit the bedroom, the sparks really fly.

    C. It's not like it used to be, but I can't complain.

    D. Sometimes I feel like we're roommates, not lovers.

3. How knowledgeable is your partner's touch?

    A. I am my own partner at the moment.

    B. He is a living and breathing Don Juan.

    C. He's like an eager student—ready and willing to receive direction.

    D. He makes me wonder if he really had sex with his past girlfriends.

4. What is talking about sex to your partner like?

    A. Good ice cream smooth and enjoyable. We love expressing our desires and taking sex to a new level.

    B. Chewing ice—it takes some work for us to open up, but we usually end up satisfied once we do.

    C. Burnt toast—my partner is brittle about any sort of criticism when it comes to our sex life, so I try to make the best of it on my own.

    D. I do not think sex should be discussed. It's best left private.

For Questions 1 through 4:

If you answered A to any of the questions, try the **Sexual Self-Discovery Kit**.

If you answered B to any of the questions, try the **Relationship Starter Discovery Kit**.

If you answered C to any of the questions, try the **Orgasm Improvement Kit.**
If you answered D to any of the questions, try the **Passion Rekindling Kit.**

5. **When you're in the heat of the moment, how pleased are you with your sexual response? Do you have a sexual concern in any of the following areas?**

Circle Yes or No

A. Desire	Yes	No
B. Lubrication	Yes	No
C. Genital sensation	Yes	No
D. General orgasm ability	Yes	No
E. Orgasm ability during intercourse	Yes	No
F. Pain (during or after sex)	Yes	No
G. Vaginal spasms (during or after sex)	Yes	No

If you answered yes to A, you may want to try either the **Sexual Self-Discovery Kit** or the **Passion Rekindling Kit.**

If you answered yes to B, C, D, or E, you may want to try the **Orgasm Improvement Kit.**

If you answered yes to F or G, you may want to try both the **Sexual Self-Discovery Kit** as well as the **Pain Alleviator Kit.**

6. **What would you like to change about your sex life?**   **Circle Yes or No**

A. I want to spice things up in my relationship.	Yes	No
B. I want to surprise my partner.	Yes	No
C. I want to try something new.	Yes	No
D. I want to incorporate fantasy into my sex life.	Yes	No
E. I want to discover new things about my partner.	Yes	No
F. I want to have an orgasm.	Yes	No
G. I want to have orgasms during intercourse.	Yes	No
H. I want to explore self-stimulation.	Yes	No
I. I want to rediscover my sexuality.	Yes	No
J. I want to get off on the right foot in a new relationship.	Yes	No

If you answered yes to A, B, C, D, or E, you may want to try the **Passion Rekindling Kit.**

If you answered yes to F or G, you may want to try the **Orgasm Improvement Kit.**

If you answered yes to H or I, you may want to try the **Sexual Self-Discovery Kit.**

If you answered yes to J, you may want to try the **Relationship Starter Discovery Kit.**

Kit Recommendations

(Note: Products without descriptions are featured on pages 29 to 39 in Chapter 2.)

The Orgasm Improvement Kit helps break down obstacles to the big "O" such as:

Low genital sensation
Difficult orgasms in general or during intercourse
Technically unknowledgeable partners

Kit contains:

❏ Hitachi *Magic Wand, AccuVibe,* or Berman Center *Aphrodite*—Use alone or as part of foreplay for difficult orgasms in general.

❏ *X-Commander* or Berman Center *Aurora*—Perfect for placing between you and your partner to provide the clitoral stimulation that many women need to reach orgasm during intercourse.

❏ *Zestra oil*—A botanical massage oil that is applied to the clitoris, labia, and vaginal opening before foreplay to help with lubrication and arousal. Zestra oil has been proven in clinical trials to enhance sexual desire, genital sensation, and the ability to have orgasms.

❏ Lubricant—as long as you're not using a silicone toy, the sky's the limit.

❏ *For Women Only: A Revolutionary Guide to Reclaiming Your Sex Life*—My first book written in conjunction with my sister, Dr. Jennifer Berman, which helps women understand sexual health and dysfunction, with an emphasis on sexual satisfaction for all women.

The Passion Rekindling Kit helps light the fire in all women who want:

More sexual desire

To add some spice

A feeling of newness with your partner

A stronger physical attraction to your partner

To incorporate fantasy into your relationship

Kit contains:

☐ *Astraea Vibrating Panties* with remote control from the Berman Center Intimate Accessories Collection

☐ Furry handcuffs and blindfold

☐ Kama Sutra *Weekender Kit* (honey dust and feather tickler, oil of love, pleasure balm, mint tree and wild clove bathing gels)

☐ Hustler's *Slippery Sex Sheets*

☐ Sinclair Intimacy Institute's *The Joy of Erotic Massage* video— Features basic and advanced techniques to explore each other's bodies. Learn to use erotic massage to heighten arousal, relax the body, and intensify intimacy.

☐ *365 Days of Sensational Sex* by Lou Paget—A handbook that gives tips on how to set the mood for sex, keep it interesting, and maintain passion in a relationship every day of the year.

☐ *52 Weeks of Naughty Nights Cards* by Lover's Choice—Like lottery tickets for your sex life, each card is scratched off for naughty IOUs, role plays, and more.

☐ *Beginner's Burlesque Kit* by SPICE—Props for turning your fantasies into reality, including striptease music, a feather boa, and fantasy mask.

The Sexual Self-Discovery Kit helps guide any woman who's interested in:

Exploring self-stimulation for the first time

Rediscovering your sexuality

Finding sexual pleasure outside of your relationship

Jump-starting your sexual desire

Kit contains:

❏ Hitachi *Magic Wand*, *AccuVibe*, or Berman Center *Aphrodite*

❏ Lubricant

❏ Handheld mirror

❏ Lavender bath oil

❏ Betty Dodson's *Self-Loving* video—Teaches women how to self-stimulate with hands-on lessons and demonstrations designed to explore their sexual expression.

❏ *Becoming Orgasmic* by Julia R. Heiman, Ph.D. and Joseph LoPiccolo, Ph.D.—A self-discovery tool that helps women understand their sexual history and how different experiences have affected it. It also guides women into self-stimulation and helps them evaluate what they are looking for in a partner.

The Relationship Starter Discovery Kit helps every woman get off on the right foot in a new relationship (no pun intended):

❏ *X-Commander* or Berman Center *Aurora*

❏ Flavored condoms

❏ Edible body paint

❏ *Totally Explicit Techniques* his and her books by Lou Paget—

Manuals that give the real deal on how men can please women and women can please men. Detailed discussion of techniques and sex aids teach what men and women are both looking for in bed.

☐ *Speak Love, Make Love* board game—A whimsical game that helps you get to know each other, sexually and otherwise.

Pain Alleviator Kit

☐ *Isis* or *Juno* pelvic floor exercisers from the Berman Center Intimate Accessories Collection—Allows you to address the dyspareunia or vaginismus in conjunction with medical treatment by working toward gradually inserting something into the vagina at your own pace and comfort level, while focusing on keeping your muscles relaxed. The practice of Kegel exercises (featured in Chapter 6) also helps, since they allow you to develop a sense of control over when your vaginal muscles tighten and relax.

☐ *Lady Finger Dilator Set*—Helps in learning to control involuntary muscle spasms. Contains four dilators that are used in conjunction with muscle control to gradually accommodate a full-sized penis without painful contractions.

☐ *Pocket Rocket, X-Commander,* or Berman Center *Aurora* or *Athena* for non-penetrative stimulation.

Genital Image Scale

I. Please read the following items and check the category that applies to YOUR feelings or thoughts about your genitals (i.e., penis, scrotum, labia, vagina, clitoris, vulva).

	Always	Often	Some-times	Never
a. I feel anxiety and worry when I think about how my genitals function.				
b. I look at my genitals.				
c. I feel confident that I understand my sexual anatomy.				
d. When I think about my genitals, I feel ashamed or embarrassed.				
e. I feel comfortable/positive about my partner seeing my genitals.				
f. I have sad and depressed feelings when I think about my genitals.				
g. I feel ashamed/embarrassed about the size of my genitals.				
h. I feel ashamed/embarrassed about the shape of my genitals.				
i. I feel ashamed/embarrassed about the look of my genitals.				
j. I feel ashamed/embarrassed about the odor of my genitals.				
k. I feel my genitals work/function as they should.				
l. I am conscious of trying to hide my genitals from being seen by my partner.				

	Always	Often	Some-times	Never
m. I feel that my genitals are attractive and would arouse my partner.				
n. As a child/adolescent, I was self-conscious or embarrassed about my genitals.				
o. I use feminine hygiene products (douches, sprays, suppositories, etc.).				
p. Growing up, my family/caregivers gave me positive messages about my genitals.				
q. Growing up, I was given the message that touching my genitals was bad or dirty.				

I. Please check whether or not the following adjectives describe your feelings about your genitals.

	Agree	Disagree
a. Unattractive		
b. Embarrassing		
c. Disgusting		
d. Attractive		
e. Malodorous (bad smelling)		
f. Offensive		
g. Inadequate		
h. Healthy		
i. Functional		
j. Desirable		
k. Well-shaped		
l. Good-sized		

Genital Image Scale: Scoring Template

CONVERT THE FOLLOWING LETTERS INTO NUMBERS PER
QUESTION CORRESPONDING TO SCALE:

Part I:

Item Number	Always	Often	Sometimes	Never
a	1	2	3	4
b	4	3	2	1
c	4	3	2	1
d	1	2	3	4
e	4	3	2	1
f	1	2	3	4
g	1	2	3	4
h	1	2	3	4
i	1	2	3	4
j	1	2	3	4
k	4	3	2	1
l	1	2	3	4
m	4	3	2	1
n	1	2	3	4
o	4	3	2	1
p	4	3	2	1
q	1	2	3	4

Part II:

	Agree	Disagree
a	0	1
b	0	1
c	0	1
d	1	0
e	0	1
f	0	1
g	0	1
h	1	0
i	1	0
j	1	0
k	1	0
l	1	0

PART I RANGE: 17 TO 68 If you have a score of 17 to 30 you should consider looking at how your feelings about your genitals are impacting your life and sexual function. If you have a score of 31 to 68 it is on the higher end. You are in pretty good shape but should always look for areas of improvement!

PART II RANGE: 0 TO 12 If you have a score of 0 to 6 you should consider looking at how your feelings about your genitals are impacting your life and sexual function. If you have a score of 7 to 12 it is on the higher end. You are in pretty good shape but should always look for areas of improvement!

References

Chapter 1

Basson, R. "The Female Sexual Response: A Different Model." *Journal of Sex and Marital Therapy* 26 (2000): 51–65.

Dodson, Betty. *Sex for One: The Joy of Selfloving*. New York: Crown, 1996.

Kaplan, Helen Singer. *Disorders of Sexual Desire and Other New Concepts and Techniques in Sex Therapy*. Philadelphia: Brunner-Mazel, 1979.

Ladas, Alice Kahn, Beverly Whipple, and John D. Perry. *The G Spot and Other Recent Discoveries About Human Sexuality*. New York: Holt, Rinehart, and Winston, 1982.

Masters, William H., and Virginia E. Johnson. *Human Sexual Response*. Boston: Little, Brown, 1966.

Masters, William H., Virginia E. Johnson, and Robert C. Kolodny. *Human Sexuality*. New York: HarperCollins, 1992.

O'Connell, H. E., J. M. Hutson, C. R. Anderson, and R. J. Plenter. "Anatomical Relationship between Urethra and Clitoris." *Journal of Urology* 159 (1998): 1892–97.

Chapter 2

Dodson, Betty. "Self-loving: Portrait of a Women's Sexuality Seminar." VHS format video.

Dodson, Betty. *Sex for One: The Joy of Selfloving*. New York: Crown, 1996.

Kaplan, Helen Singer. *The New Sex Therapy: Active Treatment of Sexual Dysfunctions*. New York: Random House, 1974.

Maines, Rachel. *The Technology of Orgasm: Hysteria, the Vibrator, and Women's Sexual Satisfaction*. Baltimore and London: The Johns Hopkins University Press, 1999.

Chapter 3

Bachmann G. A., J. Bancroft, G. Braunstein, et al. "Female Androgen Insufficiency: The Princeton Consensus Statement on Definition, Classification, and Assessment." *Fertility and Sterility* 77 (2002): 660–65.

Basson, R., R. McInnes, M. D. Smith, G. Hodgson, T. Spain, and N. Koppiker. "Efficacy and Safety of Sildenafil in Estrogenized Women with Sexual Dysfunction Associated with Female Sexual Arousal Disorder." *Obstetrics and Gynecology* 95 (2000) 4 Suppl. 1: S54.

Berman, Jennifer, and Laura Berman. *For Women Only: A Revolutionary Guide to Reclaiming Your Sex Life*. New York: Henry Holt, 2001.

Berman, J. R., L. A. Berman, T. J. Werbin, E. E. Flaherty, N. M. Leahy, and I. Goldstein, "Clinical Evaluation of Female Sexual Function: Effects of Age and Estrogen Status on Subjective and Physiologic Sexual Responses. *International Journal of Impotence Research* 11 (1999): Suppl. 1:S31–38.

Berman, J. R., L. A. Berman, T. J. Werbin, and I. Goldstein. "Female Sexual Dysfunction: Anatomy, Physiology, Evaluation, and Treatment Options." *Current Opinion Urology* 9 (1999): 563–68.

Berman, J. R., and I. Goldstein. "Sildenafil in Postmenopausal Women with Sexual Dysfunction." *Urology* 54 (1999): 578–79.

Berman, J. R., M. R. Santos, and I. Goldstein. "Relationship Between Cardiovascular Risk Factors and Female Sexual Arousal Disorder." *Menopause Review: Menopause and Sexuality* 4 (4) (1999): 43–47.

Geracioti Jr., T.D., "Persistent Depression? Low Libido? Think Testosterone Deficiency." *Current Psychiatry* (May 2004): 26.

Johns A. "Supracervical Versus Total Hysterectomy." *Clinical Obstetrics and Gynecology*, 40 (4) (1997): 903–13.

Kugaya, A., C. N. Epperson, S. Zoghi, C. H. van Dyck, Y. Hou, M. Fujita, J. K. Staley, P. K. Garg, J. P. Seibyl, R. B. Innis. "Increase in Prefrontal Cortex

Serotonin 2A Receptors Following Estrogen Treatment in Postmenopausal Women." *American Journal of Psychiatry* 160 (2003): 1522–24.

Lai, L. D., S. C. Goodwin, S. M. Bonilla, A. P. Lai, T. Yegul, S. Vott, and M. DeLeon, "Sexual Dysfunction after Uterine Artery Embolization." *Journal of Vascular and Interventional Radiology* (June 2000): 755–58.

Rako, Susan. *The Hormone of Desire: The Truth about Testosterone, Sexuality, and Menopause*. Three Rivers Press, 1999.

Rhodes, J. C., K. H. Kjerulff, P. W. Langenberg, and G. M. Guzinski, "Hysterectomy and Sexual Functioning." *Journal of the American Medical Association* 282 (1999): 1934–41.

Ross, J. K., A. Paganini-Hill, P. C. Wan, and M. C. Pike. "Effect of Hormone Replacement Therapy on Breast Cancer Risk: Estrogen Versus Estrogen Plus Progestin." *Journal of the National Cancer Institute* 92 (2000): 328–32.

Shifren, J. L., G. D. Braunstein, J. A. Simon, P. R. Casson, J. E. Buster, G. P. Redmond, R. E. Burki, E. S. Ginsburg, R. C. Rosen, S. R. Leiblum, K. P. Jones, C. A. Daugherty, K. E. Caramelli, and N. A. Mazer. "Transdermal Testosterone Treatment in Women with Impaired Sexual Function After Oophorectomy." *New England Journal of Medicine* 343 (2000): 682–88.

Sommers, Suzanne. *The Sexy Years*. New York: Crown Publishing, 2004.

Utian, W. H. et al. "Recommendations for Estrogen and Progesterone Use in Perimenopausal and Postmenopausal Women: October 2004 Position Statement of The North American Menopause Society." *Menopause: The Journal of The North American Menopause Society* 11 (6) (2004): 589–600.

Chapter 4

Kaplan, Helen Singer. *The New Sex Therapy: Active Treatment of Sexual Dysfunctions*. New York: Random House, 1974.

Luciani, Joseph. *The Power of Self-Coaching: The Five Essential Steps to Creating the Life You Want*. Hoboken: John Wiley & Sons, Inc., 2004.

MacLeod, Don, and Debra McLeod. *The French Maid: And 21 More Naughty Sex Fantasies to Surprise and Arouse Your Man*. New York: Broadway Books, 2005.

Redmond, Laure. *Feel Good Naked*. Gloucester: Fair Winds Press, 2002.

Zolbrod, Aline P. *Sex Smart: How Your Childhood Shaped Your Sexual Life and What to Do about It*. Oakland: New Harbinger Publications, 1998.

Chapter 5

Carson, Culley C., Irwin Goldstein, and Roger S. Kirby. *Textbook of Erectile Dysfunction*. Isis Medical Media, 1999.

Davis, Michele Weiner. *Sex Starved Marriage: A Couple's Guide to Boosting Their Marriage Libido*. New York: Simon & Schuster, 2003.

Fisher, Helen. *Anatomy of Love: The Natural History of Monography, Adultery, and Divorce*. New York: W. W. Norton, 1992.

Fisher, Helen. *Why We Love: The Nature and Chemistry of Romantic Love* . . . . New York: Henry Holt, 2004.

Gottman, John. *The Seven Principles for Making Marriage Work*. New York: Three Rivers Press, 1999.

Krane, Robert J., Irwin Goldstein, and Mike B. Siroky. *Male Sexual Dysfunction*. New York: Little, Brown, 1983.

Steele, R. Don. *Body Language Secrets: A Guide During Courtship and Dating*. Whittier: Steel Balls Press, 2002.

Chapter 6

Carlson, Karen, Stephanie A. Eisenstat, and Terra Ziporyn. *The New Harvard Guide to Women's Health*. Cambridge and London: Harvard University Press, 2004.

Meston, C. M., and B. B. Gorzalka. "The Effects of Sympathetic Activation on Physiological and Subjective Sexual Arousal in Women." *Behavioral Research and Therapy* 33 (1995): 651–64.

Palmore, E. B. "Predictors of the Longevity Difference: A 25-Year Follow-Up." *Gerontologist* 22 (1982): 513–8.

Roizen, Michael F., with Elizabeth Anne Stephenson. *Real Age: Are You as Young as You Can Be?* New York: Cliff Street Books/HarperCollins, 1999.

Chapter 7

Blank, Joani, ed., photographs by Tee A. Corinne. *Femalia*. San Francisco: Down There Press, 1993.

Carlson, Karen, Stephanie A. Eisenstat, and Terra Ziporyn. *The New Harvard Guide to Women's Health*. Cambridge and London: Harvard University Press, 2004.

Ebel, Charles. *Managing Herpes: How to Live and Love with a Chronic STD*. American Social Health Association, 2002.

Zhang, J., M. Hatch, D. Zhang, J. Shulman, E. Harville and A.G. Thomas. "Frequency of Douching and Risk of Bacterial Vaginosis in African-American Women." *Obstetrics and Gynecology* 104 (2004): 756-760.

Chapter 8

Eichel, E. W., J. D. Eichel, and S. Kule. "The Technique of Coital Alignment and Its Relation to Female Orgasmic Response and Simultaneous Orgasm." *Journal of Sex and Marital Therapy* 14 (1988): 129–141.

Joannides, Paul. *Guide to Getting It On!* Saline: McNaughton & Gunn, 2004.

Kinsey, Alfred, et al. *Sexual Behavior in the Human Female*. Philadelphia: W. B. Saunders, 1953.

Kitzinger, Sheila. *Woman's Experience of Sex: The Facts and Feelings of Female Sexuality at Every Stage of Life*. New York: Penguin Books, 1985.

Masters, William H., Virginia E. Johnson, and Robert C. Kolodny. *Human Sexuality*. New York: HarperCollins, 1992.

Pierce, A. P. "The Coital Alignment Technique (CAT): An Overview of Studies." *Journal of Sex and Marital Therapy* 26 (2000): 257–68.

Reinisch, June Machover. *The Kinsey Institute New Report on Sex*. New York: 1990.

Seeber, Michael, and Carin Gorrell. "The Science of Orgasm: Sex and Your Psyche." *Psychology Today* (Nov/Dec 2001).

Chapter 9

Gillespie, Larrian. *The Goddess Diet: Proven Ways to Naturally Stay Slim, Ageless, and Healthy*. Beverly Hills: Healthy Life Publications, 2000.

Salonia, Andrea et al. "Chocolate and Women's Sexual Health. An Intriguing Correlation." 7th Congress of the European Society for Sexual Medicine, London, Dec. 5–8, 2004.

Shandler, Nina. *Estrogen: The Natural Way: Over 250 Easy and Delicious Recipes for Menopause*. New York: Random House, 1998.

Chapter 10

Chia, Mantek, and Maneewan Chia. *Healing Love Through the Tao: Cultivating Female Sexual Energy*. New York: Healing Tao Books, 1986.

Chia, Mantek, and William Wei. *Sexual Reflexology: Activating the Taoist Points of Love*. Rochester: Destiny Books, 2003.

Meston, C. M., and M. Worcel. "The Effects of L-Arginine and Yohimbine on Sexual Arousal in Postmenopausal Women with FSAD." Department of Psychology, University of Texas at Austin; NitroMed, Inc., Bedford, Mass., 2000.

Watson, Cynthia Mervis. *Love Potions: A Guide to Aphrodisiacs and Sexual Pleasures*. New York: Jeremy P. Tarcher/Putnam, 2002.

Resource Guide

(Books and Web Sites for Further Reading)

■❚❚❚❚❚❚❚❚❚❚❚■

Sex: Anatomy and Masturbation

Books

- ❑ *For Women Only: A Revolutionary Guide to Reclaiming Your Sex Life.* Berman, J. & Berman, L. (2001). Henry Holt.

- ❑ *Becoming Orgasmic: A Sexual and Personal Growth Program for Women.* Heiman, J. & LoPiccolo, J. (1987). Fireside.

- ❑ *Sex For One: The Joy of Self-Loving.* Dodson, B. (1996). Three Rivers Press.

- ❑ *For Yourself: The Fulfillment of Female Sexuality.* Barbach, L. (2000). Signet.

- ❑ *Getting the Sex You Want: A Woman's Guide to Becoming Proud, Passionate and Pleased in Bed.* Leiblum, S. & Sachs, J. (2002). Crown.

- ❑ *What Your Mother Never Told You About S-e-x.* Hutcherson, H. (2003). Perigee Books.

- ❑ *Woman on Top.* Friday, N. (1993). Pocket Books.

- ❑ *My Secret Garden: Women's Sexual Fantasies.* Friday, N. (1973). Trident.

Web sites

- ❏ *drlauraberman.com,* a deeper dive into many of the topics covered in this book available online. A rich subscription environment, featuring tips, toys, and important medical information. Self-help diagnostics and treatment programs: *www.drlauraberman.com*

- ❏ Betty Dodson's Web site devoted to sexual education, erotic exploration, and masturbation: *www.bettydodson.com*

- ❏ The Clitoris.com, with links to in-depth discussions of virtually every facet of women's sexual health and pleasure: *www.the-clitoris.com*

- ❏ Bermancenter.com, a Web site devoted to ongoing discussion of women's sexual health issues, including resources for physicians specializing in female sexual function complaints: *www.bermancenter.com*

Sex: Toys, Technique, and Spicing It Up

Books

- ❏ *101 Nights of Grrreat Sex: Secret Sealed Seductions for Fun-Loving Couples.* Corn, L. (2000). Park Avenue Publishers.

- ❏ *She Comes First: The Thinking Man's Guide to Pleasuring a Woman.* Kerner, I. (2004). ReganBooks.

- ❏ *365 Days of Sensational Sex: Tantalizing Tips and Techniques to Keep the Fires Burning All Year Long.* Paget, L. (2003). Gotham Books.

- ❏ *How to Give Her Absolute Pleasure.* Paget, L. (2000). Broadway.

- ❏ *How to Be a Great Lover: Girlfriend-to-Girlfriend Totally Explicit Techniques That Will Blow His Mind.* Paget, L. (1999). Broadway.

- ❏ *For Each Other: Sharing Sexual Intimacy.* Barbach, L. (2001). Signet Books.

- ❏ *Lesbian Sex Secrets for Men.* Goddard, A. & Brungardt, K. (2000). Plume.

❏ *The Many Joys of Sex Toys: The Ultimate How-To Handbook for Couples and Singles.* Semans, A. (2004). Broadway.

❏ *Toygasms! The Insider's Guide to Sex Toys and Techniques.* Allison, S. (2003). Tickle Kitty Press.

Web sites

All of the following Web sites feature a variety of vibrators, sex toys, erotic videos, and books for both singles and couples. Online and retail store locations are listed, where appropriate.

❏ California Exotic Novelties, including the Berman Center Intimate Accessories Collection: *www.calexotics.com*

❏ Eve's Garden, also including the Berman Center Intimate Accessories Collection: *www.evesgarden.com*

❏ G-Boutique *www.boutiqueg.com*
   2131 N Damen Avenue
   Chicago, IL 60647
   (773) 235-1234

❏ Good Vibrations *www.goodvibes.com*
   603 Valencia Street
   San Francisco, CA 94110
   (415) 522-5460

   1620 Polk Street
   San Francisco, CA 94109
   (415) 345-0400

   2504 San Pablo Avenue
   Berkeley, CA 94702
   (510) 841-8987

❏ Grand Opening *www.grandopening.com*
   308A Harvard Street
   Brookline, MA 02446
   (617) 731-2626

8442 Santa Monica Blvd
West Hollywood, CA 90069
(323) 848-6970

❏ Toys in Babeland *www.babeland.com*
707 E Pike Street
Seattle, WA 98122
(206) 328-2914

43 Mercer Street
New York, NY 10013
(212) 966-2120

94 Rivington Street
New York, NY 10002
(212) 375-1701

To investigate hosting a sex-toy party for you and your friends:

❏ Safina Sex-Ed Salons: *www.safina.com*

❏ Passion Parties: *www.passionparties.com*

❏ Pure Romance: *www.pureromance.com*

Genital Health and Grooming

Books

❏ *Hot Pink: The Girls' Guide to Primping, Passion, and Pubic Fashion.* Driggs, D. & Risch, K. (2004). Just Write.

❏ *Femalia.* Blank, J. (1993). Down There Press.

❏ *Endometriosis: The Complete Reference for Taking Charge of Your Health.* Ballweg, M. (2003). McGraw-Hill.

❏ *The V Book: A Doctor's Guide to Complete Vulvovaginal Health.* Stewart, E. & Spencer, P. (2002). Bantam.

☐ *The Vulvodynia Survival Guide: How to Overcome Painful Vaginal Symptoms and Enjoy an Active Lifestyle.* Glazer, H. & Rodke, G. (2002). New Harbinger Publications.

☐ *Managing Herpes: How to Live and Love With a Chronic STD.* Ebel, C. (1998). American Social Health Association.

☐ *Sexually Transmitted Diseases: A Physician Tells You What You Need to Know.* Marr, L. (1998). Johns Hopkins University Press.

Web sites

☐ Lisa Masterson's "Butterfly" line of comfortable, seamless panties for keeping your vulva healthy: *www.mastersonmd.net*

☐ The Hanky Panky line of low-rise stretch lace thongs are comfortable and good for you: *www.herroom.com* (as well as other Web sites)

☐ The Vulvar Pain Foundation for information about pain and related disorders: *www.vulvarpainfoundation.org*

☐ The h.o.p.e. network for genital herpes, including special resources for women: *www.healthandhope.com*

☐ The Hepatitis B Foundation, a nonprofit organization dedicated to finding a cure and improving quality of life for those affected: *www.hepb.org*

☐ The Body, a comprehensive HIV/AIDS resource: *www.thebody.com*

Menopause/HRT

Books

☐ *The Sexy Years.* Sommers, S. (2004). Crown.

☐ *The HRT Solution.* Ahlgrimm, M. & Kells, J. (2003). Avery Publishing.

☐ *The Wisdom of Menopause.* Northrup, C. (2003). Bantam.

☐ *Women's Body, Women's Wisdom.* Northrup, C. (1998). Bantam.

❑ *Hormone of Desire: The Truth about Testosterone, Sexuality, and Menopause.* Rako, S. (1999). Three Rivers Press.

❑ *Natural Hormone Balance for Women: Look Younger, Feel Stronger, and Live Life with Exuberance.* Reiss, U. & Zucker, M. (2002). Atria.

❑ *Better Bones, Better Body.* Brown, S. (1996). Keats Publishing.

❑ *A Woman's Guide to Natural Hormones.* Conrad, C. (2000). Perigee.

❑ *Sex over 40.* Rosenthal, S. (2000). Jeremy P. Tarcher.

Web sites

❑ The North American Menopause Society, a nonprofit organization devoted to promoting quality of life through an understanding of menopause. Includes information on perimenopause, early menopause, and therapies to enhance long-term health and wellness: *www.menopause.org*

❑ The American Academy of Anti-Aging Medicine is a nonprofit organization with links to physicians who practice bio-identical hormone therapy, as well as other resources for treating age-related health conditions: *www.worldhealth.net*

❑ The International Academy of Compounding Pharmacies provides information for locating a compounding pharmacy in your area, for customized hormone therapy regimens: *www.iacprx.org*

Marriage and Relationships

Books

❑ *Passionate Marriage: Love, Sex, and Intimacy in Emotionally Committed Relationships.* Schnarch, D. (1998). Owl Books.

❑ *His Needs, Her Needs.* Harley, W. (2001). Revell.

❑ *The Sex-Starved Marriage.* Davis, M. (2003). Simon & Schuster.

❑ *Keeping the Love You Find.* Hendrix, H. (1993). Atria.

❏ *Getting the Love You Want.* Hendrix, H. (2001). Owl Books

❏ *The Seven Principles for Making Marriage Work.* Gottman, J. (2000). Three Rivers Press.

❏ *The Relationship Cure.* Gottman, J. (2002). Three Rivers Press.

❏ *The Five Love Languages: How to Express Heartfelt Commitment to Your Mate.* Chapman, G. (1996). Moody Publishers.

❏ *The Dance of Anger: A Woman's Guide to Changing the Patterns of Intimate Relationships.* Lerner, H. (1997). Quill.

❏ *The Dance of Intimacy: A Woman's Guide to Courageous Acts of Change in Key Relationships.* Lerner, H. (1990). Harper Perennial.

Web sites

❏ The American Association of Sex Educators, Counselors, and Therapists (AASECT) provides resources for finding a licensed professional in your area: *www.aasect.org*

❏ The American Association for Family and Marriage Therapy (AAMFT) also provides resources for finding a licensed therapist in your area: *www.aamft.org*

Fitness

Books

Pelvic Power for Men and Women: Mind/Body Exercises for Strength, Flexibility, Posture, and Balance. Franklin, E. (2003). Princeton Book Company.

Yoga, Massage, and Eastern Therapies

Books

❏ *A Woman's Guide to Tantra Yoga.* McClure, V. (1997). New World Library.

❏ *The Art of Sensual Massage.* Inkeles, G. & Foothorap, R. (2000). Arcata Arts.

❏ *Instant Calm: Over 100 Easy-to-Use Techniques for Relaxing Mind and Body.* Wilson, P. (1995). Plume.

❏ *The Relaxation & Stress Reduction Workbook.* Davis, M., Eshelman, E., & McKay, M. (2000). New Harbinger Publishers.

Web sites

❏ Sinclair Intimacy Institute offers a wide selection of videos on everything from erotic massage to Kama Sutra sex: *www.bettersex.com*

❏ The American Academy of Medical Acupuncture provides resources for finding an acupuncturist in your area: *www.medicalacupuncture.org*

❏ National Certification Commission for Acupuncture and Oriental Medicine provides resources for finding an Eastern medicine practitioner in your area, including acupuncturists: *www.nccaom.org*

❏ International Institute of Reflexology provides information about reflexology and referrals for finding a reflexologist in your area: *www.reflexology-usa.net*

❏ Reflexology Association of America provides additional resources for finding a practitioner in your area: *www.reflexology-usa.org*

Nutrition for Sexual Health

Books

❏ *The Goddess Diet.* Gillespie, L. (2000). Healthy Life Publications.

❏ *Intuitive Eating: A Revolutionary Program That Works.* Tribole, E. & Resch, E. (2003). St. Martin's Griffin.

❏ *When Your Body Gets the Blues: The Clinically Proven Program for Women Who Feel Tired, Stressed, and Eat Too Much!* Brown, M. & Robinson, J. (2002). Rodale Books.

❏ *Outsmarting the Midlife Fat Cell: Winning Weight Control Strategies for Women Over 35 to Stay Fit Through Menopause.* Waterhouse, D. (1999). Hyperion.

❏ *The Food and Mood Cookbook: Recipes for Eating Well and Feeling Your Best.* Somer, E. & Williams, J. (2004). Owl Books.

❏ *The Cortisol Connection Diet: The Breakthrough Program to Control Stress and Lose Weight.* Talbott, S. & Skolnik, H. (2004). Hunter House.

❏ *Overcoming Overeating: Living Free in a World of Food.* Hirschmann, J. & Munter, C. (1988). Ballantine Publishing.

❏ *Making Peace with Food: Freeing Yourself from the Diet/Weight Obsession.* Kano, S. (1998). Harper & Row.

❏ *Guide to Healthy Restaurant Eating.* Warshaw, H. (2002). McGraw-Hill/Contemporary.

❏ *Fight Fat After Forty: The Revolutionary Three-Pronged Approach That Will Break Your Stress-Fat Cycle and Make You Healthy, Fit, and Trim for Life.* Peeke, P. (2001). Penguin Books.

Note: All of the following categories can be addressed with the help of a licensed therapist. Consult the Web resources in **Marriage and Relationships** for how to find a therapist in your area.

Self-Esteem and Body Image

Books

❏ *Women Who Run with the Wolves.* Pinkola Estes, C. (1996). Ballantine Books.

❏ *Six Pillars of Self-Esteem.* Branden, N. (1995). Bantam.

❑ *Ten Days to Self-Esteem.* Burns, D. (1993). HarperCollins Publishers.

❑ *Women and Self-Esteem.* Sandford, L. & Donovan, M. (1984). Viking Press.

❑ *Self-Esteem: A Proven Program of Cognitive Techniques for Assessing, Improving, and Maintaining Your Self-Esteem.* McKay, M. & Fanning, P. (2000). New Harbinger Publishers.

❑ *The Body Image Workbook: An 8-Step Program for Learning to Like Your Looks.* Cash, T. (1997). MJF Books.

❑ *When Women Stop Hating Their Bodies: Freeing Yourself From Food and Weight Obsession.* Hirschmann, J. & Munter, C. (1995). Fawcett Columbine.

❑ *The Beauty Myth: How Images of Beauty Are Used Against Women.* Wolf, N. (1991). Morrow.

Anxiety and Depression

Books

❑ *Stop Obsessing: How to Overcome Your Obsessions/Compulsions.* Foa, E. & Wilson, R. (2001). Bantam.

❑ *Feeling Good Handbook.* Burns, D. (1999). Plume.

❑ *Feeling Good: The New Mood Therapy.* Burns, D. (1999). Avon.

❑ *An Unquiet Mind: A Memoir of Moods and Madness.* Redfield-Jamison, K. (1997). Vintage.

❑ *Night Falls Fast: Understanding Suicide.* Redfield-Jamison, K. (1997). Vintage.

Abuse and Trauma

Books

❑ *Getting Free: You Can End Abuse and Take Back Your Life.* Nicarthy, G. (1997). Seal Press.

❏ *It's My Life Now: Starting Over After an Abusive Relationship or Domestic Violence.* Dugan, M. & Hock, R. (2000). Routledge.

❏ *The Courage to Heal: A Guide for Women Survivors of Child Sexual Abuse.* Bass, E. & Davis, L. (1994). Harper Perennial.

❏ *I Never Told Anyone: Writings by Women Survivors of Child Sexual Abuse.* Bass, E. & Thornton, L. (1983). Harper Perennial.

❏ *Becoming Whole Again: Help for Women Survivors of Childhood Sexual Abuse.* Gallagher, V. (1991). TAB Books.

Male Sexual Dysfunction

Books

❏ *Coping with Erectile Dysfunction: How to Regain Confidence and Enjoy Great Sex.* Metz, M. & McCarthy, B. (2004). New Harbinger Publications.

❏ *Coping with Premature Ejaculation: How to Overcome PE, Please Your Partner & Have Great Sex.* Metz, M. & McCarthy, B. (2004). New Harbinger Publications.

❏ *The Viagra Myth: The Surprising Impact on Love and Relationships.* Morgentaler, A. (2003). Jossey-Bass.

❏ *The Andropause Mystery: Unraveling Truths About the Male Menopause.* Tan, R. (2001). Amred Consulting.

Index

Wait, There's More!

Free One-Week Trial
for the Passion Prescription Online Program

Sign up today and get:

- Questions and answers from Dr. Laura Berman

- Passion Coaches to help you with your own personal issues

- Self-assessments, quizzes, and other interactive tools

- Online journals and message boards

- Additional exercises and illustrations to enhance your reading

- Private e-mail newsletters delivered right to your in box

The Online Program Is the
Perfect Companion to the Book!

Exclusive offer!

Available only at **www.DrLauraBerman.com/book**

Offer good through December 2006.